WOMAN'S WEEKLY
COOK BOOK

Liz Burn

COLLINS

First published in 1986
by William Collins Sons & Co Ltd
London. Glasgow. Sydney
Auckland. Johannesburg. Toronto

British Library Cataloguing in Publication Data
Burn, Liz
  Woman's weekly cook book
  1. Cookery
  I.   Title
      641.5   TX717

ISBN 0 00 411215 6

Typeset by V & M Graphics
Printed and bound in Italy
by New Interlitho SpA, Milan

Frontispiece: Roast Pork with Sage, page 48

WOMAN'S WEEKLY
COOK BOOK

CONTENTS

INTRODUCTION

I was delighted when the idea of a *Woman's Weekly* cookery book was raised, because it gives me such a marvellous opportunity to repeat some of the lovely recipes which have appeared in the magazine in recent years. I hope that they will prove as popular with those who are new to *Woman's Weekly* as they have done with regular readers, whose countless letters arrive in the office each week. Those of you who do recognise some of the recipes here will, I trust, enjoy trying them again, and find the bright, familiar lay-out of this book indispensable in your kitchen.

I'd like to tell you a little about how the Cookery Department at *Woman's Weekly* works. Most of the week is spent creating, developing, testing and tasting all the recipes which appear in each issue of the magazine. It may surprise some people to know that we never cheat or 'mock up' food for the photographs – no plastic chickens or shaving-foam cream for us! The dishes you see in the photographs have been made up exactly to the recipes we print, so you know just what to expect.

A few days in advance of the photo session, we put our heads together and decide how we're going to illustrate the food for the forthcoming feature. Then we choose the appropriate china to use – delicate bone china for a tea party shot, earthenware for a wholesome and hearty spread, and so on. If we haven't anything suitable in our cupboards, we can borrow from department stores and cook shops. We also bring in all sorts of props – fluffy Easter bunnies, Mexican guitars, Chinese paper dragons, and other items which fit in with the theme of the week.

On the day, as usual the kitchen is a hive of activity – a constant stream of washing-up, props, pots and pans and people everywhere. Sets are built, if necessary, in the dining room next to the kitchen – it could be a cottage kitchen or a picnic scene. The food is arranged and then the photographer works his magic to create the right atmosphere.

Occasionally we pack everything and everyone into the car and go on location – to the beach, a grassy lawn, or a cornfield in the country. This may sound romantic, but it rapidly becomes less so when the flies take a liking to the food, the cream melts in the sun, or the tide comes in, threatening to wash the beach picnic clean away! Yes, photographing food can be (and often is) tiring and hectic, but on the whole it's fun and very rewarding.

Lots of readers may wonder what becomes of all the food after we've captured it on film. Well, I must admit that some of it makes an unwelcome appearance round my waist (oh, the temptation!), but the editorial staff of *Woman's Weekly* are pretty well looked after too – mistakes as well as successes are taken round and, somehow, all meet with equal approval!

In the pages that follow, I haven't quite told you how to boil an egg, but I have included lots of simple, nutritious recipes for everyday meals for you and your family. If you're feeling a bit more adventurous, there's plenty to inspire you in the chapter on entertaining, and there are lots of ideas for occasional and seasonal cooking too. Some are traditional, some are modern, but in all my recipes I've tried to reflect the trend towards fresh, wholesome ingredients which we've all come to expect. Unfortunately, lack of space has meant that some recipes have been left out, but I've included as wide a variety of recipes as possible, giving you plenty to choose from.

One note about the recipes that follow – as you'll see, both imperial and metric measurements are given. Choose either the imperial or the metric, never a combination of the two. If you don't, we can't be held responsible for the results, which could be very strange indeed!

Writing about food during my nine years as Cookery Editor of *Woman's Weekly*, collecting and swapping recipes, attending press shows and launches, meeting public relations folk, have brought me lots of good friends and many, many happy times. It's a smashing job and I enjoy every minute of it. I'd like to take this chance, too, to say a great big 'thank-you' to all my staff, both past and present, who have contributed so much, with their ideas, enthusiasm, hard work and support, to the cookery features each week and to this book.

I do hope that you'll enjoy the fruit of our labour, this superb new *Woman's Weekly* Cook Book, and that it will provide you with entertainment, enjoyment and full stomachs for years to come.

FACTS AND FIGURES

NOTES ON METRICATION

You will notice in the recipes ingredients quantities are given in both Imperial and metric measures. It is important to follow only one set of measures. Never mix Imperial and metric measures in one recipe, stick to one system or the other.

Exact conversion from Imperial to metric measures does not usually give very convenient working quantities and so the metric measures have been rounded up or down. In a few recipes it has been necessary to modify them slightly. The table shows the recommended equivalents.

Notes for American and Australian users

In America the 8 oz measuring cup is used. In Australia metric measures are now used in conjunction with the standard 250 ml measuring cup. The Imperial pint, used in Britain and Australia, is 20 fl oz, while the American pint is 16 fl oz. It is important to remember that the Australian tablespoon differs from both the British and American tablespoons; the table below gives a comparison. The British standard tablespoon, which has been used throughout this book, holds 17·7 ml, the American 14·2 ml, and the Australian 20 ml. A teaspoon holds approximately 5 ml in all three countries.

British	American	Australian
1 teaspoon	1 teaspoon	1 teaspoon
1 tablespoon	1 tablespoon	1 tablespoon
2 tablespoons	3 tablespoons	2 tablespoons
3½ tablespoons	4 tablespoons	3 tablespoons
4 tablespoons	5 tablespoons	3½ tablespoons

An Imperial/American guide to solid and liquid measures

Solid measures

IMPERIAL	AMERICAN
1 lb butter or margarine	2 cups
1 lb flour	4 cups
1 lb granulated or caster sugar	2 cups
1 lb icing sugar	3 cups
8 oz rice	1 cup

Liquid measures

IMPERIAL	AMERICAN
¼ pint liquid	⅔ cup liquid
½ pint	1¼ cups
¾ pint	2 cups
1 pint	2½ cups
1½ pints	3¾ cups
2 pints	5 cups (2½ pints)

Spoon measures

All spoon measures given in this book are level unless otherwise stated.

Can sizes

At present cans are marked with the exact metric equivalent to the Imperial weight. In some recipes measures have been rounded up when giving can sizes.

Egg sizes
Size 2 weighs 2·3–2·5 oz (65–70g)
Size 3 weighs 2–2·3 oz (60–65g)

Conversion Table

The following measures give an approximate guide when you haven't any scales at hand. The tablespoons used are the ones made according to the British Standards Institute's specifications – 1 tablespoon = 15 ml and 1 teaspoon = 5 ml. If you have not got a set of these spoons, it would be a good idea to check, using your own spoons, whether 1 oz is 2, 2½ or 3 level tablespoons and then alter the chart below accordingly.

INGREDIENTS	NUMBER OF LEVEL TABLESPOONS IN 1 oz	NUMBER OF OZ IN 1 LEVEL TEA CUP (8 fl oz/ 240 ml)
Flour	3	5 oz
Sugar (granulated, caster or soft brown)	2	8 oz
Icing sugar	2½	5 oz
Cornflour	2½	5 oz
Rice	2	8 oz
Dried breadcrumbs	3	5 oz
Dried fruit	2	5 oz
Rolled oats	3	3 oz
Chopped nuts	3	4 oz
Shredded suet	3	5 oz
Desiccated coconut	3	3 oz
Ground almonds	3	3½ oz
Jam	1	
Syrup	1	
Mixed peel	2	
Cocoa powder	4	

Liquid measures

The millilitre has been used in this book and the following table gives a few examples.

IMPERIAL FLUID OUNCES	METRIC MILLILITRES
2½	65
5 (¼ pint)	150
10 (½ pint)	300
15 (¾ pint)	450
20 (1 pint)	600
30 (1½ pints)	900
35 (1¾ pints)	1000 (1 litre)
40 (2 pints)	1100 (1·1 litres)

Solid measures

IMPERIAL OUNCES	METRIC GRAMMES	IMPERIAL OUNCES	METRIC GRAMMES
½	15	7	210
1	25	8	225
1½	40	9	250
2	50	10	275
2½	65	11	300
3	75	12	350
4	100	13	375
4½	125	14	400
5	150	15	420
6	175	1 lb	450

Note: As a general guide 1 kg (1000 g) equals 2.2 lb or about 2 lb 3 oz.

Oven Temperature Chart

OVEN HEAT	GAS MARK	ELECTRIC (FAHRENHEIT)	CENTIGRADE
Very cool	¼–½	225–250	110–120
Cool or slow	1	275	140
Cool or slow	2	300	150
Warm	3	325	160
Moderate	4	350	180
Moderately hot	5	375	190
Fairly hot	6	400	200
Hot	7	425	220
Very hot	8	450	230
Very hot	9	475	240

Measurements

⅛ inch	3 mm		5 inch	13 cm	
¼ inch	5 mm		6 inch	15 cm	
½ inch	1 cm		7 inch	18 cm	
¾ inch	2 cm		8 inch	20 cm	
1 inch	2·5 cm		9 inch	23 cm	
1¼ inch	3 cm		10 inch	25·5 cm	
1½ inch	4 cm		11 inch	28 cm	
1¾ inch	4·5 cm		12 inch	30 cm	
2 inch	5 cm		13 inch	32·5 cm	
3 inch	7·5 cm		14 inch	35 cm	
4 inch	10 cm		15 inch	37·5 cm	

GUIDELINES TO FREEZING

Where recipes are suitable for freezing we have given a note on storage time, thawing and reheating. The following gives more extensive information on how to package and successfully freeze foods.

■ Foods must be well protected and properly wrapped or packed in suitable containers – if left uncovered or badly wrapped, the low temperature will dry the food and cause 'freezer burn' which spoils the texture and flavour.

■ Where possible, pack in plastic bags and freezer foil or cling wrap. Even more economical are food containers such as yogurt, cream and margarine pots. Just wash well, dry, fill and seal with the lid, foil or cling wrap. Also use foil dishes from Chinese or Indian take aways and from commercially frozen foods. Wash well and seal with foil or cling wrap.

■ When packaging, as much air as possible should be extracted, so squeeze plastic bags gently to remove air pockets; use containers of the correct shape and size and seal completely.

■ Always label each package with date, quantity, name and storage time. It is still perfectly safe to eat frozen foods beyond the recommended storage time (although not longer than a few weeks) – the food just loses some of its original quality of colour, flavour and texture.

■ When liquids are frozen, allow for at least ½ inch (1 cm) expansion; i.e. leave ½ inch (1 cm) head-space at the top of the container.

■ The smaller the package the better. Pack in amounts generally used for home cooking. Where possible, freeze made-up dishes in containers in which they can be reheated.

■ Never put warm food into the freezer and cool hot food as rapidly as possible before packaging.

■ Never freeze too many items at once since this will raise the temperature inside the freezer. This is bad for the food in the freezer and also means food just put in will take longer to freeze and some texture and flavour will be lost.

■ Freeze foods as they come into season – when they are at their best and cheapest.

■ Partially thawed food, provided you can feel ice crystals, is safe to refreeze but the quality may deteriorate slightly.

■ If the following foods, either on their own or used in precooked dishes, have thawed you *must not refreeze* unless they have been cooked before being frozen – meat, poultry, fish, vegetables, ice-cream.

■ Most fruit and fruit dishes – unless they contain cream – and breads and cakes, if thawed, can be refrozen without much harm, although there may be some loss of colour and flavour and, in the case of fruit, some juice.

■ If you're freezing a lot of food, turn on the fast freeze switch at least 6 hours before you begin.

Remember that home-grown produce is the best, as you can select young and tender fruit and vegetables in perfect condition. If you don't grow your own, you can always 'pick your own' at farms up and down the country.

Blanch: Plunge vegetables (and some kinds of fruit) into boiling water for a short time to increase storage life and help maintain quality. The amount of time depends on the variety of vegetable.

Dry-pack: Freeze usable quantities of fruit or vegetables in plastic bags or containers without sugar or syrup. As the food will freeze in a solid mass, you'll have to use the whole of each quantity at once.

Open-freeze: A 'free-flowing' pack, where small quantities can be removed, can be produced by first spreading the prepared fruit or vegetables in a single layer on a tray and freezing until firm. Then pack and seal immediately to prevent drying.

Sugar-pack: This is the same as dry-packing, except that sugar is sprinkled over the fruit before freezing. This makes it ideal for pies, puddings or jams.

SOUP

Here are some of my favourite recipes for wholesome, hearty, home-made soups. They are perfect as starters or as satisfying snacks, served with crusty bread. All the soups have been tried out on my family and friends, who tell me that they almost look forward to the cold weather now. Why? Because they know it will mean bowls of beautiful, warming soup!

FREEZING SOUPS

All these soups can be frozen. However, if cream is to be added, do so on reheating so that the storage time of the soup is not reduced to that of the cream.

Leave ½-1 inch (1-2·5 cm) of headspace in container or bag to allow for liquid expansion during freezing. Soups will keep for 3-6 months, depending on ingredients.

Stock

Stock is the basis of a really good soup. It's so easy to make and you'll find that home-made stock certainly adds lots of extra flavour to your soups. However, the lack of home-made stock should not deter you. Soups can be made with water or, better still, vegetable cooking water.

Stock cubes are a quick-to-use base for home-made soups. They tend to be salty, so be careful when adding extra salt.

BONE STOCK

Use fresh or cooked bones or the carcass from poultry. If fresh bones are used, these can be well browned in the oven first, or fried in dripping to give a richer stock.

Makes 2 pints (1·1 litres)

1 lb (450g) bones
1 level teaspoon salt
3 pints (1·8 litres) water
2 carrots, scrubbed and sliced
Thick slice of turnip
1 onion
6 peppercorns
Bouquet garni sachet, or fresh bunch of mixed herbs

Wash the bones and put them in a pan with the salt and water. Bring to the boil and skim. Add the vegetables – leave the onion skin on if you want brown stock, peppercorns and bouquet garni sachet or fresh bunch of mixed herbs.

Simmer gently for 2 hours or cook in a pressure cooker for 1 hour. Leave to cool, then strain. Use within 3 days of making.

ITALIAN BEAN SOUP

Serves 4

1 tablespoon oil
1 medium onion, peeled and chopped
1 leek, trimmed and chopped
2 oz (50g) streaky bacon, chopped
1 clove garlic, peeled and chopped
14½ oz (400g) can canellini or white haricot beans, or butter beans
½ pint (300 ml) water
1 chicken stock cube, crumbled

Italian Bean Soup

1 bay leaf

Pepper

1 level teaspoon salt

$\frac{1}{4}$ pint (150 ml) milk

Heat the oil in a large saucepan and add the onion, leek and bacon. Cook for 5–10 minutes or until the onion and leek are soft and transparent and the fat runs from the bacon. Add the garlic, beans and liquid from the can, water, stock cube, bay leaf and seasoning.

Simmer for 15–20 minutes, remove the bay leaf and stir in the milk. Lightly mash the beans in the soup with a fork to thicken, reheat the soup and serve.

GREEN PEA SOUP

This soup is good with wholemeal bread, or with cheese on toast for a tasty and satisfying supper.

Serves 4–6

1 lb (450g) peas, frozen or fresh

2 chicken or ham stock cubes

$1\frac{1}{2}$ pints (900 ml) water

$\frac{1}{2}$ level teaspoon dried mint, or 1 teaspoon chopped fresh mint

$\frac{1}{2}$ level teaspoon sugar

1 oz (25g) margarine

1 oz (25g) flour

$\frac{1}{2}$ pint (300 ml) milk

$\frac{1}{2}$ level teaspoon salt

Pepper

Put the peas, stock cubes, water, mint and sugar into a saucepan. Bring to the boil, then cover pan with lid and simmer for 20 minutes.

Meanwhile, melt the margarine in another pan, stir in the flour, then the milk and bring to the boil, stirring all the time. Add salt and pepper to taste and simmer for about 5 minutes.

Liquidize or purée the pea mixture, then stir it into the sauce, adding more seasoning if necessary. Reheat and serve sprinkled with a little chopped fresh mint, if liked.

GOLDEN CARROT CREAM

Serves 4

$1\frac{1}{2}$ lb (700g) carrots, peeled

8 oz (225g) potatoes, peeled

Pepper

1 level teaspoon salt

$\frac{1}{4}$ level teaspoon thyme

2 bay leaves

2 pints (1·1 litres) stock, or water and stock cube

1 level teaspoon sugar

1 level tablespoon cornflour

$\frac{1}{4}$ pint (150 ml) creamy milk, or single cream

Slice the carrots and potatoes and put into a saucepan with the pepper, salt, thyme, bay leaves, stock, or water and stock cube, and the sugar. Bring to the boil, cover and simmer for about 45 minutes or until the carrots are tender. Remove the bay leaves, then sieve, liquidize or process.

Return to the pan. Blend the cornflour with a little water to a smooth paste. Stir into the pan with the milk or cream. Add seasoning to taste and reheat.

CHICKEN AND LEEK SOUP

Extra cooked chicken can be added if necessary to make this soup into a more substantial meal.

Serves 4–6

1 chicken carcass

3 pints (1·8 litres) water

1 tablespoon oil

4 rashers back bacon, derinded and chopped

2 sticks celery, cut into $\frac{1}{2}$ inch (1 cm) lengths

2 lb (900g) leeks, trimmed

2 oz (50g) pearl barley

1 level teaspoon salt

Black pepper

$\frac{1}{2}$ level teaspoon concentrated mint sauce

Break up the chicken carcass and put it into a large saucepan with at least 3 pints (1·8 litres) of water. The carcass should be completely covered.

Cover the pan, bring the liquid to the boil and simmer for 1½–2 hours. Remove from the heat and strain the stock into a jug. Leave the carcass to become cold.

Heat the oil in the pan, add the bacon and celery and fry gently for 5 minutes till the bacon becomes crisp. Meanwhile, wash the leeks thoroughly, then cut into 1 inch (2·5 cm) thick rings. Add half to the pan and continue cooking for 2 minutes.

Make the stock up to 2½ pints (1·5 litres) with extra water and add to the pan with the pearl barley, salt and pepper. Cover and simmer gently for 1 hour.

Remove any chicken meat from the carcass, then discard the bones. Stir the meat, remaining leeks and mint sauce into the soup and continue cooking for 30–40 minutes or until the pearl barley is cooked.

Chicken and
Leek Soup

POTATO, ONION & LEEK

Serves 6

1½ lb (700g) leeks

1 oz (25g) butter or margarine

4 oz (100g) onions, peeled and chopped

1 lb (450g) potatoes, peeled and cubed

1½ pints (900 ml) chicken stock, or water and 2 chicken stock cubes

Salt and pepper

¼ level teaspoon ground mace

5 fl oz (150 ml) single cream, optional

TO GARNISH:

Croutons

Trim the leeks and discard most of the dark green leaves. Wash thoroughly. Drain, then slice finely.

Melt the butter in a large saucepan, add the leeks and onion and cook gently, without browning, for about 5 minutes. Add the potatoes and then stir in the chicken stock or water and stock cubes, salt, pepper and mace. Bring to the boil, cover and simmer gently for 30 minutes.

Allow to cool slightly, then blend to a purée in a liquidizer or pass through a sieve. Reheat for a few minutes, then stir in the cream if used and season to taste.

Serve the soup garnished with a sprinkling of fried or toasted croutons.

BEAN AND TOMATO SOUP

Serves 4–6

1 oz (25g) margarine

4 oz (100g) onion, peeled and chopped

4 oz (100g) carrot, peeled and grated

15 oz (420g) can butter beans

14 oz (397g) can tomatoes

½ pint (300 ml) water

1 chicken stock cube

¼ level teaspoon thyme

Salt and pepper

Melt the margarine, add the onion and carrot and fry gently until soft.

Stir in the butter beans and liquid, tomatoes, water, stock cube, thyme, salt and pepper. Simmer for 15 minutes.

Check seasoning before serving.

HUNGARIAN SAUSAGE SOUP

Serves 4–6

2 tablespoons oil

1 lb (450g) onions, peeled and sliced

1 green pepper, de-seeded and sliced

15 oz (420g) can tomatoes

2 level tablespoons paprika pepper

½ level teaspoon caraway seeds

1½ pints (900 ml) water

1 beef stock cube

1 level teaspoon salt

Black pepper

8 oz (225g) potato, peeled and diced

8 oz (225g) packet smoked pork sausage, thickly sliced

8 oz (225g) black pudding, skinned, sliced and quartered

Heat the oil in a large saucepan, add the onion, cover and gently fry for 5 minutes. Add the green pepper, tomatoes, paprika, caraway, water, stock cube, salt and pepper. Bring the mixture to the boil, stir, cover and simmer gently for 30 minutes.

Stir in the potato, smoked sausage and black pudding, cover and continue cooking for 30 minutes.

Season to taste with salt and pepper and, if liked, serve with a spoonful of soured cream or yogurt swirled on the top of each portion.

VEGETABLE MULLIGATAWNY

Serves 4–6

1 oz (25g) margarine

1 lb (450g) onions, peeled and chopped

Bean and
Tomato Soup

| 12 oz (350g) courgettes, washed and chopped |
| 4 oz (100g) potatoes, peeled and chopped |
| 1½ oz (40g) long grain rice |
| 4 fl oz (125 ml) water |
| 7 oz (210g) can tomatoes |
| Just under ½ pint (300 ml) stock |
| 2 teaspoons Worcestershire sauce |
| 1 level teaspoon Madras curry powder |
| Pepper |
| ½ level teaspoon salt |

Melt the margarine in a large saucepan, add the onion and cook for about 7 minutes until golden brown. Stir in the courgettes and potatoes. Cover and cook over a low heat for 15–20 minutes or until vegetables are soft.

Meanwhile, place the rice and water in a small saucepan, bring to the boil, cover and cook for 10–12 minutes until liquid has been absorbed and rice is tender.

When the vegetables are soft, allow to cool slightly. Add the tomatoes, then purée either through a sieve, liquidizer or food processor. Pour back into the pan, add the stock, Worcestershire sauce, curry powder, pepper and salt. Reheat for 10 minutes, stirring occasionally. Serve with poppadums.

CULLEN SKINK

Serves 4–6

1 lb (450g) smoked haddock

1 large onion, peeled and thinly sliced

1 lb (450g) cooked mashed potato

1 pint (600 ml) milk

1 level tablespoon cornflour

$\frac{1}{2}$ level teaspoon salt

White pepper

TO GARNISH:

Chopped parsley

Place the haddock and onion in a large saucepan and just cover with water. Simmer for 10 minutes until the fish is cooked. Drain fish and onion. Retain liquid.

Remove all skin and any bones from the fish and flake the flesh into large pieces.

In a pan mix the potato with the fish liquid until smooth. Stir in the milk and onion.

Blend the cornflour to a smooth paste with a tablespoon of water, then add to the pan. Bring to the boil, stirring, and cook for 1 minute. Reduce heat, add the fish and season to taste. Simmer very gently for 10–15 minutes – do not allow to boil. Serve garnished with parsley.

RED PEPPER SOUP

Serves 4–6

2 oz (50g) margarine

8 oz (225g) onions, peeled and chopped

8 oz (225g) red peppers, de-seeded and chopped

1 clove garlic, peeled and crushed

3 level tablespoons flour

1 level tablespoon paprika pepper

2 level tablespoons tomato purée

$1\frac{1}{2}$ pints (900 ml) stock, or water and 2 chicken stock cubes

1–2 teaspoons vinegar

Salt and pepper

Melt the margarine, add the onions and peppers and fry gently, without browning, for 5–8 minutes until the onions are soft. Stir frequently. Mix in the garlic, then the flour and paprika and cook for 1 minute.

Stir in the tomato purée, then the stock or water and stock cubes.

Bring to the boil, stirring. Reduce the heat, add the vinegar and salt and pepper to taste. Simmer for 20 minutes.

CELERY AND BLUE CHEESE SOUP

This is also good made with Stilton cheese.

Serves 4

1 oz (25g) butter or margarine

1 large onion, peeled and finely chopped

1 head of celery, trimmed and finely chopped

1 level tablespoon flour

1 pint (600 ml) water

1 chicken stock cube, crumbled

$\frac{1}{2}$ pint (300 ml) milk

Salt and pepper

2 oz (50g) Danish Blue cheese, crumbled

Melt butter or margarine in a pan, add onion and celery and fry gently until soft. Stir in the flour, then add water. Bring to the boil, stirring, and cook for 1 minute. Stir in the stock cube and simmer until the celery is soft – about 30 minutes.

Stir in the milk and season to taste. Heat again but don't boil.

Serve with the cheese crumbled on top.

VEGETABLES AND SALADS

Versatile, colourful, healthy – vegetables work wonders in a variety of ways, and need never be boring. Marvellous in money-stretching meals, they are full of vitamins, minerals and fibre – it's really a case of the more you have, the better!

I've also put together some tasty salad recipes, each one dressed to suit the season.

VEGETABLES

Here is a brief guide to some of the more unusual vegetables

Celeriac: is similar in appearance to the turnip. Choose the smoothest-looking ones. Cut in quarters, then peel. Celeriac discolours when cut, so if it is to be left for any length of time submerge it in a basin of water and add 1–2 tablespoons of vinegar.

Celeriac has a mild celery flavour and is easy to chew.

Fennel: looks like a pale green, giant bulb with fingers. Delicious eaten raw like celery in salads. Has a slight aniseed flavour. As the outer layer is usually a bit stringy it's best to remove it and cut back the stems. Keep the fine, ferny leaves; chop and scatter them over a cooked dish or salad. Allow 1 large head per person. Cut in half or quarter to cook.

Salsify and Scorzonera: long carrot-shaped roots – salsify has a whitish skin and scorzonera a brownish-black one; both have a similar delicious flavour. Top and tail, then scrub under cold running water. Either peel before cooking – adding lemon juice and water to prevent discolouration – or cook and then rub off skin. Don't cut the roots unless they won't fit into the pan. Cook carefully as these vegetables can overcook.

Bean sprouts: can be grown at home, but are being sold by more and more shops. Best eaten on the day they are bought as they lose crispness and freshness quickly. Rinse and drain well. Can be eaten on their own as a salad. Also delicious as a sandwich filling like mustard and cress or in stir-fry dishes.

Spinach: one of the most delicious of all leaf vegetables. Should look bright and lively – not limp and wilted. Pick over the leaves discarding any blemished ones and tough stalks. Wash them in several changes of water. Cook with no extra water.

Courgettes: should look firm and fresh. They do not need to be peeled. Slice away the stalk and any small, brown patch at the other end of the courgette before cutting into desired size. The larger the courgettes the less tender and tasty they are.

Aubergines: should look shiny and tight. The flavour is not affected by size. Unless making a purée, do not peel. Slice, cube or halve and stuff. Sprinkle 1 tablespoon of salt over the prepared aubergine and leave for half an hour. This will extract some of the slightly bitter juice which is then rinsed away under cold water. Dry the vegetables before use.

Peppers: should look shiny and sleek. Red are sweeter and more mellow in flavour than green. Yellow and white peppers are similar in flavour to the red ones.

Green peppers that have red and yellow patches on them are beginning to ripen. Under favourable conditions they will ripen fully, but often they just wrinkle and deteriorate.

The pepper should be de-seeded before use. Either halve and scoop out the seeds, or cut in rings; if the pepper is to be used whole, cut off the top and scoop out the seeds.

THE BEST WAY TO COOK NEW POTATOES

Serves 2–3

1 tablespoon oil

$\frac{1}{2}$ oz (15g) butter

1 lb (450g) new potatoes, washed and scrubbed

2 sprigs fresh mint

$\frac{1}{2}$ level teaspoon salt

Melt oil and butter in a saucepan with a tight-fitting lid. Add the potatoes, mint and salt, cover with lid and cook over a low heat, shaking the pan occasionally for 20–25 minutes.

Serve hot with more fresh mint, if liked.

Not suitable for freezing.

NEW POTATOES IN A CURRY CREAM SAUCE

Serve on their own or with lamb chops, poached white fish, hard-boiled eggs, or even with Sunday lunch!

Serves 4

$1\frac{1}{2}$ lb (700g) new potatoes

2 tablespoons oil

1 onion, peeled and chopped

1 small cooking apple, peeled and diced

2 oz (50g) sultanas

2 level teaspoons curry powder

1 level teaspoon flour

$\frac{1}{4}$ pint (150 ml) water

1–2 level tablespoons mango chutney

4–5 tablespoons single cream

2 teaspoons lemon juice

Salt and pepper

Scrub the potatoes. Cook in their skins until tender, about 10–15 minutes.

Heat the oil and gently fry the onion until it begins to soften. Add the apple, sultanas and curry powder. Gently fry for about 5 minutes, stirring all the time to prevent sticking. Stir in the flour and cook for $\frac{1}{2}$

minute. Add the water and chutney and bring to the boil, stirring. Stir in the cream, lemon juice and salt and pepper to taste.

Drain the potatoes and put into a serving dish or dishes. Spoon over the sauce and serve.

Not suitable for freezing.

HOT POTATO AND SAUSAGE SALAD

Serves 3–4

1 lb (450g) new potatoes, scrubbed and boiled

1 lb (450g) beef sausages, cooked

8 oz (225g) new carrots, coarsely grated

FOR THE DRESSING:

2 tablespoons oil

1 tablespoon malt vinegar

2 level teaspoons horseradish sauce

$\frac{1}{2}$ level teaspoon salt

$\frac{1}{2}$ level teaspoon prepared English mustard

1 bunch spring onions, finely chopped

Cut the potatoes into 1 inch (2.5 cm) cubes. Cut the cooked sausages into 1 inch (2.5 cm) thick chunks; mix both with the carrot.

Make the dressing: put all the ingredients into a screw-topped jar. Screw the lid on tightly and shake vigorously. Pour the dressing over the potato mixture and stir to coat. Turn into a serving dish.

Not suitable for freezing.

NEW POTATO SUPPER

Serves 4

1–$1\frac{1}{2}$ lb (450–700g) new potatoes, scrubbed

$1\frac{1}{2}$ oz (40g) margarine or butter

$1\frac{1}{2}$ oz (40g) flour

$\frac{3}{4}$ pint (450 ml) milk

1 level teaspoon French mustard

$\frac{1}{8}$ level teaspoon nutmeg

Salt and pepper

4 oz (100g) boiled ham, diced

4 oz (100g) mushrooms, sliced

3 oz (75g) grated cheese

Cook the potatoes in boiling water until tender, about 15 minutes. Drain, peel if liked and cut into cubes.

Melt the margarine or butter in a large saucepan. Stir in the flour, then the milk. Bring the sauce to the boil stirring all the time, and cook for 1 minute. Reduce the heat, add the mustard, nutmeg and salt and pepper to taste.

Add the potatoes, ham, mushrooms and 2 oz (50g) of the cheese; stir and heat gently for 4–5 minutes. Pour the mixture into a 2 pint (1·1 litre) shallow, ovenproof dish. Sprinkle the rest of the cheese over the top; place under hot grill to brown.

Not suitable for freezing.

CRUNCHY CRACKER BEANS

Serves 4

1 lb (450 g) French beans

2 oz (50g) butter

1 oz (25g) cream crackers, crushed

$\frac{1}{2}$ oz (15g) flaked almonds

Salt and pepper

Top and tail the beans and cut in half if large. Cook them in boiling, salted water for 8–10 minutes or until tender. Drain.

Meanwhile, melt the butter, add the almonds and fry them until golden brown, stirring frequently. Add the crushed crackers and cook until golden. Add seasoning and sprinkle over the French beans to serve.

Not suitable for freezing.

POTATOES IN PARCELS

Serves 4

1–1$\frac{1}{2}$ lb (450–700g) new potatoes, small ones if possible

2 rashers unsmoked bacon, derinded

2 large sprigs of mint

Black pepper

1 oz (25g) butter

Scrub or scrape the potatoes, choosing fairly small ones as near the same size as possible.

Cut 4 squares of foil of approximately 8 inches (20 cm) each and butter them well. Put about 6 potatoes in each square, add half a rasher of bacon cut into squares, and a few mint leaves. Season with pepper.

Wrap up each parcel and place in the centre of a moderately hot oven, gas mark 5 or 375°F/190°C and bake for 30 minutes, or a little longer, depending on size.

Not suitable for freezing.

CREAMY CARROT FLAN

Serves 4–5

FOR THE PASTRY:

6 oz (175g) plain flour

$\frac{1}{2}$ level teaspoon salt

1$\frac{1}{2}$ oz (40g) margarine

1$\frac{1}{2}$ oz (40g) lard

5–6 teaspoons water

FOR THE FILLING:

1 lb (450g) new carrots

3 eggs, size 3, hard-boiled

3 oz (75g) cream cheese

5 oz (150g) carton plain yogurt

$\frac{1}{2}$ level teaspoon salt

Black pepper

$\frac{1}{2}$ level teaspoon sugar

Good pinch of ground ginger

Sift the flour and salt into a bowl. Add the fats and rub them in until the mixture resembles breadcrumbs. Stir in the water to give a soft, not sticky, dough. Knead lightly, then wrap and chill for 20 minutes.

From top:
Mushrooms in
Lemon Sauce,
page 23;
Creamy Carrot
Flan, page 21;
New Potato
Supper, page
20; Potatoes in
Parcels, page
21; Crunchy
Cracker Beans,
page 21

Meanwhile, trim and wash the carrots, scrape or peel as necessary. Boil in salted water for 15 minutes or until just tender. Drain and rinse under cold water. Drain again. Set the oven to fairly hot, gas mark 6 or 400°F/200°C.

On a lightly-floured surface roll out the pastry and line an 8 inch (20 cm) flan ring. Prick the base well with a fork and line with a piece of crumpled foil or greaseproof paper and baking beans. Bake above the centre of the oven for 20 minutes, then remove the lining and bake for a further 10 minutes. Leave to cool.

Cut the carrots into 2 inch (5 cm) sticks; roughly chop one of the hard-boiled eggs.

In a basin, beat the cream cheese to soften and gradually beat in the yogurt. Add salt and pepper, sugar and ginger, then stir in the chopped egg and carrots. Spoon the mixture into the baked pastry flan. Garnish with the remaining eggs cut into quarters.

To freeze: the baked flan will freeze for up to 4 months. Thaw and crisp in moderate oven for 15 minutes. Fill as in recipe.

CARROT AND APPLE SAUTÉ

Serve with brown rice or with roast or grilled pork.

Serves 4–6

1½ lb (700g) carrots, peeled and cut into thin sticks
2 oz (50g) butter
12 oz (350g) onions, peeled, halved and sliced
12 oz (350g) dessert apples, peeled, cored and sliced
1 oz (25g) raisins

½ **level teaspoon salt**

Pepper

½ **level teaspoon sugar**

2 level teaspoons mint jelly

Cook the carrots in boiling, salted water for about 15 minutes or until tender.

Meanwhile, melt the butter in a large frying pan and gently fry the onion for 10 minutes, stirring frequently.

Drain the carrots and add to the onion with the sliced apples, raisins, salt, pepper, sugar and mint jelly. Continue cooking for about 5 minutes, stirring to coat the vegetables evenly with the juices.

Not suitable for freezing.

MUSHROOMS IN LEMON SAUCE

Serve these hot as a vegetable dish or as a starter.

Serves 4–6

2 oz (50g) butter

¼ **pint (150 ml) milk plus 2 tablespoons**

1 lb (450g) medium-large mushrooms, wiped and trimmed

1 lemon

2 level teaspoons cornflour

Salt and pepper

Melt the butter in a medium-sized saucepan; add the ¼ pint (150 ml) milk and the mushrooms, leaving them whole. Pare the rind off the lemon and cut into small diamond shapes; add to the pan. Bring to the boil, cover and simmer gently for 5 minutes. Remove from the heat.

Blend the cornflour with the 2 tablespoons milk and stir into the mushrooms. Bring to the boil, stirring. Cook until thick. Season with salt and pepper. Remove from the heat and stir in the lemon juice.

Not suitable for freezing.

HOT CREAMY MUSHROOMS

Serve as a lunch with a salad or as a substantial starter.

Serves 2

2 oz (50g) butter

1 small onion, peeled and finely chopped

8 oz (225g) mushrooms, wiped and sliced

5 oz (150g) double cream

1 egg, size 3, beaten

Grated rind and juice of 1 lemon

½ **level teaspoon salt**

Black pepper

Grated nutmeg

1 tablespoon chopped parsley

FOR THE TOPPING:

1 clove garlic, peeled and crushed

3 slices white bread

Set the oven to moderate, gas mark 4 or 350°F/180°C.

Melt 1 oz (25g) of butter in a frying pan and gently fry the onion for 2 minutes. Add the mushrooms and turn in the butter for ½ minute. Remove from the heat and allow to cool slightly.

Pour the cream into a basin and beat in the egg. Add the lemon juice and rind, salt, pepper, nutmeg and parsley. Add the mushroom mixture to the cream, mix together and then divide between two individual, buttered gratin dishes.

Cream the remaining 1 oz (25g) of butter with the garlic then use to spread over each slice of bread. Remove the crusts then cut each slice into nine squares. Overlap the bread in a circle on top of the mushrooms.

Bake in centre of oven for 30 minutes.

Not suitable for freezing.

COURGETTE AND CREAM CHEESE BAKE

Serves 4

2 oz (50g) butter

1$\frac{1}{2}$ lb (700g) courgettes, cut into $\frac{1}{2}$ inch (1 cm) chunks

8 oz (225g) onions, peeled and sliced

4 oz (100g) button mushrooms, wiped and halved

6 oz (175g) cream cheese

4 oz (100g) wholemeal breadcrumbs

$\frac{1}{2}$ level teaspoon sage

$\frac{1}{2}$ level teaspoon rosemary

1 level teaspoon salt

Black pepper

1 oz (25g) mixed chopped nuts

Melt the butter in a large saucepan. Add the courgettes, onion and mushrooms and fry gently for 10 minutes, stirring often.

Set the oven to moderately hot, gas mark 5 or 375°F/190°C.

Beat the cream cheese until soft then stir in the breadcrumbs, sage, rosemary, salt and pepper.

Remove the vegetables from the heat and stir in the cream cheese mixture. Stir carefully as the cheese melts and coats the vegetables. Spoon into a 2$\frac{1}{2}$ pint (1·5 litre), shallow, ovenproof dish and sprinkle the nuts over.

Cover with greaseproof paper and cook above the centre of the oven for 30–40 minutes, removing the paper 10 minutes before the end of cooking.

To freeze: freeze when cold for up to 2 months. Reheat from frozen in a moderately hot oven for 30–40 minutes.

RED CABBAGE AND CORN MEDLEY

This medley goes well with poached eggs or sausages.

Serves 4–6

1$\frac{1}{2}$ lb (700g) red cabbage, trimmed and thinly sliced

1$\frac{1}{2}$ level teaspoons salt

1 oz (25g) butter

12 oz (350g) cooked beetroot, skinned and diced

7 oz (210g) can sweetcorn, drained

1 tablespoon oil

3 tablespoons vinegar

Black pepper

$\frac{1}{8}$ level teaspoon ground allspice or nutmeg

Place the cabbage in a large, deep frying pan. Cover with water and add 1 teaspoon of salt. Bring to the boil then cook for 5 minutes or until just tender. Drain.

Push the cabbage to one side of the pan, add butter and heat to melt. Add remaining ingredients and cook over a medium heat, stirring frequently, until well mixed and hot – about 3 minutes.

Not suitable for freezing.

PEPERONI RIPIENI

Serves 2–4

1 aubergine weighing about 12 oz (350g)

2$\frac{1}{2}$ level teaspoons salt

2 red peppers weighing 4–6 oz (100–175g) each

2 green peppers weighing 4 oz (100g) each

2 tablespoons oil

1 small onion, peeled and sliced

8 oz (225g) streaky bacon cut into 1 inch (2.5 cm) pieces

1 courgette approx. 4 oz (100g), cut into $\frac{1}{4}$ inch (5 mm) slices

1 large clove garlic, peeled and crushed

7 oz (210g) can tomatoes

$\frac{1}{2}$ level teaspoon mixed herbs

Pepper

Trim the stalk from the aubergine. Dice aubergine into $\frac{1}{2}$ inch (1 cm) cubes, sprinkle with two level teaspoons salt and leave for 30 minutes. Rinse aubergines in cold water and pat dry.

Set the oven to moderately hot, gas mark 5 or 375°F/190°C.

From top:
Carrot and
Apple Sauté,
page 22;
Courgette and
Cream Cheese
Bake; Hot
Creamy
Mushrooms,
page 23; Red
Cabbage and
Corn Medley

Peperoni
Ripieni, page 24

From the stem end of the peppers, cut a lid $\frac{1}{2}$–$\frac{3}{4}$ inch (1–2 cm) down. Carefully remove the seeds and membrane. Place the pepper shells and lids in a pan of boiling water, bring water back to the boil and blanch (i.e., boil for 2 minutes). Remove from heat, drain and cool.

Heat the oil in a large heavy frying pan and gently fry the onion and bacon for 2–3 minutes. Remove from heat, stir in the aubergines, courgettes, garlic, tomatoes, mixed herbs, remaining salt and pepper.

Return filling to the heat, cover and cook for 10–15 minutes until just cooked.

If necessary, trim the base of the peppers very slightly to make them flat. Stand the pepper shells in a heatproof dish containing 1 tablespoon of vinegar and 1 tablespoon of water. Divide up filling and spoon into each shell. Replace lids and bake uncovered for 30 minutes until peppers have softened.

To freeze: do not cook. Freeze for up to 1 month. Thaw for 1 hour then cook as recipe, increasing the time as necessary.

SWEET AND SOUR STIR-FRY

From top:
Sweet and Sour
Stir-Fry;
Crunchy Topped
Ratatouille,
page 28; Fennel
Florence Style,
page 28

Serves 4

FOR THE SAUCE:

8 oz (225g) can pineapple chunks

1 level tablespoon cornflour

2 tablespoons malt vinegar

3 tablespoons soy sauce

$\frac{1}{2}$ level teaspoon ground ginger

1 level tablespoon sugar

FOR THE VEGETABLE MIXTURE:

2 tablespoons oil

6 spring onions, trimmed and sliced into rings

12 oz (350g) carrots, peeled and cut into 2 inch (5 cm) long strips

4 sticks celery, cut into 2 inch (5 cm) long strips

$\frac{1}{4}$ cucumber, cut into 2 inch (5 cm) long strips

4 oz (100g) fresh or frozen green beans

4 oz (100g) button mushrooms, sliced

8 oz (225g) can bean sprouts

Drain the juice from the pineapple and use some of it to blend the cornflour to a smooth paste in a pan. (Reserve pineapple chunks.) Then stir in the rest of the juice together with the malt vinegar, soy sauce, ginger and sugar. Bring to the boil, stirring, and cook for $\frac{1}{2}$ minute. Keep the sauce hot over a low heat until ready to serve.

Heat the oil in a large frying pan or wok. Add the spring onion and fry for a minute. Then add the prepared carrots, celery, cucumber and green beans and fry over a high heat, stirring constantly with a wooden spoon for about 3 minutes. Add the mushrooms and pineapple and cook for a further minute, then stir in the bean sprouts and cook for $\frac{1}{2}$ minute.

Pour over the sauce, stir to mix well and reheat. Serve immediately.

Not suitable for freezing.

FENNEL FLORENCE STYLE

Serves 4

2 large heads fennel, each about 1 lb (450g)

FOR THE SAUCE:

8 oz (225g) onion, peeled and chopped

2 tablespoons oil

14 oz (397g) can tomatoes

1 rounded tablespoon tomato purée

6 stuffed green olives, sliced

$\frac{1}{2}$ level teaspoon marjoram

1 bay leaf

$\frac{1}{4}$ pint (150 ml) water

Pepper

$\frac{1}{2}$ level teaspoon salt

$\frac{1}{4}$ level teaspoon sugar

1 level tablespoon cornflour

FOR THE TOPPING:

2 oz (50g) cream cheese

3 oz (75g) Cheddar cheese, grated

1 tablespoon grated Parmesan cheese

Trim the fennel tops to 1–2 inches (2·5–5 cm).

Place the fennel in a pan of boiling, salted water and cook for about 30 minutes. Drain, then cut in half and place in a shallow, ovenproof dish.

Set the oven to fairly hot, gas mark 6 or 400°F/200°C.

Meawhile make the sauce. Gently fry the onion in the oil until it begins to soften. Stir in the canned tomatoes, tomato purée, green olives, marjoram, bay leaf, water, pepper and salt, sugar and cornflour which has been blended to a smooth paste with a little water. Bring to the boil and simmer for 1–2 minutes. Pour over the fennel in the dish.

To make the topping, blend all three cheeses together and dot in lumps over the fennel.

Bake towards the top of the oven for 30 minutes, until the cheese has browned.

Not suitable for freezing.

CRUNCHY TOPPED RATATOUILLE

Serves 4–6

8 oz (225g) aubergine

1 level tablespoon salt

1 oz (25g) margarine

8 oz (225g) onion, peeled and sliced

1 clove garlic, peeled and crushed

14 oz (397g) can tomatoes

5 oz (130g) can tomato purée

$\frac{1}{2}$ pint (300 ml) water

1 level teaspoon basil

$1\frac{1}{2}$ level teaspoons salt and pepper, mixed

1 lb (450g) courgettes, trimmed and thickly sliced

1 green pepper, weighing about 8 oz (225g), de-seeded and sliced

1 small cauliflower

FOR THE TOPPING:

1–2 oz (25–50g) margarine

1 clove garlic, peeled and crushed

3–4 slices bread, diced

Wipe the aubergine, cut in half lengthwise and slice thickly. Spread the aubergine slices on a plate and sprinkle with the salt. Leave to one side for 15 minutes.

Meanwhile melt margarine in a large saucepan. Add onion and gently fry for 3 minutes. Stir in the garlic, then tomatoes, tomato purée, water, basil, salt and pepper.

Add the sliced courgettes and green pepper. Bring to the boil, stir, reduce the heat and gently simmer, covered, for 10 minutes.

Meanwhile, under cold running water, rinse the aubergine free of salt. Divide the cauliflower into small sprigs and add, together with the aubergine, to the pan. Stir and simmer for a further 15 minutes. Taste and add further seasoning as necessary.

During last few minutes of cooking melt margarine, stir in crushed garlic, then fry bread cubes until golden and crisp. Sprinkle them over the ratatouille to serve.

To freeze: freeze without the topping for up to 3 months. Thaw for 1 hour then reheat gently in saucepan, stirring with a fork. Add water if necessary. Add topping as above.

SALADS

GRATED CARROT AND PEAR SALAD

Serve with cold sliced meats and crusty bread.

Serves 4

1 lb (450g) carrots, peeled and grated

6 spring onions, trimmed and sliced finely

2 dessert pears, peeled, cored and diced

4 oz (100g) sultanas

2 oz (50g) salted peanuts

Grated rind and juice of 1 orange

1 level tablespoon runny honey

1 tablespoon oil

1 tablespoon lemon juice

$\frac{1}{4}$ level teaspoon salt

Good pinch of black pepper

Place grated carrot, spring onions, diced pear, sultanas and peanuts into a bowl. Mix the grated rind and juice from the orange, honey, oil, lemon juice, salt and pepper together. Pour over the salad and toss to coat.

Not suitable for freezing.

EASTERN TWO BEAN SALAD

Serves 2–3

14 oz (397g) can red kidney beans

14 oz (397g) can chick peas

Lettuce leaves

6 sticks celery

1 large onion, peeled and chopped

4 oz (100g) button mushrooms, sliced

1 tablespoon lemon juice

1 tablespoon oil

2 level tablespoons curried mayonnaise

2 level tablespoons chopped parsley

Drain the kidney beans and chick peas and rinse away all the brine in a colander. Drain well and place in a serving bowl lined with lettuce leaves.

Chop the celery into strips widthways, then mix into the beans with the onion and mushrooms. Mix the lemon juice with the oil and mayonnaise and toss the salad in it.

Sprinkle the parsley over and serve.

Not suitable for freezing.

ORIENTAL CHICKEN SALAD

Serves 4

10 oz (275g) bean sprouts

8 oz (225g) carrots, peeled and grated or cut into thin sticks

4 sticks celery, cut into thin sticks

2 level tablespoons garlic mayonnaise

$1\frac{1}{2}$ tablespoons soy sauce

$\frac{1}{4}$ level tablespoon ground ginger

8 oz (225g) boned and cooked chicken, cut into $\frac{1}{2}$ inch (1 cm) cubes

Place all the vegetables in a large bowl and toss them together.

Mix the garlic mayonnaise, soy sauce and ginger together, then add to the salad and mix well.

Add the cubed chicken and lightly mix into the salad.

Not suitable for freezing.

CAESAR SALAD

Serves 4–6

1/4 **pint (150 ml) oil**

1 clove garlic, peeled and crushed

8 oz (225g) streaky bacon, coarsely chopped

4 slices brown bread, crusts removed

1 egg, size 3

1 teaspoon Worcestershire sauce

1 tablespoon lemon juice

Pepper

2 oz (50g) can anchovy fillets

1 iceberg lettuce

2 oz (50g) walnuts, coarsely chopped

TO GARNISH:

Garlic croutons

Mix the oil and garlic together and leave for 30 minutes to flavour the oil.

Fry the bacon in 1 tablespoon of garlic oil until lightly brown and crispy. Remove from the pan with a slotted spoon and place to one side.

Cut the bread into 1 inch (2·5 cm) cubes. If necessary, add a little more oil to the pan, then fry the bread until golden brown on all sides. Remove from the pan, place to one side. Do not discard any oil or bacon juices left over.

Put the egg in a pan of boiling water and cook for 1 minute. Cool quickly in cold water then put the semi-cooked egg in a liquidizer or food processor. Add the remaining garlic oil, any strained juices from the frying pan, Worcestershire sauce, lemon juice, pepper and four anchovy fillets. Process until mixture is well blended and any pieces of cooked egg have been broken down.

Cut the lettuce into 1 inch (2·5 cm) chunks and place in a bowl with the walnuts and bacon. Pour the dressing over the top and mix well, seasoning with pepper if liked.

Turn into a serving dish, garnish with the remaining anchovies and garlic croutons.

Not suitable for freezing.

HOLIDAY SALAD

Serves 6

FOR THE DRESSING:

5 tablespoons oil

1 tablespoon lemon juice

1 tablespoon vinegar

1/2 **level tablespoon made English mustard**

1 level tablespoon parsley, finely chopped

Pepper

FOR THE SALAD:

8 oz (225g) mozzarella or Edam cheese

8 oz (225g) onion, peeled and sliced

12 oz (350g) tomatoes, sliced

1 avocado pear

Sprig of parsley

Mix all the dressing ingredients together, and season with pepper to taste.

Cut the cheese into 1/2 inch (1 cm) cubes. Place the onion, tomato and cheese in a bowl, add half the prepared dressing and toss.

Arrange the onion and tomato salad in a serving dish. Peel, then cut the avocado pear in half lengthways, remove the stone. Thinly slice the avocado pear lengthways and arrange on top of the salad.

Spoon the remaining dressing over the avocado and garnish the centre with a sprig of parsley.

Not suitable for freezing.

STUFFED PEPPER SLICES

Serves 4–6

8 oz (225g) cream cheese

2 level tablespoons lemon mayonnaise

2 oz (50g) mixed chopped nuts

3 level tablespoons chives, finely chopped

Pepper

1 red pepper [approx. 6 oz (175g)]

1 green pepper [approx. 6 oz (175g)]

Lettuce

Mix the cheese, mayonnaise, nuts and chives together; season with pepper.

From top:
Grated Carrot
and Pear Salad,
page 29;
Eastern Two
Bean Salad,
page 29;
Oriental
Chicken Salad,
page 29;
Holiday Salad;
Stuffed Pepper
Slices

Cut the stalk end from the peppers and carefully remove the seeds. Fill the peppers with the cheese mixture, pressing down well. Wrap in cling wrap and chill for 30 minutes.

To serve, slice the peppers into $\frac{1}{4}$ inch (5 mm) slices and arrange on a bed of lettuce

Not suitable for freezing.

FENNEL, FETA AND BLACK OLIVE SALAD

Serves 2

1 bulb fennel

6–8 black olives, stoned

1 spring onion, trimmed and sliced

3 oz (75g) feta cheese

2 tablespoons oil

Juice of $\frac{1}{2}$ lemon

Salt and pepper

Trim the roots of the fennel, wash if necessary, and slice thinly across the bulb.

Place in a glass serving dish with the stoned olives and sliced spring onion. Cut 2 oz (50g) of the cheese into dice and add to the fennel.

Put the rest of the cheese, oil and lemon juice in a basin and beat with a fork until well mixed. Add salt and pepper to taste.

Pour over the salad and toss ingredients until well coated.

Not suitable for freezing.

Fennel, Feta and Black Olive Salad

AVOCADO AND CHICKEN SALAD

Serves 3–4

FOR THE DRESSING:

Grated rind and juice of $\frac{1}{2}$ lemon

3 tablespoons mayonnaise

2 tablespoons natural yogurt

Pepper

FOR THE SALAD:

8 oz (225g) cooked chicken

1 pink grapefruit, skin and pith removed

2 avocados, peeled, stoned and diced

4 inches (10 cm) cucumber, diced

2 oz (50g) sultanas

2 bunches watercress

Mix all the dressing ingredients together and season with pepper.

Cut the chicken into strips about $\frac{1}{4}$ inch (5 mm) thick and 1 inch (2·5 cm) wide. Put chicken, segmented grapefruit, avocado, cucumber and sultanas in a bowl, add the dressing and mix together. Line individual serving dishes with watercress, spoon the salad on top and garnish with a slice of lemon.

Not suitable for freezing.

MEDITERRANEAN SUMMER SALAD

Serves 4

FOR THE SALAD:

2 red peppers, de-seeded and sliced

1 green pepper, de-seeded and sliced

8 oz (225g) courgettes, sliced thinly

12 oz (350g) onions, peeled and sliced

2 beefsteak tomatoes, sliced

FOR THE DRESSING:

6 tablespoons oil

3 tablespoons vinegar

2 level tablespoons tomato purée

1 teaspoon soy sauce

Mediterranean
Summer Salad

1 level tablespoon fresh tarragon, chopped, or 1
level teaspoon dried tarragon

1 level teaspoon sugar

Pepper

FOR THE TOPPING:

$4\frac{1}{2}$ oz (125g) can sardines in oil

2 oz (50g) Cheddar cheese, grated

1 teaspoon lemon juice

Pepper

$\frac{1}{2}$ French stick, sliced thickly

TO GARNISH:

Fresh parsley sprigs

Put all the salad ingredients in a bowl and
mix together. Blend the dressing ingredients
well, then pour over the salad and leave to
marinate for 30 minutes.

Mash the sardines, cheese and lemon juice
together, then season with pepper. Grill the
French stick slices until lightly browned on
both sides. Spread one side with the topping
and grill for 5–10 minutes until lightly
browned.

Spoon the salad on to one side of a serving
plate, arrange the sardine slices on the other
side, and garnish with parsley.

Not suitable for freezing.

SPICY RAISIN AND POTATO SALAD

Serves 4

$1\frac{1}{2}$ lb (700g) new potatoes

2 tablespoons oil

1 tablespoon malt vinegar

2 level tablespoons tomato ketchup

$\frac{1}{2}$ teaspoon tabasco sauce

2 oz (50g) raisins

1 level teaspoon paprika

1 red pepper, de-seeded and finely chopped

$\frac{1}{4}$ level teaspoon salt

Good pinch of pepper

Cook potatoes in boiling salted water until tender. Meanwhile, mix together oil, vinegar, ketchup, tabasco, raisins, paprika, red pepper, salt and pepper. Drain the potatoes when cooked. Holding the hot potatoes in a kitchen towel, peel them quickly and toss in the dressing. Serve cold if liked, or, to serve hot, return salad to pan and heat through.

Not suitable for freezing.

CRISPY SPROUT SALAD

Serves 4

4 oz (100g) streaky bacon, rind removed and cut into $\frac{1}{2}$ inch (1 cm) pieces

1 lb (450g) Brussels sprouts, cleaned and sliced

8 oz (225g) leeks, trimmed, washed and sliced

1 bunch watercress, trimmed

4 sticks celery, sliced

FOR THE DRESSING:

6 tablespoons oil

2 tablespoons vinegar

1 clove garlic, peeled and crushed

$\frac{1}{4}$ level teaspoon salt

Good pinch of pepper

Fry the bacon over a gentle heat until golden brown and crispy. Remove and drain on absorbent paper.

Place the Brussels sprouts, leeks, watercress and celery in a bowl. Make the dressing by mixing the oil, vinegar, garlic, salt and pepper together. Before serving, toss the salad in the dressing. Sprinkle over the cooked bacon.

Not suitable for freezing.

Crispy Sprout Salad; Herby Tomato Salad; Cauliflower Salad

HERBY TOMATO SALAD

Serves 4

8 oz (225g) onion, peeled and sliced

6 tablespoons oil

2 tablespoons vinegar

2 level teaspoons marjoram

8 oz (225g) tomatoes, sliced

2 oz (50g) black olives

4 oz (100g) Red Leicester cheese, cut into cubes

2 triangles of processed cheese, cut into cubes

Place the sliced onion in a serving bowl. Heat the oil and vinegar until hot.

Stir in the marjoram and pour over the onion and mix well. Cut each tomato slice in half and add to the salad with the olives and cheeses and toss well before serving.

Not suitable for freezing.

CAULIFLOWER SALAD

Serves 4

1 medium-sized cauliflower

$\frac{1}{2}$ cucumber, diced

1 green pepper, de-seeded and sliced

2 tomatoes, skinned

1 bunch spring onions, trimmed and finely chopped

FOR THE DRESSING:

6 tablespoons each of oil and vinegar

2 level tablespoons tomato ketchup

Pepper

$\frac{1}{2}$ level teaspoon salt

Cut the cauliflower into small florets and place in a bowl with the cucumber. Add the pepper. Cut each tomato into eight segments; add to the bowl with the spring onion.

Make up the dressing by combining all the remaining ingredients. Pour over the salad and toss. Allow to stand for about 1 hour before serving.

Not suitable for freezing.

Red Cabbage Salad with Apple

RED CABBAGE SALAD WITH APPLE

Serves 4

1 lb (450g) red cabbage, finely shredded

2 green apples

2 oranges

FOR THE DRESSING:

5 oz (150g) carton natural yogurt

4 tablespoons oil

4 tablespoons vinegar

1 clove garlic, peeled and crushed

¼ level teaspoon salt

Good pinch of pepper

Place the cabbage in a bowl. Core the apples and cut into cubes.

Peel the oranges with a sharp knife, removing as much pith as possible, and cut into segments. Place the apples and oranges in the bowl.

Mix all the dressing ingredients together, and pour over the salad. Toss before serving.

Not suitable for freezing.

FISH

I can never understand why fish isn't more popular. There are so many different types you can buy, it's comparatively cheap and easy to prepare, it's nutritious and it doesn't take long to cook, as my recipes prove. Fish is very tasty too – served with an unusual sauce or stuffing, it's hard to beat, so why not take my advice and rediscover fish? You'll be glad you did.

PLAICE AND ORANGE SUPREME

Serves 4

1½ lb (700g) plaice fillets

Salt and pepper

Lemon juice

1 lb (450g) leeks, trimmed and washed

1 medium cauliflower

1 oz (25g) margarine or butter

1 small onion, peeled and finely chopped

2 tablespoons oil

1 level tablespoon flour

½ pint (300 ml) milk and water, mixed

Grated rind and juice of half an orange

2–3 tablespoons single cream (optional)

Ask the fishmonger to skin and fillet the fish.

Cut each fillet in half lengthways. Season with a little salt and pepper, and lemon juice if liked. Roll up, skin-side inside, and secure with a wooden cocktail stick.

Cut the leeks into ½ inch (1 cm) thick slices. Trim and wash the cauliflower and divide into tiny sprigs.

Heat the margarine or butter and oil in a frying pan, add the leeks, cauliflower and onion. Fry gently for 2 minutes, then cover with a lid and cook for 4–5 minutes, until almost done. Stir in the flour and cook for one minute. Stir in the milk and water, orange rind and juice, and bring to the boil, stirring constantly. Add salt and pepper to taste. Reduce the heat to a simmer. Place the rolled fish on top of the vegetables. Cover tightly with lid and cook for about 25 minutes, or until the fish and cauliflower are cooked. Remove the cocktail sticks. Gently stir in the cream if used. Adjust seasoning.

Not suitable for freezing.

Plaice and Orange Supreme

SOLE VERONIQUE

Serves 6

6 lemon or Dover sole fillets each weighing about 4–5 oz (100–150g)

4 oz (100g) peeled prawns

Salt and pepper

1 tablespoon lemon juice

½ pint (300 ml) water

4 tablespoons white wine

A large blade of mace

6 black peppercorns

1 bay leaf

2 oz (50g) butter

3 level tablespoons flour

6 oz (175g) grapes, halved and de-seeded

Set the oven to moderate, gas mark 4 or 350°F/180°C.

Skin the fish if the fishmonger has not done it: lay the fillet skin side down on a work surface. Hold the tail end firmly in the fingers of the left hand (a little salt sprinkled on the tail will help you grip) and using a small knife make a sawing action to separate the flesh from the skin, holding the knife almost upright as you work.

Sprinkle a few prawns, a little seasoning and a dash of lemon juice over the skinned side of each fillet, then roll each one up from head to tail.

Place the fish rolls in an ovenproof dish, add the water, wine, rest of lemon juice, mace, peppercorns and bay leaf. Cover the dish with foil and poach in the centre of the oven for 20 minutes. The fish is cooked when it turns opaque and looks milky.

Carefully lift the fish rolls out of the dish, arrange on a serving dish and keep warm. Strain the liquid and reserve.

Melt the butter in a pan, stir in the flour and cook gently for ½ minute, then stir in the strained fish liquor. Bring to the boil, stirring, and cook for 1 minute. Add the grapes and heat for a moment or two then carefully pour over the fish and serve. Garnish with whole prawns, if liked.

Not suitable for freezing.

FISH IN PUFF PASTRY

Serves 4

6 fillets of whiting, total weight 1¼–1½ lb (600–700g)

1 bunch watercress

3 tablespoons soured cream

Grated rind of ½ large lemon

Salt and pepper

12 oz–1 lb (350–450g) puff pastry

Beaten egg or milk

Set the oven to hot, gas mark 7 or 425°F/220°C.

Remove any skin and bones from the fish.

To make the filling: trim watercress and chop roughly. Stir in the soured cream, lemon rind, and seasoning.

Roll out the pastry to a rectangle, approx. 15 × 11 inches (37·5–28 cm). Then place this on a baking sheet.

Place 3 fillets at one end of the pastry, then season with salt and pepper. Spread the filling over the top.

Cover with rest of fish. Brush edges of pastry with beaten egg or milk. Fold over pastry and press edges together. Trim and 'knock up' edges with the blade of a knife. Roll out trimmings and cut into ¼ inch (5 mm) wide strips, or little fish shapes if liked. Brush pie with egg or milk, and arrange trimmings in a decorative pattern on the top. Brush again with egg or milk.

Bake above the centre of the oven for 30–40 minutes, until the pastry is cooked to a golden brown.

To freeze: freeze when cold for up to 1 month. Thaw and eat cold or reheat in moderate oven for 20–25 minutes.

FISH AND POTATO PIE

Serves 4

1½ oz (40g) margarine

1 medium onion, chopped

1 oz (25g) flour

½ pint (300 ml) milk

3 gherkins, chopped

2 tablespoons malt or white vinegar

1 level teaspoon made English mustard

1 lb (450g) white fish, such as coley, skinned and cubed

Salt and pepper

1 lb (450g) potatoes, peeled and thinly sliced

Set the oven to moderately hot, gas mark 5 or 375°F/190°C. Grease a 2 pint (1.1 litre) shallow, ovenproof dish.

Melt 1 oz (25g) margarine, add the onion and fry it gently for 2–3 minutes. Stir in the flour and milk, then bring to the boil, stirring all the time, and cook for 1 minute. Remove pan from heat and add the gherkins, vinegar, mustard, fish and seasoning.

Arrange half the sliced potatoes in the bottom of the dish and season them well, then spoon over the fish mixture. Cover with the remaining potatoes, season them, then dot with the remaining margarine.

Cook the pie towards the top of the oven for about 1 hour or until the potatoes are cooked.

Not suitable for freezing.

SMOKY GOLDEN RICE POT

Serves 4

2 oz (50g) margarine

8 oz (225g) onions, peeled and chopped

6 oz (175g) bacon, derinded and chopped

6 oz (175g) long grain rice

1 level teaspoon curry powder

Juice of ½ lemon

1 pint (600 ml) water

Pepper

1 lb (450g) smoked cod, or other smoked fish

7 oz (210g) can sweetcorn niblets, drained

TO GARNISH:

Fresh, chopped parsley

3 lemon slices

Melt the margarine in a large saucepan. Add the onion and bacon, and fry gently until cooked. Stir in the rice and curry powder, and cook for 1 minute, stirring constantly. Pour the lemon juice and water into the pan, season with pepper, then cover and simmer gently for 10 minutes.

Meanwhile remove skin and bones from fish, and cut into 1½ inch (4 cm) pieces.

Stir into the rice mixture with the drained sweetcorn. Cover and cook for 10 minutes or until the fish is cooked.

Turn into a serving dish, and garnish with parsley and lemon slices.

Not suitable for freezing.

SMOKED FISH CAKES

Makes 6

1 lb (450g) potatoes

4 oz (100g) onion

8 oz (225g) smoked mackerel

2 eggs, size 3

3 level tablespoons flour

½ level teaspoon baking powder

1 level teaspoon salt

½ teaspoon pepper

Oil for frying

Fish and Potato Pie

Smoked Fish Cakes

Generous pinch of caster sugar

½ level teaspoon dry mustard powder

A few finely chopped herbs

Drain the fish, then flake it with a fork and put in a serving dish. Top and tail the beans. If using runner beans, slice them thinly, but cut French beans into 2 inch (5 cm) lengths. Have ready a pan of boiling salted water and cook the beans for about 10 minutes, until tender.

Drain in a sieve or colander and run under cold water to cool before arranging over the tuna fish.

Peel the tomatoes. The skins should come off easily if you plunge them into boiling water for the count of 20, and transfer immediately into cold water.

Cut the tomatoes into quarters and remove pips and centres. Keep several pieces aside for decoration and arrange the rest on top of the beans. Slice the cucumber thinly, peeling it if preferred, and arrange a layer over the tomatoes.

Briefly soak the anchovy fillets in a little milk to remove any excess saltiness, then halve each fillet lengthways and arrange in a criss-cross design over the salad. Halve the olives and lay them in the anchovy diamond shapes. Place the reserved tomatoes around edge of dish.

To make the French dressing, place all the ingredients in a screw-topped jar. Shake well, then pour the dressing over the salad about 15 minutes before serving. This dressing keeps very well in a screw-topped jar, but always shake it well before using.

Not suitable for freezing.

Peel the potatoes and onion and grate them into a bowl. Leave for 10 minutes then squeeze out excess liquid.

Skin the fish and break it into small pieces. Mix the fish and potato with the eggs, flour, baking powder and seasoning, stirring together well.

Mark the mixture into six, spoon each portion into the hot oil and fry for about 4 minutes on each side or until cooked and golden brown.

Not suitable for freezing.

SALAD NIÇOISE

Serves 5–6

Two 7 oz (210g) cans tuna fish in oil

1 lb (450g) runner or French beans

1 lb (450g) tomatoes

½ large cucumber

2 oz (50g) can anchovy fillets

8 black olives, stoned

FOR THE FRENCH DRESSING:

2 tablespoons cooking oil

1 tablespoon vinegar

Pepper

1 level teaspoon salt

COLD MACKEREL WITH TANGY HORSERADISH SAUCE

Serves 2

2 medium-sized mackerel, prepared

1 small lemon, quartered

1 bay leaf

Few sprigs of parsley

½ level teaspoon mixed herbs

Summer
Mackerel

1 small onion, peeled and sliced

1 carrot, peeled and sliced

10 black peppercorns

FOR THE SAUCE:

3 oz (75g) cream cheese

1 level tablespoon creamed horseradish

2 gherkins, finely chopped

Pepper

$\frac{1}{2}$ level teaspoon salt

Wash the mackerel, remove the heads and trim the tails and fins.

Place the lemon quarters, bay leaf, parsley, mixed herbs, onion, carrot and peppercorns in a large frying pan and add water to a depth of $1\frac{1}{2}$ inches (4 cm). Bring to the boil, cover with a lid and simmer for 5 minutes.

Place the mackerel on top of the vegetables, cover with lid and poach the fish gently for 15–20 minutes. Remove from the heat and leave mackerel to cool in stock.

When cold, remove the mackerel and, using a round-bladed knife, carefully peel away skin. Arrange fish on a serving plate.

To make the sauce, cream the cheese in a small basin until soft and then beat in the horseradish until smooth. Stir in 3 tablespoons of strained fish stock, half the chopped gherkin and the seasoning.

Spoon the sauce over the mackerel and sprinkle with the rest of the chopped gherkin.

To freeze: freeze for up to 1 month. Thaw and serve, adding garnish.

SUMMER MACKEREL

Serves 4

3 lb (1·35 kg) whole fresh mackerel

1 lb (450g) carrots, peeled and cut into sticks

1 lb (450g) leeks, washed, trimmed and sliced

4 oz (100g) onion, peeled and sliced

2 lemons, sliced

2 sprigs fresh thyme or 1 level teaspoon dried thyme

1 bay leaf

8 peppercorns

4 whole cloves

$1\frac{1}{2}$ pints (900 ml) water

2 level teaspoons salt

1 tablespoon vinegar

FOR THE DRESSING:

5 oz (150g) carton natural yogurt

6 level tablespoons mayonnaise

2 tablespoons lemon juice

Remove the heads from the mackerel. Hold the fish firmly with the backbone towards the palm of your hand, and push the entrails out of the body with your thumb.

Cut off the fins with kitchen scissors. Rinse the fish under cold running water to remove any blood and pieces of gut. When the inside of the fish is completely cleaned, pat dry.

Place the fish on a board and, using a very sharp knife, remove the head then cut across the body into 2–2½ inch (5–6 cm) pieces. Cut off the tail from each fish.

Place the carrots, leeks, onion and half the lemon slices in a 5 pint (3·2 litre) flameproof dish and mix in the herbs, spices, water, salt and vinegar. Bring to boil, cover then simmer for 15–20 minutes. Add the mackerel pieces to the vegetables in the pan and cover with a lid or foil. Poach gently for 8–10 minutes, depending on the size of the pieces. Leave to cool in the pan.

Strain the vegetables and arrange them on a serving dish. Arrange the fish pieces on top. Pour a little of the fish stock over, then add the remaining lemon slices.

Mix together the yogurt, mayonnaise and lemon juice and pour over the fish, vegetables and lemon slices in the serving dish.

Not suitable for freezing.

GOLDEN HADDOCK PASTRY PLAIT

Serves 4

1 lb (450g) smoked haddock

Milk

4 oz (100g) cottage cheese

1 bunch spring onions, chopped

Salt and pepper

8 oz (225g) packet frozen puff pastry, thawed

Poach the fish in ¼ pint (150 ml) of milk and water mixed, then drain, reserving the liquid.

Remove any skin and bones and flake the fish, then put it in a bowl with the cottage cheese, spring onion, and some seasoning.

Set the oven to hot, gas mark 7 or 425°F/220°C.

On a lightly-floured working surface, roll pastry out into a 12 × 12 inch (30 × 30 cm) square and transfer it to a baking sheet. Spoon the filling down the centre of the pastry, leaving about 1 inch (2·5 cm) clear at the top and the bottom, then fold these edges up over the filling. With a sharp knife or a pair of scissors, cut the sides diagonally at 1 inch (2·5 cm) intervals and to within ½ inch (1 cm) of the filling, then fold alternate strips of the pastry from either side over the filling.

Brush the plait with a little milk and bake above the centre of the oven for 40–45 minutes until the pastry is golden brown.

If liked, served the Haddock Plait with a **fish sauce.** Make the reserved fish liquor up to ½ pint (300 ml) with milk. In a small pan, blend 1 tablespoon of cornflour with a little of the liquor, then stir in the rest; bring to the boil, stirring all the time, and cook until thick. Season to taste and serve separately.

Not suitable for freezing.

CHEESE TOPPED COD

Serves 4–6

1 lb (450g) new potatoes

2 oz (50g) margarine

1½ oz (40g) flour

¾ pint (450 ml) milk

4 oz (100g) Red Leicester cheese, grated

Salt and pepper

1 lb (450g) white fish, such as cod or coley, skinned and cut into cubes

1 oz (25g) browned breadcrumbs

Scrub the new potatoes and boil them in salted water for about 15 minutes or until tender, depending on their size; drain.

Melt the margarine in a pan and stir in the flour then the milk, then bring to the boil, stirring all the time, and cook for 1 minute. Add three-quarters of the cheese and some seasoning to taste. Stir the fish into the sauce, bring to the boil and simmer for 2 minutes. Remove the pan from the heat, cover and leave to stand for 10 minutes. Reheat the mixture quickly.

Cheese Topped Cod; Golden Haddock Pastry Plait; Kipper Rice Ring, page 44

Either divide the fish mixture between 4–6 individual dishes or spoon it into a 2½ pint (1·5 litre) shallow, ovenproof dish. Slice the potatoes and lay the slices over the fish. Mix the rest of the cheese and crumbs together, then sprinkle them over the potatoes.

Place under medium to hot grill, cook until golden brown and heated through.

Garnish with a sprig of watercress.

Not suitable for freezing.

SARDINE TOAST TOPPER

Makes 4

4·4 oz (125g) can of sardines in oil

6 level tablespoons mayonnaise

2 oz (50g) grated Cheddar cheese

1 oz (25g) grated onion

1 teaspoon lemon juice

1 level tablespoon fresh chopped parsley

⅛ level teaspoon black pepper

4 thick slices bread

Butter

Drain the oil from the sardines and remove the bones. Place sardines in a basin with the mayonnaise, cheese, onion, lemon juice, chopped parsley and pepper. Mix well.

Toast the bread on both sides. Spread one side lightly with butter, then spread the sardine mixture thickly over the top. Place under a medium-hot grill for 2–3 minutes until bubbling and light golden brown.

KIPPER RICE RING

Serves 4–6

6 oz (175g) boil-in-the-bag kippers

8 oz (225g) long-grain rice

2 eggs, size 3, hard-boiled

1 tablespoon chopped parsley

2 tomatoes, cut into segments

FOR THE DRESSING:

1 tablespoon oil

2 tablespoons vinegar

1 level teaspoon dry mustard powder

½ level teaspoon salt

¼ level teaspoon pepper

A pinch of sugar

A pinch of cayenne pepper

Cook the kippers as directed on the packet.

Cook the rice in boiling salted water for 11–12 minutes until just tender. Drain in a colander, then cool under cold running water and drain again thoroughly.

Put the rice into a bowl with the flaked kipper. Chop the hard-boiled eggs and add to the rice with the parsley.

To make the dressing, put all the ingredients into a screw-topped jar, put on the lid and shake well to mix them. Pour the dressing over the rice and stir to coat.

Grease the ring mould. Arrange the tomato segments round the base of the ring mould, then carefully spoon the rice on top, pressing the mixture down gently but firmly as the mould is filled. Chill in the fridge for about 30 minutes before serving.

Not suitable for freezing.

SCAMPI PROVENÇALE

Serves 6

2 oz (50g) butter

4 oz (100g) onion, peeled and chopped

1 lb (450g) scampi (see note)

2 tablespoons white wine

4 tomatoes, skinned, de-seeded and chopped

2 oz (50g) black olives, stoned

1 level teaspoon tomato purée

2 cloves garlic, peeled and crushed

Salt and pepper

TO GARNISH:

Chopped parsley

Melt the butter in the pan and gently fry the onion until soft, about 15 minutes. Add the scampi and cook, stirring gently for 2 minutes. Add all the remaining ingredients except parsley. Cover the pan with a lid and simmer gently for 5–8 minutes. Add seasoning to taste and serve immediately, sprinkling a little chopped parsley over the top.

Note: As scampi is expensive we tested this recipe using the less expensive monkfish instead, and the result was excellent. Skin the fish and cut into 1 inch (2·5 cm) cubes.

To freeze: freeze when cold for up to 1 month. Thaw and reheat quickly. Garnish.

Baked Stuffed Trout

SARDINE SIZZLERS

Serves 4

| 1 lb (450g) potatoes |
| 1 can sardines in tomato sauce |
| 2 oz (50g) plain flour |
| 1 tablespoon vinegar |
| Salt and pepper |
| Oil for frying |

Peel the potatoes and cook in boiling salted water for about 20 minutes until tender, depending on size. Drain well, then mash.

Mash the sardines thoroughly in the sauce, then add to the potatoes together with the flour and vinegar and beat until well mixed. Add salt and pepper to taste.

Divide mixture into twelve, roll each piece into a ball then flatten into a round cake.

Chill the sardine cakes in the fridge until firm, then fry them quickly in hot oil for 3–5 minutes on each side or until golden brown; drain on kitchen paper.

To freeze: do not fry. Carefully wrap to avoid flavour transfer. Freeze for up to 1 month. Cook from frozen.

BAKED STUFFED TROUT

Serves 4

| 4 rainbow trout, frozen or fresh |
| Salt and pepper |
| 2 oz (50g) butter or margarine |
| 4 oz (100g) onion, peeled, halved and thinly sliced |
| ½ green pepper, de-seeded and sliced |
| 4 oz (100g) mushrooms, sliced |
| 2 teaspoons soy sauce |
| 2 tomatoes, chopped |
| Finely grated rind and juice of ½ large lemon |
| ½ level teaspoon dill (optional) |
| Parsley |

Set oven to fairly hot, gas mark 6 or 400°F/200°C.

Cut off fins and trim tail on each trout. Rinse and dry fish. Open out the fish and place skin side down. With a sharp knife, cut along either side of the backbone through the ribs.

Snip through the backbone at the head then cut under it and as closely as possible to the backbone, down to the tail. Remove the complete backbone in one piece.

Slip the knife under the small bones, holding a few at a time against the blade with the thumb, then pull away. Rub the flesh to make sure all small bones are removed. Season.

In 1 oz (25g) butter fry onion, pepper and mushrooms to soften. Add the rest of the ingredients, but using only half the soy sauce, except the parsley. Add the seasoning and chopped parsley to taste. Allow to cool.

Divide the stuffing between the fish. Place in a buttered ovenproof dish.

Melt the rest of the butter with the remaining soy sauce, then brush it over the fish. Bake above the centre of the oven for 20–25 minutes or until cooked. Baste once with the butter mixture during cooking.

Not suitable for freezing.

MEAT AND CHICKEN

'What shall we have for dinner today?' You'll find the answer to that eternal question in this chapter, with recipes ranging from the cheap and cheerful, or those with the gourmet touch, and from recipes which are quick to make to those which take a little more time and effort.

MEAT

Choosing a joint of beef

A joint of top rib of beef is a relatively cheap roasting joint. The butcher sells it partially boned and rolled which makes for easier carving.

When buying beef the lean meat should be plum red in colour; very bright meat denotes beef that has not been hung sufficiently and will not be tender when cooked.

Remember that top rib of beef is best when slow roasted and should never be overcooked as the more it is cooked the drier and tougher it becomes – ideally it should be pink to red in the middle.

ROAST BEEF

Serves 5–6

3½–4 lb (1·6–1·8 kg) boned and rolled top rib of beef

1–2 tablespoons oil or dripping

1 large carrot, peeled and sliced

1 onion, peeled and sliced

1 bay leaf

Pepper

Remove the meat from the fridge about 1 hour before cooking or allow extra time for cooking.

Set the oven to moderate, gas mark 4 or 350°F/180°C.

Weigh the meat and calculate the cooking time; for rare beef allow 20 minutes per lb (450g) plus 20 minutes; for medium cooked beef allow 30 minutes per lb (450g) plus 30 minutes.

Brush a small roasting tin, just large enough to hold the joint comfortably, with oil or dripping. Put the vegetables and bay leaf in the centre with the meat on top, placing it so that the thickest layer of fat is on the top. The meat can be placed on a trivet or stand but the advantage of vegetables is that they flavour the juices for the gravy and are also delicious served with the meat.

Sprinkle pepper over the meat. Roast, uncovered, just above the centre of the oven, basting occasionally.

About 30 minutes before the meal, remove the meat from the oven or, if it isn't cooked, move it to the floor of the oven and raise the temperature in readiness for the Yorkshire puddings.

Gravy

Remove the meat from the roasting tin, place on a warm serving plate and leave to "set" before carving. Remove the vegetables to a serving plate.

Stir 1 level tablespoon flour into the meat juices in the pan. Place the roasting tin over the heat and cook for about 1 minute, stirring. Gradually stir in 1 pint (600 ml) of water – the cooking liquor from the carrots and potatoes can be used – then add a crumbled beef stock cube. Bring to the boil, stirring, and cook for 1–2 minutes. Add salt and pepper to taste.

Roast Beef and
Yorkshire
Puddings

To freeze: any leftover beef should be sliced and interleaved with squares of waxed paper. Wrap and freeze for up to 3 months. Thaw and eat cold or reheat in gravy.

INDIVIDUAL YORKSHIRE PUDDINGS

Makes 12

4 oz (100g) plain flour

Pinch of salt

1 egg, size 3

¼ pint (150 ml) milk

¼ pint (150 ml) water

Sift the flour and salt into a bowl, make a well in the centre and drop in the egg. Add a little of the milk and stir carefully with a wooden spoon, gradually incorporating the flour from the sides. Add the rest of the milk and the water and beat well.

Grease 12 deep patty tins with about 1 oz (25g) lard or dripping.

When the beef has been removed from the oven, raise the temperature to hot, gas mark 7 or 425°F/220°C. Put the greased patty tins at the top of the oven to get hot (about 2 minutes). Remove from the oven and fill each hole almost to the top with batter. Bake at the top of the oven for 20–25 minutes or until risen and well-browned.

If preferred, a large Yorkshire pudding can be made by heating lard in a small roasting tin, pouring in the batter and baking as above but for 30–35 minutes.

Not suitable for freezing.

Horseradish Sauce

Serve either the bottled variety or make your own fresh Horseradish Sauce. The bottled variety is very good with a tablespoon of double cream stirred in before serving.

To make your own, peel a small root of horseradish then coarsely grate 2 table-

Roast Pork with Sage

spoons into a basin together with 1 table-spoon vinegar, $\frac{1}{2}$ level teaspoon dry mustard, and 1 level teaspoon caster sugar.

Beat 5 oz (150g) double or whipping cream until thickened, stir in the horseradish mixture. Add salt and pepper to taste.

HIGHLAND LAMB

Serves 6

5–6 lb (2·3–2·7 kg) leg of lamb

FOR THE GLAZE:

4 level tablespoons French mustard

1 tablespoon soy sauce

2 level teaspoons rosemary

$\frac{1}{4}$ level teaspoon ground ginger

1 tablespoon oil

FOR THE GRAVY:

$\frac{1}{2}$ pint (300 ml) stock

1 level tablespoon cornflour

Salt and pepper

Weigh the meat.

Mix all the glaze ingredients together, adding the oil little by little to make a thick cream-like consistency. Spread the glaze over the lamb then place it in a roasting tin. Leave in a cool place for an hour or more – the longer the better – before cooking.

Set the oven to moderate, gas mark 4 or 350°F/180°C.

Cook the meat allowing 25–35 minutes per lb (450g). Baste two or three times during cooking.

Allow the meat to stand for about 15 minutes before carving.

Make the gravy. In a pan blend the cornflour with a little of the stock then stir in the rest. Add the skimmed juices from the meat pan. Bring to the boil, stirring, and cook for 1–2 minutes. Add seasoning to taste.

To freeze: slice and freeze as for Roast Beef (page 47).

ROAST PORK WITH SAGE

Serve with red cabbage and parsley potatoes.

Serves 6–8

5 lb (2·3 kg) hand of pork, unscored and boned

1–2 cloves garlic, peeled and crushed, optional

12 sage leaves, or 1 level teaspoon dried sage

Pepper

1 level teaspoon salt

12 oz (350g) onions, peeled and sliced

1 oz (25g) breadcrumbs

4 tablespoons orange juice

A day ahead, wipe and trim the meat. Remove the rind and cut into thin strips. If used, spread the garlic evenly over the meat. Cover with sage leaves and season well. Roll up and secure with string. Cover and refrigerate overnight.

Set the oven to fairly hot, gas mark 6 or 400°F/200°C.

Three hours before required, place the onion in the bottom of a casserole dish. Place meat on top. Cover and cook for 30 minutes per lb (450g) plus 30 minutes.

Half-way through the cooking, remove the lid and press the breadcrumbs into the fat. Complete the cooking uncovered, basting occasionally.

At the same time place the crackling in a tin and cook until crisp and puffy.

When cooked, place the pork on a dish. Garnish with the onion. Pour the juices into a pan, add the orange juice and boil to reduce. Add seasoning.

To freeze: slice and freeze as for Roast Beef (page 47) for up to 1 month.

From top: Oxtail Goulash Hot Pot, page 50; Spicy Beef and Bean Casserole, page 50; Hot Pot of Lamb

HOT POT OF LAMB

Serves 4

1½ lb (700g) middle neck of lamb chops

2 level tablespoons flour

Salt and pepper

1 tablespoon oil

1 large onion, cut into quarters

½ pint (300 ml) water

1 herb stock cube

1 tablespoon redcurrant jelly

½ level teaspoon or 2 small sprigs of rosemary

1 teaspoon vinegar

4 oz (100g) mushrooms, halved

8 oz (225g) packet of peas

Set the oven to moderate, gas mark 4 or 350°F/180°C. Trim the meat and remove the spinal cord as this would give a bitter flavour to the dish.

Season the flour, then use to coat the meat. Fry the meat in the oil until deep brown on both sides, then transfer to a 2½–

3 pint (1·5–1·8 litre) casserole dish. Fry the onion quarters in the remaining fat for a minute, then add to the casserole with the water, crumbled stock cube, redcurrant jelly, rosemary and vinegar. Cover with the lid or foil and cook the casserole in the centre of the oven for 45 minutes.

Add the mushrooms, peas and further seasoning as necessary and cook for a further 30 minutes.

To freeze: cook for 1 hour – do not add the mushrooms or peas. Cool quickly, then pack and freeze. Thaw at cool room temperature. Add the peas and the mushrooms and cook in a covered casserole in a moderate oven for ¾–1 hour.

SPICY BEEF AND BEAN CASSEROLE

Serves 4

4 oz (100g) dried butter beans (see note)
1 lb (450g) stewing steak, such as chuck
1 beef stock cube
FOR THE MARINADE
4 level tablespoons brown sugar
2 tablespoons oil
1 tablespoon Worcestershire sauce
2½ oz (60g) can tomato purée
1–2 level tablespoons made English mustard
1 tablespoon malt vinegar
2 large onions, sliced
Salt and pepper

Cover the butter beans with cold water and soak them overnight.

Next day, trim the excess fat from the meat and cut the meat into finger-shaped pieces. Place in a 2½ pint (1·5 litre) casserole dish with all the marinade ingredients, turning the meat in the marinade to coat. Leave for 2–3 hours.

Set oven to moderate, gas mark 4 or 350°F/180°C.

Drain the beans, reserving ½ pint (300 ml) of the liquor. Add the beans, liquor and crumbled stock cube to the meat mixture and stir to mix. Cover the casserole with the lid or foil and cook in the centre of the oven for about 2 hours or until cooked.

Just before serving, thicken if required by first blending 1 level tablespoon of cornflour with 2–3 tablespoons water to a smooth paste, then stirring into the casserole until the juices thicken.

Note: Use fresh dried beans, as beans kept for nine months or more may take a great deal of cooking and may not soften at all.

To freeze: do not thicken with cornflour, but cool, pack and freeze. Thaw overnight and reheat in a pan on top of the stove, thickening with the cornflour and adding a little extra stock if required.

OXTAIL GOULASH HOT POT

Serves 4

1 large or 2 small oxtails, weighing about 3 lb (1·35 kg) in all
2 tablespoons oil
2 large onions, peeled and sliced
1 lb (450g) carrots, peeled and sliced
1 oz (25g) flour
2 level tablespoons paprika
14 oz (397g) can tomatoes
½ pint (300 ml) water
1 beef stock cube
1 level teaspoon caraway seeds
Salt and pepper

Set the oven to warm, gas mark 3 or 325°F/160°C.

Fry the oxtail pieces, a few at a time, in the oil until brown all over, then transfer to a 4½ pint (2·7 litre) casserole dish. Turn the onions and carrots in the remaining fat for 1–2 minutes, then add to the oxtail. Stir the flour into the fat in the pan, then add the paprika, tomatoes, water, stock cube, caraway seeds, salt and pepper.

Cover the casserole with the lid or foil and cook in the centre of the oven for 3 hours. Skim the surface to remove excess fat if to be eaten immediately, and serve with boiled potatoes.

Note: This hot pot is best prepared and cooked the day before, then cooled and refrigerated overnight. The excess fat can be scraped off before the hot pot is reheated for 45 minutes in a moderately hot oven, gas mark 5 or 375°F/190°C; or turn the oxtail into a pan, bring slowly to the boil and simmer for 10 minutes.

To freeze: after cooling, skim, pack and freeze. Thaw overnight at cool room temperature, then reheat in a covered casserole dish in the oven, as above.

LAMB RATATOUILLE

Serves 4

1 aubergine, cubed
1½ level teaspoons and 1 level tablespoon salt
½ oz (15g) flour
Black pepper
1½ lb (700g) best end neck of lamb, cut into thin chops (trim bone if very long)
2 tablespoons oil
2 level tablespoons tomato purée
2 tablespoons water
1 lb (450g) courgettes, sliced
2 green peppers, de-seeded and cut into thin strips
6 oz (175g) mushrooms, halved
1 lb (450g) tomatoes, skinned and halved
8 oz (225g) onions, peeled and sliced
2 level tablespoons fresh mint, finely chopped
2 level teaspoons dried basil

Sprinkle the cubed aubergine with a level tablespoon of salt, cover with absorbent kitchen paper and leave for 15 minutes.

Set the oven to moderate, gas mark 4 or 350°F/180°C.

Season the flour with 1 teaspoon of salt and some pepper and toss the meat in it. Heat the oil in a frying pan, add the chops and brown evenly on all sides. Remove from the pan. Stir the tomato purée into the remaining fat, together with 2 tablespoons water. Leave to one side.

Rinse the aubergines under cold water to remove excess salt and pat dry. Layer all the

Lamb Ratatouille

vegetables and the chops in a 4 pint (2·4 litre) casserole dish, seasoning each layer with salt, pepper, mint and basil, piling the vegetables high. **Note:** The volume will reduce considerably during cooking.

Pour the tomato purée over the vegetables, cover the dish with a lid or foil and cook in the middle of the oven for 1½ hours.

To freeze: freeze when cold for up to 3 months. Partially thaw and reheat on top of stove until hot.

WAYS OF USING WINE

Dishes with wine won't make you drunk! When it's cooked, wine loses its alcoholic content but leaves behind a subtle flavour that adds something very special to the dish.

■ Add wine instead of some of the stock or water when cooking casseroles.

■ Tenderize meat by pouring wine over the pieces of meat. Add a sliced onion and a few herbs of choice and leave to marinate for an hour or two. Then use in casseroles, etc.

■ Soak dried fruits in sherry or sweet white wine, then use in puddings or in fruit cakes.

Steak Diane;
Boeuf à la
Bourguignonne

STEAK DIANE

Serves 4

4 fillet steaks each weighing 4–6 oz (100–175g)

1 oz (25g) butter

2 tablespoons oil

2 tablespoons Worcestershire sauce

1 tablespoon lemon juice

1 heaped tablespoon grated onion

1 tablespoon chopped parsley

Black pepper

1 level teaspoon salt

If necessary flatten the steaks to about ½ inch (1 cm) thickness by hitting gently with a rolling pin.

Heat the butter and oil, add the steaks and fry for 3–4 minutes on each side. Remove on to a serving plate and keep hot.

Add Worcestershire sauce, lemon juice, onion and parsley to pan juices and cook for 1 minute, stirring. Taste, and season.

Spoon sauce over the steaks and serve, or return the steaks to the pan for a few seconds to reheat, if necessary.

Not suitable for freezing.

BOEUF À LA BOURGUIGNONNE

Serves 6

2 lb (900g) topside or 2½–3 lb (1·2–1·35 kg) braising steak

4 oz (100g) streaky bacon, in one piece, cut into ½ inch (1 cm) cubes

8 oz (225g) onions

2 tablespoons oil

1 oz (25g) flour

½ pint (300 ml) red wine

¼ pint (150 ml) water

1 clove garlic, peeled and crushed

Pepper

½ level teaspoon salt

FOR THE BOUQUET GARNI (SEE NOTE):

2 small bay leaves

1 sprig thyme

Bunch of parsley stalks

TO SERVE:

12 small onions, peeled

1 oz (25g) butter

6 oz (175g) button mushrooms, wiped

Set the oven to moderate, gas mark 4 or 350°F/180°C.

Cut the meat into about 1½ inch (4 cm) cubes. Fry the bacon in a large frying pan until the bacon starts to crisp. Add the onion and fry for 1–2 minutes to soften. Transfer the bacon and onion to a 4 pint (2·4 litre) casserole dish.

Add the oil to the frying pan and when hot add the meat, a few pieces at a time, and fry until brown all over – this will take about 10–15 minutes. Sprinkle over the flour and cook for 2–3 minutes, stirring.

Stir in the wine and water and bring to the boil. Remove from the heat and stir in the garlic, pepper and salt and the bouquet garni (tie the fresh herbs together in a bunch).

Transfer to the casserole dish. Cover and cook in the centre of the oven for $1\frac{1}{2}$–2 hours depending on the meat used.

Half an hour before the end of cooking, fry the small whole onions in the butter for 10–15 minutes until beginning to brown. Stir in the mushrooms. Add the onions and mushrooms for the last 15 minutes of cooking.

Note: If fresh herbs are unobtainable use 2 bouquet garni sachets.

To freeze: freeze when cold for up to 1 month. Partially thaw before reheating.

BEEF OLIVES

Serves 4

3 oz (75g) streaky bacon, derinded and finely chopped

1 small onion, peeled and finely chopped

1 level tablespoon chopped parsley

4 oz (100g) fresh breadcrumbs

2 oz (50g) shredded suet

$\frac{1}{2}$ level teaspoon dried mixed herbs

Grated rind of $\frac{1}{2}$ lemon

1 egg, size 3

Salt and pepper to taste

$1\frac{1}{2}$ lb (700g) thinly sliced topside

1 level tablespoon made English mustard

3 level tablespoons seasoned flour

4 tablespoons oil

$\frac{3}{4}$ pint (450 ml) beef stock

8 oz (225g) onions, peeled and sliced

TO GARNISH:

Chopped parsley

Mix the first nine ingredients together to make a stuffing.

Beat the meat thinly between sheets of cling wrap. Cut into about eight equal oblong shapes. Spread mustard thinly over the meat and divide stuffing equally between the pieces. Roll up and secure with fine string. Spoon seasoned flour into a plastic bag, add beef olives and shake until evenly coated.

Set the oven to warm, gas mark 3 or 325°F/160°C.

Heat the oil and fry the beef olives until well browned all over. Remove and place in a shallow casserole into which they just fit. Stir remaining flour into the pan and brown lightly. Add the stock and bring to the boil. Add seasoning to taste.

Place onion over olives and pour over the gravy. Cover and bake in centre of oven for about $1\frac{1}{2}$ hours. Garnish with parsley.

To freeze: cool, pack and freeze. Thaw overnight at a cool room temperature. Reheat in fairly hot oven for about 40 minutes.

STEAK AND KIDNEY PIE

Serves 4–6

1–$1\frac{1}{2}$ lb (450–700g) shoulder or chuck steak

8 oz (225g) lamb's kidney

3 level tablespoons flour

Pepper

$\frac{1}{4}$ level teaspoon salt

3 tablespoons oil

12 oz–1 lb (325–450g) onion, peeled and sliced

$\frac{3}{4}$ pint (450 ml) beef stock, or water and a stock cube

2 bay leaves

1 teaspoon Worcestershire sauce

4 oz (100g) mushrooms

FOR THE PASTRY:

4 oz (100g) margarine and lard mixed

8 oz (225g) plain flour

$\frac{1}{2}$ level teaspoon salt

1 egg, size 3, beaten

4 tablespoons water

Trim the meat then cut into $\frac{3}{4}$–1 inch (2–2·5 cm) cubes. Remove the membranes from the kidney, cut in half and then, with scissors, snip away the white core.

Steak and
Kidney Pie

Cut each kidney into half again.

Dip the meat and kidneys into seasoned flour. Heat the oil in a large frying pan then fry the meat and kidneys until well browned all over. Add the onions and fry until brown. Stir in any remaining flour.

Stir in the water, bay leaves, crumbled stock cube, and Worcestershire sauce. Bring to the boil, stirring. Reduce the heat, cover with lid and simmer for about 1 hour. Stir in the mushrooms. Leave until cold.

Meanwhile, make the pastry: rub the fats into the flour and salt. Beat the egg with the water then, reserving about 1 tablespoon to glaze the pastry, use the rest to bind the pastry ingredients together. Knead lightly then roll into a rectangle. Fold in three, wrap and chill in the fridge.

Set the oven to hot, gas mark 7 or 425°F/220°C. Roll out the pastry 2–3 inches (5–7·5 cm) larger than the rim of a 2–2½ pint (1·1–1·5 litre) pie dish. Place the pie dish on top and cut round. Cut a ¾ inch (2 cm) wide strip from the outer trimmings.

Transfer meat mixture to pie dish. Brush dish edge with glaze, cover with pastry strip, brush pastry strip with glaze before placing pastry lid on top. Press edges together and decorate with a small knife.

Roll out trimmings and cut out 12 large and 12 small 'leaves'. Arrange on top and make a cut in the centre of lid to let steam out. Brush with glaze and bake above the centre of the oven for about 45 minutes or until the meat is tender.

To freeze: freeze with uncooked pastry for 2 months. Thaw and cook as above.

MOUSSAKA

Serves 8

3 lb (1·35 kg) aubergines, sliced
3 level teaspoons salt
6 tablespoons oil
FOR THE MEAT SAUCE:
8 oz (225g) onion, chopped
1½ lb (700g) minced lamb
1 tablespoon oil
14 oz (397g) can tomatoes
1 level teaspoon oregano
2 cloves garlic, peeled and crushed
1 level teaspoon salt
⅛ level teaspoon cayenne pepper
⅛ level teaspoon pepper
¼ pint (150 ml) red wine

FOR THE CHEESE SAUCE:

2 oz (50g) butter or margarine
2 oz (50g) flour
1 pint (600 ml) milk
Pepper
¼ level teaspoon salt
4 oz (100g) feta cheese
2 eggs, size 3

Layer aubergine in a large dish, sprinkle layers with salt and leave for 1 hour. Rinse well and pat dry. Heat half the oil and fry half the aubergines for 5 minutes, turning all the time. Remove from pan. Repeat with rest of oil and aubergines.

Meanwhile, make the meat sauce: fry the onion and the mince in the oil until the onion is soft and the mince is brown.

Pour off any excess liquid and stir in all the remaining meat sauce ingredients. Bring to the boil and simmer gently for 15 minutes.

Use one 5 pint (3·2 litre) or two 2½ pint (1·5 litre) ovenproof dishes. Place a third of the meat mixture in the bottom of the dish and cover with a third of the aubergines until both of these have been used up.

Make the cheese sauce. Melt the butter or margarine in a small saucepan and stir in the flour, then cook for 1 minute. Stir in the milk and bring to the boil, stirring, and cook for 1 minute. Mix two thirds of the cheese with the eggs, stir into the sauce, and season.

Set oven to moderate, gas mark 4 or 350°F/180°C.

Cover with the cheese sauce and sprinkle with the remaining cheese. Cover the Moussaka with foil and cook in the centre of the preheated oven for 1½ hours. Remove the foil 30 minutes before the end of cooking to allow the topping to become golden brown. For an even browner top, place the dish under the grill for a few minutes if desired.

To freeze: follow recipe up to but not including the cheese sauce. Cover with foil and bake as in recipe for 1 hour. Cool quickly, then place a large piece of foil on a baking sheet, and turn the cooked mixture out on to it. Seal the foil round the meat. Leave on the baking sheet and freeze. Return to dish and thaw overnight in fridge. Make cheese sauce and continue as in recipe, cooking for 1–1½ hours.

OSSO BUCO

Serves 8

6 veal shank bones – see note
2 oz (50g) flour, seasoned with pepper and ½ level teaspoon salt
3 level tablespoons oil
2 cloves garlic, peeled and crushed
1 large onion, peeled and finely chopped
1 large carrot, peeled and diced
1 stick celery, trimmed and chopped
¾ pint (450 ml) beef or veal stock
2 level teaspoons grated lemon rind
1 lb (450g) tomatoes, skinned and chopped
Salt and pepper

Note: Ask your butcher to cut 2–2½ inch (5–6 cm) thick slices across the hind shank, you will then get more marrow from the bones. Use one or two large frying pans to cook the meat so that the bones stand upright and close together and thus prevent the marrow falling out.

Snip the meat around the bones with kitchen scissors to prevent it from curling up. Coat the meat pieces with the seasoned flour. Heat the oil in the pan, then add the meat pieces and fry until brown on both sides. Remove meat from the pan, and leave on one side. Lower the heat, add garlic, onion, carrot and celery, and cook for about 5 minutes, stirring, until starting to soften.

Pour in ¼ pint (150 ml) stock, stirring to mix in bits from the sides and base of the pan. Return the veal to the pan with the vegetables, being careful to keep the meat upright, so that you will not lose the marrow from the bones.

Bring to the boil, add the lemon rind and tomatoes, and pour over the remainder of the stock. Stir in plenty of seasoning. Cover the pan and simmer for 1 hour.

Turn the pieces of meat over carefully and if there is a lot of liquid in the pan, leave the lid off so that it can reduce. Continue to cook for 30–45 minutes.

When it is ready, the meat should be so tender it parts easily from the bones. Taste and add salt and pepper as necessary. Arrange on a hot serving dish.

To freeze: freeze when cold for up to 1 month. Thaw and reheat in pan.

Frikadellers

FRIKADELLERS

Delicious accompanied by crusty fresh bread.

Serves 4

FOR THE MEAT BALLS:

2 slices white bread, diced

$\frac{1}{4}$ pint (150 ml) hot water

8 oz (225g) minced pork

8 oz (225g) minced lamb

1 egg, size 3

1 clove garlic, peeled and crushed

$\frac{1}{2}$ level teaspoon marjoram

Pepper

1 level teaspoon salt

2 tablespoons oil

FOR THE VEGETABLE MIXTURE:

1 large onion, peeled and sliced

3 sticks celery, trimmed and sliced

1 red and 1 green pepper, de-seeded and sliced

1 large clove garlic, peeled and crushed

4 tomatoes, skinned

$\frac{3}{4}$ pint (450 ml) water and chicken stock cube

2 tablespoons tomato purée

1 level teaspoon marjoram

Pepper

1 level teaspoon salt

Two 15 oz (420g) cans red kidney beans

Mix the bread and water together. Leave to soak, then mash until pulpy. Stir in the minced meats and other ingredients for meat balls except the oil.

Divide the bread and meat mixture into 16 pieces and shape each one into a ball on a lightly-floured surface. Place on a board or plate.

Quickly brown the meatballs all over in the oil, then remove from the pan. Keep aside in a warm dish.

Add the onion, celery and peppers to the fat in the pan and fry for 10 minutes until the vegetables begin to soften. Stir frequently. Remove any excess fat from the pan. Stir in the garlic, tomatoes, cut into wedges, the water and stock cube, tomato purée, marjoram, seasoning and the drained red kidney beans.

Replace the meatballs. Cover and simmer for 30 minutes. Serve at once.

To freeze: freeze for up to 2 months. Partially thaw and reheat carefully in a saucepan.

LIVER PÂTÉ

What's the difference between a pâté and a terrine?

These days the two have come to mean identical mixtures, so that Pâté du Chef or Terrine du Chef featured on restaurant menus are quite often the same.

However, a pâté is a mixture of meats baked in a pastry crust. A terrine is that same mixture baked in an earthenware, glass or enamelled cast iron dish.

So this Liver Pâté is really Liver Pâté en Terrine because the terrine or cooking dish has replaced the pastry crust as the case in which the pâté is cooked.

Liver Pâté

Serves 6

8 oz (225g) lamb's or pig's liver
6 rashers streaky bacon, derinded
3 oz (75g) onion, peeled
4 anchovies or $\frac{1}{2}$ teaspoon anchovy essence
$\frac{1}{2}$ oz (15g) butter or margarine
$\frac{1}{2}$ oz (15g) flour
$\frac{1}{4}$ pint (150 ml) milk
Black pepper
$\frac{1}{2}$ level teaspoon salt
$\frac{1}{4}$ level teaspoon ground bay leaves
$\frac{1}{4}$ level teaspoon mace
$\frac{1}{4}$ level teaspoon ground allspice
1 egg, size 3

Cut the liver, 4 rashers of bacon and onion into pieces. Either put in a food processor or mince twice through a mincer together with the anchovies.

Melt butter, stir in flour and cook for $\frac{1}{2}$ minute without browning. Gradually whisk in milk. Bring to boil, whisking, and cook for $\frac{1}{2}$ minute.

Remove the pan from the heat and stir the salt, pepper, bay leaves, mace and allspice into the white sauce. Then mix in the egg thoroughly.

Add the liver and bacon mixture. Taste for flavour and add further seasoning as necessary.

Pour the mixture into a $1\frac{1}{2}$ pint (900 ml) ovenproof dish. Cut remaining bacon into small pieces and scatter over pâté.

Cover with foil then place in a 'bain marie' i.e. a larger shallow tin containing about 1 inch (2·5 cm) of cold water. Bake in a moderately hot oven, gas mark 5 or 375°F/ 190°C, for about $1\frac{1}{4}$ hours, removing foil after about 1 hour.

Note: Cooking in a 'bain marie' ensures that the ingredients cook gently and slowly. The water prevents over-cooking, particularly around outer edges.

To freeze: wrap and freeze when cold for up to 1 month. Thaw and eat cold.

Devilled
Kidneys

SAUTÉED LIVER WITH RED PEPPER

Serves 3–4

12 oz (350g) sliced lamb's liver

1 small red pepper, de-seeded

1 level tablespoon plain flour

1 oz (25g) butter

2 oz (50g) onion, chopped

¼ pint (150 ml) Noilly Prat or other dry vermouth

¼ pint (150 ml) water

1 level tablespoon tomato purée

½ level teaspoon dried thyme

⅛ level teaspoon pepper

Cut the liver and red pepper into strips. Coat the liver in the flour and fry in the butter for about 2 minutes. Add the onion and the red pepper and fry for a further 2 minutes. Stir in the Noilly Prat, water, tomato purée, thyme and pepper.

Bring to the boil, stirring, then lower the heat, cover, and cook for a further 15–20 minutes, covered.

Not suitable for freezing.

DEVILLED KIDNEYS

Serves 4

1 oz (25g) margarine or butter

2 oz (50g) onion, peeled and chopped

1 oz (25g) flour

¼ level teaspoon salt

Good pinch of pepper

1 lb (450g) lambs' kidneys, cores removed

2 tablespoons brandy

¼ pint (150 ml) water or stock

1–1½ level teaspoons made English mustard

2 teaspoons Worcestershire sauce

1 level tablespoon tomato purée

2 level tablespoons chopped parsley

Melt the margarine or butter in a frying pan and fry the onion for 5 minutes until soft. Mix the flour with the salt and pepper and roll the kidneys in it to coat. Add kidneys to the pan, fry for 2 minutes, then add all the remaining ingredients except the parsley. Cover, bring to the boil and simmer for 10 minutes or until cooked.

Sprinkle with parsley before serving.

Not suitable for freezing.

CHICKEN

LEMON ROAST CHICKEN

Serves 4

3½ lb (1·6 kg) chicken, jointed, or 4 large joints of chicken

1 oz (25g) butter

1 level teaspoon salt

Black pepper

Pared rind and juice of 1 lemon

3 oz (75g) packet parsley and thyme stuffing

4 rashers streaky bacon, derinded

TO GARNISH:

Lemon

Parsley

Set the oven to hot, gas mark 6 or 400°F/200°C.

Remove the skin from the chicken joints. Rub the dish with a quarter of the butter and place the chicken, flesh side down, in it. Sprinkle the chicken with salt, pepper and lemon juice and dot with the remaining butter. Cut the pared lemon rind into thin strips and arrange on top of the chicken.

Roast in the oven for 1¼ hours.

Stir 7 fl oz (210 ml) of boiling water into the stuffing mix and leave for 15 minutes, then shape into 12 balls.

Stretch the bacon with the flat of a knife, cut each rasher in half and roll it up.

30 minutes before the end of cooking turn the chicken pieces over, add the stuffing balls, rolling them in the chicken juices, and place the bacon rolls on top of the chicken. Finish cooking.

Garnish with lemon and parsley before serving.

To freeze: freeze when cold for up to 1 month. Thaw and reheat gently but thoroughly in covered frying pan.

CROFTER'S CHICKEN

Serves 4–6

3½ lb (1·6 kg) oven-ready roasting chicken

Salt and pepper

FOR THE STUFFING:

4 oz (100g) carrots, peeled and grated

2 oz (50g) dried apricots, finely chopped

1 oz (25g) raisins

1 small onion, peeled and finely chopped

½ level teaspoon marjoram

¼ level teaspoon salt

Good pinch of pepper

FOR THE POTATO BASE:

1 clove garlic, optional

½ oz (15g) butter

2 lb (900g) potatoes, peeled

Salt and pepper

1 lb (450g) leeks, washed and sliced

½ pint (300 ml) boiling milk

2 oz (50g) Cheddar cheese, grated

Lemon Roast Chicken

Set oven to moderately hot, gas mark 5 or 375°/190°C.

Season the inside of the bird with salt and pepper. Mix together the grated carrot, apricots, raisins, onion, marjoram, salt and pepper and use to stuff the chicken.

Cut clove of garlic in half, if used, and rub around a 3½ pint (2·1 litre) dish, then grease with the butter. Cut potatoes into ¼ inch (5 mm) slices and place half in bottom of dish. Season with salt and pepper, cover with sliced leeks and then cover with remaining sliced potatoes. Season again with salt and pepper. Pour over boiling milk and sprinkle with cheese. Weigh chicken and calculate cooking time, allowing 25 minutes per lb (450g).

Place chicken on top of vegetables and cook in oven for allotted time or until chicken is cooked and vegetables are golden brown.

Not suitable for freezing.

COQ AU VIN

Serves 4

4–6 chicken joints
4 oz (100g) back bacon, derinded and cut into strips
¾ pint (450 ml) red wine
4 oz (100g) mushrooms
2 large onions, peeled and sliced
2 cloves garlic, peeled and crushed
2 tablespoons oil
¼ pint (150 ml) stock
1 bouquet garni
2 bay leaves
Black pepper
1 oz (25g) butter
½ oz (15g) flour

Skin the chicken joints. Put the bacon in a large frying pan and cook gently until the fat starts to run and the bacon starts to brown. Raise the heat, add the oil and then fry the chicken joints until they are a deep golden brown on all sides.

Add the onions and garlic and fry for 3–4 minutes until the onions start to soften. Add the stock, bouquet garni, bay leaves, pepper and wine. Cover and simmer for 30 minutes until the chicken is tender.

Meanwhile, make some kneaded butter: put the butter and flour into a cup and cream together until it forms a paste.

Remove the chicken from the pan. Dot small knobs of the kneaded butter over the surface of the sauce, then gradually stir them in with a wooden spoon – the liquid will thicken as it is stirred.

Replace the chicken in the sauce, add the mushrooms, cover and cook for a further 15 minutes.

Adjust seasoning to taste before serving.

To freeze: freeze when cold for up to 1 month. Thaw and reheat thoroughly.

SPICY CHICKEN AND BEAN TOP POT

Serves 4

4–6 chicken joints
Salt and pepper
1 oz (25g) butter or margarine
2 tablespoons oil
1 large onion, peeled and sliced
15 oz (420g) can tomatoes
4 level tablespoons cornflour
¾ pint (450 ml) hot water
1 chicken stock cube
2 teaspoons Worcestershire sauce
1 level tablespoon chilli seasoning
1 teaspoon sugar
1 large bay leaf
1 tablespoon tomato purée
15 oz (420g) can red kidney beans, drained

Skin the joints and season well with salt and pepper.

Heat the butter and oil in a large frying pan and fry the chicken joints and onions until they start to brown – this will take about 5 minutes.

Drain a little of the tomato juice from the can, blend with the cornflour and leave to one side. Add the tomatoes, water, stock cube, Worcestershire sauce, chilli seasoning, sugar, bay leaf, tomato purée and drained kidney beans to the chicken and onions and simmer with the lid on for 30 minutes.

Remove the joints, add the blended cornflour, then stirring all the time, bring back to the boil and simmer for 1 minute. Replace the joints, cover and cook for a further 10 minutes. Taste the sauce and adjust the seasoning if necessary, before serving.

To freeze: freeze when cold for up to 3 months. Thaw and reheat gently and thoroughly on top of the stove.

SOUTH AMERICAN CHICKEN

Serve with rice.

Serves 4

8 chicken drumsticks or 4 chicken portions
2 tablespoons oil
1 large green pepper, de-seeded and cut into 4
3 tomatoes, skinned
2 cloves garlic, peeled
$\frac{1}{2}$ pint (300 ml) water
1 chicken stock cube
$1\frac{1}{2}$ level tablespoons chilli seasoning
1 level teaspoon salt
$\frac{1}{4}$ level teaspoon ground cinnamon
$\frac{1}{8}$ level teaspoon ground black pepper
A pinch of ground cloves
2 level teaspoons cornflour
2 cubes plain cooking chocolate

Set oven to moderate, gas mark 4 or 350°F/180°C.

Fry the chicken pieces in oil until golden on both sides. Drain off the oil and place in a 3 pint (1·8 litre) casserole dish. Discard oil.

Place all the remaining ingredients in a blender or food processor and blend until smooth. Pour over chicken, cover and cook in the centre of the oven for $1\frac{1}{4}-1\frac{1}{2}$ hours or until chicken is cooked.

To freeze: after the chicken is cooked, allow to cool and place with sauce in a container. Cover, label and freeze for up to 2 months. Allow chicken to defrost completely in the fridge (this may take up to 28 hours). Pour into an ovenproof dish and reheat in a moderate oven for about $1\frac{1}{4}-1\frac{1}{2}$ hours.

CHICKEN DHAL

Serves 6–8

3 oz (75g) butter
2 level teaspoons garam masala
$3\frac{1}{2}$ lb (1·6 kg) chicken
2 level tablespoons desiccated coconut
FOR THE DHAL:
$\frac{1}{2}$ oz (15g) butter
1 large onion, peeled and sliced
1 large carrot, peeled and sliced
1 red pepper, de-seeded and sliced
1 clove garlic, peeled and crushed
8 oz (225g) red lentils
15 fl oz (450 ml) water and 1 chicken stock cube
1 level tablespoon tomato purée
$\frac{1}{2}$ level teaspoon mixed spice
$\frac{1}{4}$ level teaspoon ginger

Set the oven to moderately hot, gas mark 5 or 375°F/190°C.

Beat together the butter and garam masala and spread the mixture over the chicken. Place the chicken in a $3\frac{1}{2}$ pint (2·1 litre) ovenproof dish. Sprinkle the coconut over the top and cook in the preheated oven for 45 minutes.

Meanwhile, make the dhal: melt the butter and fry the onion, carrot, red pepper and garlic until the onion is soft. Stir in the red lentils, water, stock cube, tomato purée and spices. Bring to the boil, stirring.

When the chicken has cooked for 45 minutes, remove from the oven. Lift chicken out on to a plate or board. Pour the lentil and vegetable mixture into the bottom of the dish. Place the chicken on top. Return to the oven and cook for a further 45 minutes or until the chicken is cooked.

Not suitable for freezing.

Chicken
Jambalaya

CHICKEN JAMBALAYA

Serves 4

2 tablespoons oil

8 small chicken joints

1 large onion, peeled and sliced

1 red pepper, de-seeded and sliced

1 clove garlic, peeled and crushed

6 oz (175g) long grain rice

14 oz (397g) can tomatoes

1 level teaspoon dried thyme

1 level teaspoon salt

Good pinch of pepper

$\frac{3}{4}$ pint (450 ml) water

1 chicken stock cube

4 oz (100g) piece of ham, cut into $\frac{1}{2}$ inch (1 cm) cubes

4 oz (100g) frozen peas

4 oz (100g) courgettes, washed and sliced

4 oz (100g) carrots, peeled and sliced

Set oven to moderately hot, gas mark 5 or 375°F/190°C.

Heat oil in a 5 pint (3·2 litre) flameproof casserole, or paella pan, and fry the chicken until golden brown on both sides. Remove from casserole, add onion and fry for 5 minutes. Add red pepper, garlic and rice and cook for 2 minutes. Stir in all the remaining ingredients. Place the chicken on top then bring to the boil. Cover with a lid or foil and place in the centre of the oven.

Cook for 45 minutes or until the chicken is tender and the rice is fluffy.

To freeze: freeze when cold for up to 2 months. Thaw and reheat gently in covered saucepan on top of the stove.

ORIENTAL CHICKEN

Serve with bean sprout salad and rice.

Serves 4–6

8–12 small chicken joints or thighs

3 tablespoons soy sauce

1 tablespoon oil

1 oz (25g) margarine

8 oz (225g) onion, peeled and finely sliced

1 level tablespoon flour

$\frac{1}{2}$ level teaspoon ginger

2 level teaspoons French mustard

2–3 teaspoons lemon juice

$\frac{1}{4}$ pint (150 ml) stock or water

Pepper

$\frac{1}{2}$ level teaspoon salt

Remove the skin from the chicken. Place the joints in a basin, add soy sauce and marinate for 2 hours, turning occasionally.

Set the oven to warm, gas mark 3 or 325°F/160°C.

Heat the oil and margarine, drain the chicken joints, then fry quickly to brown. Remove the chicken joints to a 2 pint (1·1 litre) shallow casserole and set aside in a warm place.

Add the onion to the fat and fry for a couple of minutes. Stir in the flour, ginger, mustard, lemon juice, stock or water, seasoning and any leftover soy sauce. Bring to the boil, stirring, then pour over the chicken.

Cover chicken with foil and bake in the centre of the oven for $1\frac{1}{2}$ hours or until the chicken is very tender.

To freeze: freeze when cold for 1 month. Thaw and reheat thoroughly in covered saucepan on top of the stove.

TANDOORI CHICKEN

Serves 4

$2\frac{1}{2}$ lb (1·2 kg) oven-ready roasting chicken or 4 large or 8 small joints

1 large clove garlic

1 level teaspoon ginger

1 level tablespoon mild paprika pepper

Tandoori Chicken

1 level teaspoon ground coriander

$\frac{1}{2}$ level teaspoon turmeric

$\frac{1}{2}$ level teaspoon ground cumin

2 level teaspoons salt

Juice of $\frac{1}{2}$ lemon

5 oz (150g) single cream

Note: Ready-made tandoori mixture can be bought. Follow directions on label, adding lemon juice and cream.

Wipe chicken and remove any feathers. Halve the chicken by cutting along the breast bone with scissors or a knife.

Hold the chicken firmly and cut either side of the back bone: a strong sharp knife may be needed as well as scissors.

Cut each chicken piece in half, following the natural line between the joints – one breast and one leg, i.e. four joints in all. Slash the skin 3 or 4 times to allow the spicy mixture to penetrate to the flesh.

Peel and crush the garlic and add to the spices, strained lemon juice and single cream. Mix well with a metal spoon.

Spicy Chicken
and Fruit Curry

Turn the chicken pieces in the spicy cream and leave in a cold place for 4–6 hours. Turn occasionally to allow chicken time to soak up flavour.

Set the oven to hot, gas mark 7 or 425°F/220°C. Bake skin side up in oiled tin towards top of oven for 35–40 minutes. Baste occasionally.

Not suitable for freezing.

SPICY CHICKEN AND FRUIT CURRY

Lots of ingredients but very simple to cook.

Serves 4

8 small chicken joints

Salt and pepper

2 tablespoons oil

1 oz (25g) margarine

$2\frac{1}{2}$ lb (1·2 kg) onions, peeled and sliced

2 sticks celery, sliced

1 green pepper, de-seeded and sliced

1 red pepper, de-seeded and sliced

2 tomatoes, skinned and quartered

2 eating apples, peeled and diced

Grated rind and juice of 1 orange

2 cloves garlic, peeled and crushed, optional

2–3 level tablespoons medium curry powder

2 level tablespoons flour

$\frac{1}{2}$ pint (300 ml) chicken stock, or water and half a stock cube

1 oz (25g) sultanas

2 bananas, thickly sliced

2 level tablespoons desiccated coconut

Remove the skin from the chicken joints and season the joints with salt and pepper.

Heat the oil in a large frying pan and fry the joints until golden brown on all sides. Reduce the heat and cook for about 10 minutes. Remove the joints to a plate. Heat the margarine in the same pan, add all the vegetables, apples and orange rind and juice and gently fry for about 5 minutes to start to soften the vegetables.

Add the garlic, curry powder, and flour and stir over a low heat for a few minutes.

Stir in the stock or water and stock cube. Bring to the boil. Reduce the heat to a simmer then add the chicken joints. Cover and simmer for 1 hour.

Add the sultanas and thickly sliced banana and cook for a further 10 minutes.

Serve with coconut sprinkled over the top.

To freeze: do not add sultanas, bananas or coconut. When cold freeze for up to 1 month. Partially thaw then reheat in large frying pan. Complete as in recipe.

DUCK À L'ORANGE

Serves 4

$4\frac{1}{2}$–5 lb (2–2·3 kg) oven-ready duck, fresh or frozen

$\frac{1}{2}$ level teaspoon salt

3 large oranges

2 tablespoons lemon juice

2 level tablespoons cornflour

$\frac{1}{2}$ pint (300 ml) stock, approx.

1 teaspoon vinegar

1 level tablespoon demerara sugar

Thaw the frozen duck thoroughly. Set the oven to moderately hot, gas mark 5 or 375°F/190°C.

Remove the giblets then prick the duck well on the underside with a fine skewer. Weigh the duck and calculate the cooking time allowing 30 minutes per lb (450g). Place the duck in a roasting tin and cook in centre of the oven.

To make the giblet stock, wash the giblets then place in a small pan with the salt and cover with water. Simmer for 20 minutes.

To make the sauce, with a potato peeler pare off the rind of 2 oranges, then squeeze the juice. Put the pared rind and orange and lemon juice into a pan, cover and simmer for 10 minutes to extract the flavour. Strain.

Cut half pared rind into thin matchlike sticks. Discard rest. If liked, cut decoration into skin of third orange; slice to garnish.

When the duck is cooked lift out on to a serving plate and keep hot.

Drain off all but 2 tablespoons of fat from the tin – leave the small amount of juice in the tin as well. Stir in the cornflour, scraping up all the bits from the tin, then add the orange and lemon juice, orange shreds, $\frac{1}{2}$ pint (300 ml) giblet stock and vinegar. Stir in the sugar and orange slice garnish and simmer for 2–3 minutes. Taste and season.

Lift out the orange slices and arrange over the duck. Either pour the sauce over the duck or serve separately. Cut the duck into quarters and garnish with watercress sprigs if liked.

To freeze: freeze the duck and sauce separately for up to 2 months. Thaw completely. Reheat together in pan or covered dish in oven.

PUDDINGS - HOT AND COLD

Even in these calorie-conscious days, most families like puddings and feel hard-done-by if they aren't served one. In Britain, we've a rich tradition of delicious desserts. Hot, cold, simple, sumptuous, here are some exciting ways to round off a meal, whether it's a straightforward family supper, or something altogether more special.

Tips for Steamed Puddings

Puddings need room to rise so cover the top with either a double thickness of greased greaseproof paper or greased foil and make a $1\frac{1}{2}$ inch (4 cm) deep pleat across the centre to allow for expansion. Tie the paper or foil tightly under the rim with string. It's a good idea to make a handle over the basin so that the hot pudding is easier to lift out.

Choose greaseproof or foil coverings for puddings needing up to 2 hours' steaming, and foil for puddings requiring longer cooking.

If you don't have a steamer you can 'boil' the pudding by standing the basin on two skewers or on an upturned saucer. The boiling water should reach about halfway up the basin. Cover the pan tightly with a lid.

Keep the water boiling briskly and steadily, all the time, adding more boiling water as needed. 'Sad' puddings happen because the water has gone off the boil or leaked into the pudding.

To prevent aluminium pans discolouring, add 1 tablespoon of lemon juice or vinegar or a piece of lemon rind to the water.

Puddings can be steamed in a pressure cooker – check manufacturer's instructions.

To unmould, ease round the edge with a knife, invert on a hot plate and shake gently. Leave the basin inverted to keep the heat and moisture in.

TREACLE PUDDING

Serves 6

FOR THE TOPPING:

4 tablespoons treacle

4 teaspoons orange juice

2 level tablespoons fresh breadcrumbs

FOR THE PUDDING:

4 oz (100g) margarine

4 oz (100g) caster sugar

2 eggs, size 3

Finely grated rind and juice of 1 orange

8 oz (225g) self-raising flour

Mix the treacle, orange juice and breadcrumbs together then spoon into a well-greased 2 pint (1·1 litre) pudding basin.

Cream the margarine and sugar together. Add the eggs, one at a time, beating well after each addition. Beat in the orange rind, then fold in the flour and orange juice. Spoon the mixture on top of the treacle. Cover with a double sheet of greaseproof paper with a $1\frac{1}{2}$ inch (4 cm) pleat down the centre. Secure with string. Steam or boil for 2 hours, topping up the saucepan with boiling water as necessary.

Serve with extra black treacle and custard.

Pressure cooking: Put $1\frac{1}{2}$ pints (900 ml) boiling water in cooker. Steam pudding for 15 minutes then cook for 30 minutes at low pressure. Reduce pressure slowly.

To freeze: freeze when cold for up to 2 months. Steam from frozen for $1-1\frac{1}{2}$ hours.

Treacle Pudding

Tangy Bread
and Butter
Pudding, page
68

TANGY BREAD AND BUTTER PUDDING

Serve this delicious pudding with cream for an extra special treat.

Serves 4

6 medium slices bread

2–3 oz (50–75g) butter or margarine

3 level tablespoons lemon curd

2 oz (50g) dried mixed fruit

1½ oz (40g) sugar

2 eggs, size 3

1 pint (600 ml) milk

If liked, remove the crusts from the bread. Spread bread with butter or margarine then lemon curd and cut each slice into 4 triangles or squares.

Arrange half the bread over the bottom of a 2 pint (1·1 litre) dish and sprinkle over most of the fruit and half the sugar. Top with remaining bread, arranging it butter side up in an attractive pattern.

Beat the eggs then stir in the milk and beat again. Strain first, if preferred, to remove the egg threads then pour the mixture over the bread. Sprinkle on the rest of the fruit and sugar. Leave to stand for 15–20 minutes.

Set the oven to moderate, gas mark 4 or 350°F/180°C.

Bake the pudding in the centre of the oven for 45–50 minutes until the pudding is firm and set.

Not suitable for freezing.

SPOTTED DICK

Serve with custard.

Serves 4

4 oz (100g) self-raising flour

4 oz (100g) fresh white breadcrumbs

4 oz (100g) suet

3 oz (75g) caster sugar

3 oz (75g) currants

Spotted Dick

Grated rind of 1 lemon

Salt

About $\frac{1}{4}$ pint (150 ml) milk to mix

Mix together the flour, breadcrumbs, suet, sugar, currants, lemon rind and a pinch of salt. Stir in enough milk to form a medium soft dropping consistency.

Spoon the mixture into a well-buttered $1\frac{1}{2}$ pint (900 ml) pudding basin. Pleat a double thickness of greaseproof and place over the pudding – the pleat gives room for the pudding to rise – and tie it securely round the basin with string. Steam for 2 hours, adding more boiling water to the pan as required.

Pressure cooking: Put $1\frac{1}{2}$ pints (900 ml) of water into the pressure cooker. Pre-steam the pudding for 15 minutes then steam at 5 lb (2·3 kg) pressure for 35 minutes.

To freeze: freeze as for Treacle Pudding (page 66).

SPOTTED DATE PUDDING

Eat hot as a pudding, or cold as a cake.

Serves 5–6

4 oz (100g) chopped dates

4 oz (100g) fresh breadcrumbs

$\frac{1}{2}$ level teaspoon salt

3 oz (75g) shredded suet

3 oz (75g) caster sugar

Grated rind of 1 lemon

1 egg, size 3

7–8 tablespoons milk

1 tablespoon golden syrup

Set the oven to moderate, gas mark 4 or 350°F/180°C.

Grease a deep 2–$2\frac{1}{2}$ pint (1·1–1·5 litre) dish. Press some dates against the side of the dish to give a spotted look.

Mix the flour, breadcrumbs, salt, suet, sugar, lemon rind and remaining dates together. Beat the egg and add to the flour with enough milk to give a soft dropping consistency. Spoon the syrup into the dish, then pour the date mixture on top.

Bake for about 1 hour until firm and springy to the touch.

To freeze: freeze as for Treacle Pudding (page 66). Thaw and serve cold.

AN UPPER CRUST PIE

Serve hot with custard.

Serves 4

FOR THE SHORTCRUST PASTRY:

6 oz (175g) plain flour

Pinch of salt

$1\frac{1}{2}$ oz (40g) lard

$1\frac{1}{2}$ oz (40g) margarine

1 egg yolk, size 3

2 tablespoons cold water

FOR THE FILLING:

1 lb (450g) rhubarb, after trimming

1 orange

8 oz (225g) dried prunes, soaked overnight

3 oz (75g) granulated sugar

1 level tablespoon cornflour

1 egg white, size 3

Caster sugar to dredge

Sift the flour and salt into a bowl and rub in the fats until the mixture resembles fine breadcrumbs. Mix in the egg yolk and water to a smooth dough. Roll in cling wrap and chill.

Set the oven to fairly hot, gas mark 6 or 400°F/200°C.

Chop rhubarb into 1 inch (2·5 cm) pieces. Grate the rind from the orange, remove the white pith and cut the flesh into small segments. Mix prunes, orange rind and flesh, rhubarb, sugar and cornflour.

Roll out the pastry on a floured surface and cut a lid shape to fit a $2\frac{1}{2}$ pint (1·5 litre) deep pie dish. Arrange the trimmings neatly round the sides of the dish and place the filling in the dish. Dampen the pastry edges with water, place the lid on top and press edges together. Re-roll any remaining pastry scraps and make a pastry plait to decorate the lid. Whisk egg white with a fork until foamy and paint on to the pastry, taking care not to break the bubbles. Dredge heavily with caster sugar as this gives a crunchy topping. Make a slit in the centre of the pie to let out the steam, then place on a baking sheet and bake for 35 minutes.

To freeze: cool and freeze for up to 3 months. Thaw and serve cold, or reheat in a moderately hot oven for 20–30 minutes.

RICH RICE PUDDING

Serves 4

| 1½ oz (40g) butter or margarine |
| 4 oz (100g) pudding (round-grain) rice, washed and drained |
| Grated rind of 1 lemon |
| 2 oz (50g) sugar |
| 1 egg, size 3 |
| 1 pint (450 ml) milk |
| 2 oz (50g) sultanas |
| 1 oz (25g) glacé cherries, chopped neatly |
| 1 oz (25g) angelica, chopped |
| Nutmeg |

Set the oven to warm, gas mark 3 or 325°F/160°C.

Rub ½ oz (10g) margarine or butter round the rim of a 2 pint (1·1 litre) ovenproof dish.

Mix rice, lemon rind and sugar and place in the dish. Beat the egg with milk and strain on to the rice. Stir in sultanas, glacé cherries and angelica. Sprinkle nutmeg on top and dot with rest of butter.

Bake in the centre of the oven for 2 hours until the middle of the pudding is soft but firm and the skin golden brown.

Not suitable for freezing.

CRUNCHY APRICOT UPSIDE-DOWNER

Serves 6

| 2 level tablespoons golden syrup |
| 7 oz (200g) can apricot halves |
| 3 glacé cherries, halved |
| 1 oz (25g) crunchy muesli or muesli bar |
| 6 oz (175g) margarine |
| 6 oz (175g) caster sugar |
| 3 eggs, size 3 |
| ¼ teaspoon almond essence |
| 5 oz (150g) self-raising flour |
| 1 oz (25g) ground almonds |

Set the oven to fairly hot, gas mark 6 or 400°F/200°C.

Grease a 2½–3 pint (1·5–1·8 litre) ring tin. Spoon the golden syrup over the base of the tin. Drain the apricots, reserving the juice. Place half a cherry in each apricot half before arranging them in the ring tin. Sprinkle the muesli or crushed bar between the apricots.

Cream the margarine and sugar until light and fluffy. Add the eggs one at a time, beating well after each addition. Beat in the essence and 2 tablespoons apricot juice. Fold in the flour and almonds.

Carefully spoon mixture over the apricots and bake just above the centre of the oven for about 35 minutes until well risen and springy to the touch.

Turn out and serve with custard made with milk and any leftover apricot juice.

To freeze: freeze when cold for up to 2 months. Thaw and serve cold.

CHOCOLATE MARBLE LOAF

Serves 4–6

| 2–3 oz (50–75g) plain chocolate |
| 4 oz (100g) margarine |
| 4 oz (100g) sugar |
| 2 eggs, size 3 |
| 5 oz (150g) self-raising flour |
| 2–3 tablespoons water |
| 1 macaroon |
| CHOCOLATE SAUCE: |
| 2 oz (50g) sugar |
| ½ pint (300 ml) water |
| 1 oz (25g) cocoa powder |

From top:
Upper Crust Pie,
page 69;
Spotted Date
Pudding, page
69; Rich Rice
Pudding;
Crunchy Apricot
Upside-Downer;
Chocolate
Marble Loaf;
Butterscotch
Pie

Set the oven to moderate, gas mark 4 or 350°F/180°C. Grease and base-line a 1½ pint (900 ml) loaf tin.

Break the chocolate into pieces and place in a basin in the oven for 5 minutes to melt, then remove.

Cream the margarine and sugar until soft and fluffy. Add the eggs, one at a time, beating well after each addition. Fold in the flour and water. Spoon half the mixture into another basin and mix in the cooled chocolate.

Place two layers of chocolate and plain mixture in the tin, alternating the flavours. With a knife, cut through the mixture in a criss-cross fashion to give the pudding its marble effect. Cut the macaroon into cubes and sprinkle over the top.

Bake above the centre of the oven for 40–50 minutes until firm and springy to the touch.

Make the chocolate sauce: boil the sugar, water and cocoa powder together for 5 minutes, stirring all the time, until smooth. Serve in a jug with the chocolate loaf.

To freeze: wrap and freeze when cold for up to 3 months. Thaw and serve cold. The sauce is unsuitable for freezing.

BUTTERSCOTCH PIE

Serves 6–8

FOR THE BISCUIT CASE:

6 oz (175g) digestive biscuits

3 oz (75g) margarine or butter

FOR THE FILLING:

2 oz (50g) plain flour

6 oz (175g) brown sugar

8 fl oz (240 ml) milk

1 oz (25g) butter

4 tablespoons cold water

1 teaspoon vanilla essence

2 eggs, size 3, separated

2 oz (50g) caster sugar

Place biscuits in a plastic bag and crush with a rolling pin. Melt margarine or butter in a saucepan, then quickly stir in biscuit crumbs. Press mixture evenly into a 9 inch (23 cm) pie plate or flan dish, then chill.

Mix flour and sugar in a bowl. Heat milk and add to mixture with butter and water. Pour into a saucepan and heat very slowly until mixture begins to thicken, then add vanilla and egg yolks. Cook until very thick and glossy, beating well with a wooden spoon to prevent lumps forming. Cool slightly and pour into the biscuit case. Make a swirl on top with a round-bladed knife.

Set the oven to cool, gas mark 2 or 300°F/150°C.

Beat egg whites until they form stiff peaks, then fold in caster sugar. Pipe or spoon meringue on top of the flan and bake for 10–15 minutes until lightly browned.

Not suitable for freezing.

GOOSEBERRY TART

Serves 6–8

FOR THE PASTRY:

6 oz (175g) plain flour

3 oz (75g) margarine and lard, mixed

2 level tablespoons icing sugar, sifted

Water to mix

FOR THE FILLING:

1½ lb (700g) large, ripe gooseberries

1 egg, size 3

3 oz (75g) caster sugar

5 oz (150g) single cream

Sift the flour into a bowl, add the fats and rub in until the mixture resembles fine breadcrumbs. Add the icing sugar and then stir in enough water to give a soft but not sticky dough. Knead lightly then cover and chill in the refrigerator for 30 minutes.

Set the oven to moderately hot, gas mark 5 or 375°F/190°C.

Roll out the pastry on a floured surface and use to line a 9 inch (23 cm) fluted flan tin or ring.

Top and tail the gooseberries and arrange them, standing on end, over the base of the flan. Beat together the egg, sugar and cream and pour over the gooseberries.

Gooseberry Tart

Apple Almond
Pie

Stand the flan case on a baking sheet and bake above the centre of the oven for 35–40 minutes or until the filling has set.

To freeze: freeze for up to 2 months. Thaw and serve.

APPLE ALMOND PIE

Serves 6

FOR THE PASTRY:

8 oz (225g) plain flour

3 oz (75g) margarine

1 oz (25g) caster sugar

1 egg yolk, size 3

3–4 tablespoons cold water

FOR THE FILLING:

4 oz (100g) almond paste or marzipan

3 oz (75g) butter

2 oz (50g) caster sugar

1½ lb (700g) eating apples, peeled

2 egg whites, size 3

TO GLAZE:

1 egg yolk, size 3, beaten

1 teaspoon water

Sift flour into a bowl and rub in margarine. Stir in sugar, egg yolk and enough water to give a soft, not sticky, dough. Wrap in cling wrap and chill for 30 minutes.

Set oven to hot, gas mark 7 or 425°F/ 220°C. Roll out two-thirds of pastry and line a 9 inch (23 cm) flan dish or tin. Trim edges. Prick base with fork. Knead trimmings into rest of pastry. Roll out and cut into ½ inch (1 cm) wide strips, to be used for the lattice on top. Grate almond paste over pastry case.

Cream butter and sugar until fluffy. Grate

apples and stir into creamed mixture. Whisk egg whites until stiff, then fold into mixture. Spread apple meringue over almond paste and smooth level.

Cover and edge with lattice of pastry strips. Brush pastry with glaze. Bake above centre of oven for 40–45 minutes.

To freeze: wrap and freeze when cold for up to 3 months. Thaw and eat cold. Pastry can be crisped in oven for 10 minutes if liked.

STRAWBERRY CLOUD

Serve with digestive biscuits.

Serves 6–8

8 oz (225g) ripe strawberries

1 egg white

2–3 oz (50–75g) icing sugar, sifted

1 tablespoon lemon juice

Hull the strawberries (wash only if dirty then dry thoroughly on kitchen towel); mash them roughly with a fork.

Pour egg white into a large bowl, add icing sugar and whisk gently with an electric or rotary whisk. Add strawberries and continue to whisk gently to mix, then increase the speed to high and whisk for about 7–10 minutes with the electric mixer, or briskly for 15–20 minutes with the rotary whisk until light, foamy and thick. Whisk in the lemon juice, then spoon into a serving bowl or individual dishes.

Not suitable for freezing.

From top:
Bobbly
Blackcurrant
Bake; Luscious
Fruit Medley,
page 76;
Strawberry
Cloud;
Raspberry and
Vanilla Ring,
page 77;
Summer Fruit
Pudding;
Gooseberry and
Almond
Amulets, page
76

SUMMER FRUIT PUDDING

Serves 4–6

8 oz (225g) strawberries

6–8 oz (175–225g) raspberries

3–4 oz (75–100g) icing sugar

1 tablespoon lemon juice

5½–6 trifle sponges

5 fl oz (150 ml) double or whipping cream

Hull the strawberries then slice or cut in half; pick over the raspberries and remove any bad ones. Transfer the fruit to a basin and sprinkle over the icing sugar and lemon juice, then leave the fruit for 30 minutes to 1 hour to extract the juice.

Split the sponges in half and cut each half into two triangles. Line the base and sides of a 1 lb (450g) loaf tin with the trifle sponges, reserving two sponges (eight triangles) for the top. Spoon the fruit and juice into the lined tin and cover the top with the rest of the sponge triangles. Cover with cling wrap or foil, press down firmly and weight down with a can of food. Stand the tin in a shallow dish and leave overnight in the fridge.

Turn the pudding out on to a serving dish.

Whisk cream until thick then spoon some into a piping bag with large star nozzle attached and decorate the top of the pudding. Serve the rest of the cream separately.

Not suitable for freezing.

BOBBLY BLACKCURRANT BAKE

Serves 6

FOR THE PASTRY:

10 oz (275g) plain flour

½ level teaspoon cinnamon

A pinch of salt

6 oz (175g) margarine

4 oz (100g) caster sugar

1 egg, size 3, beaten

FOR THE FILLING:

12 oz (350g) blackcurrants

5–7 oz (150–200g) granulated sugar

2 tablespoons water

Sift the flour, cinnamon and salt into a mixing bowl. Cut the margarine into pieces then rub them into the flour until it resembles breadcrumbs. Stir in the sugar and beaten egg, and bind them together into a firm dough. Wrap in foil or cling wrap and chill in the fridge overnight or until the pastry is a hard block.

Remove the blackcurrant stalks. If necessary, wash the fruit then drain thoroughly. Put the fruit in a pan and, if it has not been washed, add the water. Simmer for about 10 minutes then stir in the sugar and boil gently to a fairly thick consistency; leave to cool.

Cut the pastry in half. Grate half into an 8½ inch (21·5 cm) spring clip tin (see note). Spread over the base and press down gently but firmly. Spread the blackcurrants over the pastry and grate the rest of the pastry over the top, making sure the topping is taken right to the edge of the tin to prevent the filling bubbling up. However, do not flatten the top pastry layer.

Bake in a fairly hot oven, gas mark 6 or 400°F/200°C for 35–40 minutes, until the pastry is an even brown. Cool in the tin for about 5 minutes to allow the pastry crusts to harden before easing away from the sides of the tin. Leave to cool completely, then remove the base.

Note: Alternatively, use an 8 inch (20 cm) round cake tin with a loose base.

To freeze: freeze when cold for up to 2 months. Thaw and eat cold.

GOOSEBERRY AND ALMOND AMULETS

Serves 6

12 oz (350g) gooseberries

1 level tablespoon cornflour

½ pint (300 ml) water

2–4 oz (50–100g) brown sugar

FOR THE AMULETS:

1 egg white, size 3

1 oz (25g) ground almonds

1 oz (25g) plain flour

2 oz (50g) caster sugar

TO SERVE:

1 large block vanilla ice-cream

Top and tail the gooseberries.

Blend the cornflour with a little of the water in a pan then stir in the rest of the water and the sugar. Bring to the boil, stirring all the time, and boil for about ½

minute. Add the gooseberries and cook until tender but still whole, then leave to cool.

To make the Amulets: set the oven to hot, gas mark 6 or 400°F/200°C. Put the egg white into a bowl and break it up lightly with a fork. Sprinkle the almonds, flour and sugar over the egg white and mix to a smooth paste.

Cut a sheet of non-stick Bakewell paper in half. Draw three rectangles, 9×2 inches (23×5 cm), on each half of the paper. Brush 2 baking sheets with a little fat then place non-stick paper on top. Divide the almond mixture equally into 6, then spread ⅙th over each rectangle with a palette knife. Place one baking sheet in the oven and bake for 6 minutes.

Remove the biscuits from the oven and, as each one becomes cool enough to handle, peel each strip off paper and roll into a 'bracelet' shape. Place on cooling rack to harden completely, then repeat with the other two strips.

Put other baking sheet in oven, bake and roll into 'bracelets' as before. If the mixture hardens before you have a chance to roll it up, return the sheet to the oven for 15–20 seconds to soften slightly.

To serve, stand each amulet on an individual serving plate or dish, spoon in a scoopful or two of ice-cream and pour over the gooseberry sauce.

Not suitable for freezing.

LUSCIOUS FRUIT MEDLEY

For a special occasion, stir 3–4 tablespoons brandy or sherry into the cooled fruit or, alternatively, flavour the cream with brandy or sherry.

Serves 8

8 oz (225g) gooseberries

8 oz (225g) blackcurrants

8 oz (225g) strawberries

8 oz (225g) raspberries

8 oz (225g) granulated sugar

1 pint (600 ml) water

4 level teaspoons arrowroot

Top and tail the gooseberries; remove the stalks from the blackcurrants, wash if necessary, and drain well. Hull the strawberries and wash if necessary; pick over the raspberries.

Dissolve the sugar in the water in a medium-sized pan, then boil gently for about 5 minutes.

Blend the arrowroot to a smooth paste with a little extra water, then stir into the sugar syrup. Bring to the boil, stirring all the time, and cook until the mixture clears. Add the gooseberries and blackcurrants and simmer until the fruit is tender but still whole (about 5–8 minutes), then remove from the heat. Stir in the strawberries, cut in half if large, and the raspberries. Leave to cool completely before pouring into a serving bowl or individual glasses. Serve with cream and sponge finger biscuits.

Note: if you grow soft fruits in your garden, different weights of each fruit can be used, as long as the total amounts to 1 lb (450g) for 4 people and 2 lb (900g) for 8 people.

Not suitable for freezing.

RASPBERRY AND VANILLA RING

Serves 6

2 oz (50g) sugar

2 level tablespoons redcurrant jelly

1/4 pint (150 ml) water plus 1 tablespoon

2 level teaspoons gelatine

8 oz (225g) raspberries

FOR THE VANILLA LAYER:

2 eggs, size 3, separated

2 level tablespoons cornflour

2 oz (50g) sugar

1 pint (600 ml) milk

1/2 oz (15g) (1 sachet) gelatine

2 tablespoons water

1 teaspoon vanilla essence

3 tablespoons double cream

Dissolve the sugar and redcurrant jelly in the water and bring to the boil, then remove from the heat. Soak the gelatine in 1 tablespoon water then stir into the jelly syrup to dissolve; leave to cool.

Pick over the raspberries, removing any bad fruit, then stir them into the syrup. Rinse a 2½ pint (1·5 litre) ring mould with cold water and pour in the raspberry syrup. Leave on one side to set.

Meanwhile, make the vanilla layer. Blend the egg yolks, cornflour and sugar with 1 tablespoon of milk. Heat the rest of the milk to just below simmering, then gradually stir into the egg yolk mixture. Return to the pan and cook gently until the milk has thickened then remove from the heat. Soak the gelatine in 2 tablespoons of cold water, add to the sauce and stir to dissolve; add the vanilla essence. Leave to cool until on the point of setting then stir in the cream.

Whisk the egg whites until stiff then fold them into the vanilla cream and pour over the raspberry layer. Leave the ring mould in a cool place to set completely. When ready to serve, turn the Raspberry and Vanilla Ring out on to a serving plate.

Not suitable for freezing.

PASSION FRUIT SYLLABUB

Serves 4

2 passion fruits

5 oz (150g) double cream

1 oz (25g) caster sugar

2 egg whites, size 3

Milk

1/2 teaspoon lemon juice

Cut the passion fruits in half and scoop out the pulp and seeds. Press through a sieve. You will get only a small amount of juice – about 2 tablespoons – from the fruit, but this has a strong flavour so do not worry.

Whip the cream until it stands in soft peaks, then fold in the sugar. Whisk the egg whites until stiff, then fold into the cream.

Make the juice up to 1/4 pint (150 ml) with milk, then fold this into the cream and egg-white mixture. Stir in the lemon juice.

Divide between four stemmed glasses and serve at once.

Not suitable for freezing.

BASIC VANILLA ICE-CREAM

Makes 1 pint (600 ml)

6 oz (175g) caster sugar

2 eggs, size 3

$\frac{1}{2}$ pint (300 ml) milk

$1\frac{1}{2}$ teaspoons vanilla essence

$14\frac{1}{2}$ oz (410g) can evaporated milk

Place 5 oz (150g) caster sugar with the eggs in a bowl and beat together with a wooden spoon until light and fluffy. Heat milk to just below simmering point and pour over egg mixture, stirring all the time. Place bowl of custard over pan of boiling water and cook, stirring until the mixture coats the back of the spoon.

Remove from the heat, stir in the vanilla essence, then sprinkle surface with remaining sugar and allow to become cold. Meanwhile, chill evaporated milk in the fridge. When custard is cold stir in the evaporated milk, then pour into a foil container and freeze.

Allow to freeze for about $2\frac{1}{2}$ hours and then remove from freezer and break up the ice-cream to stop large ice crystals from being formed. This can be done in a food processor, with electric beaters or simply by using a wooden spoon. (At this stage the flavouring of your choice can be added.) Return ice-cream to freezer.

To serve, remove from freezer 15 minutes before needed.

CHOCOLATE ICE-CREAM

2 oz (50g) plain chocolate, melted

1 pint (600 ml) Basic Vanilla Ice-Cream (see above)

Ice-cream wafers

Stir melted chocolate into the half-set ice-cream. Return to the freezer to freeze completely. When required scoop into small balls using a melon baller and serve with wafers.

MUESLI AND HONEY ICE-CREAM

2 oz (50g) toasted muesli

2 tablespoons honey

1 pint (600 ml) Basic Vanilla Ice-Cream (see above)

Stir most of the crushed muesli and all the honey into the half-set ice-cream. Return to the freezer to freeze completely. Scoop into balls and serve with extra crushed muesli.

Basic Vanilla
Ice-Cream and
Variations

TUTTI FRUTTI ICE-CREAM

2 oz (50g) glacé cherries

2 oz (50g) angelica

1 pint (600 ml) Basic Vanilla Ice-Cream (see page 78)

2 oz (50g) chopped mixed peel

Chop the cherries and angelica. Add to the half-set ice-cream with the mixed peel.

Stir well to distribute the fruit throughout the ice-cream and place in the freezer to become fully frozen.

MAGIC MARSHMALLOW ICE-CREAM

2 oz (50g) marshmallows

1 pint (600 ml) Basic Vanilla Ice-Cream (see page 78)

Dip the blades of a pair of scissors in hot water and cut marshmallows into $\frac{1}{4}$ inch (5 mm) cubes.

Stir cubed marshmallows into the half-set ice-cream. Return to the freezer to freeze completely. Cut ice-cream into cubes and serve with biscuits of your choice.

SHERRY AND RATAFIA ICE-CREAM

2 oz (50g) ratafia biscuits or macaroons, crushed

1 tablespoon sherry

1 pint (600 ml) Basic Vanilla Ice-Cream (see page 78)

Stir crushed biscuits and sherry into the half-set ice-cream. Return to the freezer to freeze completely. Scoop into balls and serve with extra ratafia biscuits.

CHOCOLATE CHIP ICE-CREAM

2 oz (50g) peppermint Matchmakers, chopped

$\frac{1}{2}$ teaspoon peppermint essence

1 pint (600 ml) Basic Vanilla Ice-Cream (see page 78)

Stir chopped Matchmakers and peppermint essence into the half-set ice-cream. Return to the freezer to freeze completely. Scoop into balls and serve with extra Matchmakers.

PINA COLADA ICE-CREAM

12 oz (350g) can pineapple slices

1 pint (600 ml) Basic Vanilla Ice-Cream (see page 78)

2 oz (50g) desiccated coconut

2 tablespoons dark rum

Glacé cherries

Reserve one slice of pineapple for decoration and liquidize remaining pineapple slices with juice to make a purée. Stir into the half-set ice-cream with the coconut and rum. Refreeze. Cut reserved pineapple into cubes and place a cube on each cocktail stick with two glacé cherries.

Scoop into balls and serve decorated with pineapple and cherry sticks.

CRANBERRY AND ORANGE FROZEN WHIP

Serves 6

15 oz (420g) carton natural yogurt

$6\frac{1}{2}$ oz (185g) jar cranberry and orange sauce

3 oz (75g) caster sugar

Stir yogurt, cranberry and orange sauce and caster sugar together. Pour into a foil container and place in freezer to become completely frozen.

MANGO ICE-CREAM

Serves 4–6

1 ripe mango

10 oz (275g) soured cream

3 oz (75g) caster sugar

Peel the mango and remove the flesh from the stone. Mash with a fork or blend in a processor, stir in soured cream and caster sugar, and mix well.

Pour into a plastic container, leaving a $\frac{1}{2}$ inch (1 cm) head-space and cover with lid. Freeze until the mixture is half frozen.

Remove from the container and beat well with a wooden spoon or in a processor to break up the large ice crystals.

Return to the container and freeze until firm.

COOKING FOR ONE OR TWO

In this chapter, I've come up with lots of ideas on how to make eating on your own, or cooking for just two or three, a more enjoyable experience. No one wants to spend hours in the kitchen in order to produce a single-serving supper, and it's all too easy to join the tea and toast brigade. You'll find these meals interesting and appetising without being too much bother, and a good basis for maintaining a healthy, balanced diet. Remember, as well, that with only yourself to please, you'll be able to experiment with different flavours and more exotic dishes. Lucky you! And just because there are only one or two in the family doesn't mean you have to forego the Sunday Roast – see the recipes at the end of this chapter!

MEALS FOR ONE

CREAMY CRUNCH MUSHROOMS

2 spring onions, trimmed and chopped
1 small clove garlic, peeled and crushed
2 oz (50g) cottage cheese
Salt and pepper
3 large flat mushrooms [2–3 oz (50–75g) total weight]
1 crispbread
$\frac{1}{2}$ oz (15g) Edam cheese, grated

Set the oven to fairly hot, gas mark 6 or 400°F/200°C.

Mix the spring onions, garlic and cottage cheese, with salt and pepper to taste.

Place the mushrooms in a small oven-proof dish and spoon some cottage cheese mixture on the top of each. Break the crispbread into crumbs and mix with the cheese and a little salt and pepper. Sprinkle over the cottage cheese. Bake towards the top of the oven for 15 minutes.

Not suitable for freezing.

SPICED CAULIFLOWER CHEESE

1 small cauliflower [12 oz (350g) prepared weight]
1 tablespoon vinegar
$\frac{1}{2}$ pint (300 ml) water
$\frac{1}{4}$ level teaspoon salt
2 cheese spread triangles
1 dessertspoon salad dressing
$\frac{1}{8}$ teaspoon ground nutmeg
Pepper
1 rasher back bacon, derinded

Place prepared cauliflower, vinegar, water and salt in a pan. Bring to the boil, cover and simmer for 10 minutes. Drain.

Meanwhile, cream the cheese spread with the dressing, then stir in the nutmeg and salt and pepper. Spread the cheese mixture over the cauliflower. Cut the bacon into six thin strips and arrange in a lattice fashion over the top of the cauliflower.

Place the cauliflower under the grill for 5 minutes until the bacon is cooked and the cheese lightly browned.

Not suitable for freezing.

From left: Salad Bowl; Creamy Crunch Mushrooms, page 81; Chicken Stir Fry; Frankfurter Ratatouille; Spiced Cauliflower Cheese, page 81; Fish Stack

SALAD BOWL

1 ripe pear, quartered, cored and cubed

1 slice [1 oz (25g)] ham, cut into $\frac{1}{2}$ inch (1 cm) squares

1 stick celery sliced

2 oz (50g) cottage cheese

1 tablespoon lemon juice

$\frac{1}{2}$ level teaspoon curry powder

Salt and pepper

Mix the pear, ham and celery and place in the serving bowl. Mix the cottage cheese with lemon juice, curry powder and salt and pepper to taste and spoon over the fruit and ham.

Not suitable for freezing.

CHICKEN STIR FRY

4 oz (100g) chicken

$\frac{1}{2}$ oz (15g) butter

2 spring onions, trimmed and chopped

1 tablespoon soy sauce

$\frac{1}{4}$ level teaspoon ginger

$\frac{1}{4}$ level teaspoon salt

Pepper

4 radishes, sliced

$\frac{1}{2}$ green pepper, de-seeded and chopped

3 oz (75g) bean sprouts

If necessary, remove the meat from the chicken joint and cut into thin strips.

Heat the fat in a frying pan, and cook the chicken quickly for 1 minute, stirring all the time. Stir in the spring onions, soy sauce, ginger, salt and pepper, radishes and green pepper and cook for 3 minutes, stirring. Add the bean sprouts and cook for a further 1–2 minutes. Serve immediately.

Not suitable for freezing.

FRANKFURTER RATATOUILLE

8 oz (225g) aubergines, cut into $\frac{1}{2}$ inch (1 cm) cubes

Pepper

2 level teaspoons salt

1 oz (25g) onion, chopped

2 oz (50g) courgettes, sliced

2 tomatoes, sliced

$\frac{1}{2}$ level teaspoon dried mint

2 tablespoons water

2 oz (50g) frankfurter, sliced

Place the cubed aubergine on a plate and sprinkle with salt. Stand for 1 hour, then rinse with cold water and drain well.

Place the aubergines and the rest of the ingredients in a pan. Bring to the boil, cover and simmer for 20–25 minutes, stirring occasionally.

Add pepper to taste and serve hot.

To freeze: freeze when cold for up to 1 month. Thaw for 30 minutes then reheat in pan adding a little more water.

FISH STACK

1 tomato, sliced
Salt and pepper
1 oz (25g) sweetcorn
3 oz (75g) cod portion
1 teaspoon lemon juice
1 oz (25g) Edam cheese, grated
1 teaspoon chopped parsley

Set the oven to fairly hot, gas mark 6 or 400°F/200°C.

Place the sliced tomato in the centre of a 12 inch (30 cm) square of foil. Season with salt and pepper. Sprinkle the corn over, then place the fish on top. Sprinkle with lemon juice and season well. Top with the cheese and parsley.

Secure the edges of the foil to form a loose parcel then bake above the centre of the oven for 30 minutes.

Not suitable for freezing.

COD WITH CORN

2 oz (50g) sweet corn, canned or frozen
1 tomato, sliced
Pepper and salt
4 oz (100g) cod fillet
1 teaspoon lemon juice
Half bunch watercress
1 oz (25g) Cheddar cheese, grated

Set the oven to fairly hot, gas mark 6 or 400°F/200°C.

Layer the corn, tomato and seasoning on a 12×12 inch (30×30 cm) square of foil. Place the fish on top. Sprinkle with lemon juice and a little more seasoning. Coarsely chop a few sprigs of watercress, and sprinkle over the fish. Cover with the grated Cheddar cheese.

Close and secure the foil, place on a baking tray and bake for 20 minutes.

To steam: prepare as above, wrap in foil, then place in a steamer over a pan of hot water and steam for 15 minutes.

Not suitable for freezing.

SAGE AND ONION PORK

$\frac{1}{2}$ small onion, peeled and sliced
2 level tablespoons frozen peas
1 medium raw potato, peeled and cubed
1 small cooking apple, peeled, cored and sliced
Pepper
$\frac{1}{4}$ level teaspoon salt
1 level teaspoon sage
4 oz (100g) lean pork, i.e., pork fillet or a thin pork chop

Set the oven to fairly hot, gas mark 6 or 400°F/200°C.

Layer the onion, peas, potato and apple with seasoning on a 12×12 inch (30×30 cm) square of foil. Sprinkle the sage over, then top with thin slices of pork or the pork chop. Close the foil, pressing the edges together, and cook above the centre of the oven for about 45 minutes. The pork can be quick fried to brown first, if liked.

Not suitable for freezing.

CHEESY JACKET POTATO

1 potato, washed and halved lengthways
Pepper
$\frac{1}{4}$ level teaspoon salt
4 spring onions, sliced
2 oz (50g) mushrooms, wiped and sliced
4 tablespoons soured cream or yogurt
1 level teaspoon cornflour
1 oz (25g) blue cheese

Set the oven to fairly hot, gas mark 6 or 400°F/200°C.

Score a criss-cross pattern on the cut-side of the potato halves, then place in the centre of a 12×12 inch (30×30 cm) square of foil. Sprinkle seasoning over the top.

Add the onion and mushrooms. Mix together the soured cream or yogurt and cornflour, then dab over the vegetables. Crumble the cheese over the top. Close the foil, securing the edges. Cook above the centre of the oven for 30–40 minutes or until tender.

To steam: prepare the potato halves as for baking, wrap in foil and steam over a high heat in a steamer for 30 minutes.

Not suitable for freezing.

CHICKEN AND PEPPERS

2 level teaspoons flour
2 level teaspoons paprika pepper
$\frac{1}{4}$ level teaspoon salt
$\frac{1}{8}$ level teaspoon pepper
1 chicken breast or drumstick, skinned
$\frac{1}{2}$ small onion, peeled and sliced
4 oz (100g) carrots, peeled and very finely sliced
1 small red pepper, de-seeded and sliced
$\frac{1}{2}$ oz (15g) margarine
2 tablespoons cider or orange juice

Set the oven to fairly hot, gas mark 6 or 400°F/200°C.

Mix the flour, paprika, salt and pepper together, then use to coat the chicken. Place the onion, carrots, red pepper and margarine on a 12×12 inch (30×30 cm) square of foil and add more seasoning. Place the chicken on top. Spoon over the cider or orange juice. Close the foil loosely. Place on a baking sheet and bake above the centre of the oven for 1 hour.

To steam: prepare as above. Wrap in foil, then place in a steamer over a pan of hot water and steam for 45 minutes.

To freeze: freeze when cold. Thaw completely before reheating.

From top: Devilled Beefburger; Liver with Bacon; Chicken and Peppers; Sage and Onion Pork, page 83; Cheesy Jacket Potato, page 83; Cod with Corn, page 83

DEVILLED BEEFBURGER

4 oz (100g) courgettes, washed and sliced
1 small green pepper, de-seeded and thinly sliced
2 spring onions, chopped
$\frac{1}{2}$ oz (15g) margarine
Pepper and a pinch of salt
1 level tablespoon tomato purée
1 teaspoon Worcestershire sauce
$\frac{1}{2}$ level teaspoon curry powder
1 beefburger

Set oven to fairly hot, gas mark 6 or 400°F/200°C.

Layer the courgettes, green pepper and onion on a 12×12 inch (30×30 cm) square of foil with the margarine and seasoning. Mix the tomato purée, Worcestershire sauce, and curry powder together. Spread on both sides of the beefburger, and place on top of the vegetables. Close and secure the foil. Place on a baking sheet and bake for 25 minutes.

To steam: prepare as above, wrap in foil, then place in a steamer over a pan of hot water and steam for 20 minutes.

To freeze: freeze when cold for up to 3 months. Reheat from frozen in fairly hot oven, or in a steamer.

LIVER WITH BACON

1 small carrot, peeled and sliced
1 small stick celery, sliced
$\frac{1}{2}$ onion, peeled and sliced
2 oz (50g) mushrooms, wiped and sliced
1–2 level tablespoons frozen peas
Pepper
$\frac{1}{4}$ level teaspoon salt
1 level teaspoon gravy granules
4 oz (100g) lamb's liver
1 tablespoon parsley, chopped
1 rasher lean bacon, derinded

Set the oven to fairly hot, gas mark 6 or 400°F/200°C.

Put the carrot, celery and onion into a pan and just cover with salted water. Bring to the boil and cook for 5 minutes. With a slotted spoon place the blanched vegetables in the centre of a 12×12 inch (30×30 cm) square of foil and add the mushrooms and peas. Season well. Mix the gravy granules with about 2 tablespoons of the cooking liquor. Pour over the vegetables in the foil.

Remove any skin or tubes from the liver, then slice thinly. Arrange the sliced liver over the top of the vegetables. Sprinkle with the parsley. With scissors snip the bacon over the top, close the foil. Bake for about 30 minutes.

To steam: prepare as above, wrap in foil tightly and steam for 15–20 minutes over a pan of hot water.

To freeze: freeze when cold for up to 1 month. Thaw and reheat in fairly hot oven for 20–30 minutes.

TROUT WITH TOMATOES

1 trout or mackerel, filleted
1 level tablespoon flour
Salt and pepper
1–2 tablespoons oil
1 small onion, peeled and finely chopped
1 oz (25g) mushrooms, chopped
1 level tablespoon chopped parsley
1 teaspoon vinegar
½ oz (15g) butter
2 tomatoes, skinned and sliced

Trim the fish fillets. Coat the fillets in the flour mixed with the salt and pepper. Heat 1 tablespoon of the oil and then fry the fish in it until golden brown on both sides. Arrange on a serving plate and keep warm.

Cook the onion for 2–3 minutes in the pan, adding another tablespoon of oil if necessary. Add the mushrooms and cook for a further 5 minutes. Stir in the parsley and vinegar, season to taste. Push to one side of the pan. In the empty side of the pan, melt the butter and fry tomatoes gently for about 2 minutes.

Spoon the onion mixture over the fish and arrange the tomato slices on top.

Not suitable for freezing.

STEAK AND ONION BAKE

Serves 2

1 lb (450g) chuck steak
1 level teaspoon tomato purée
12 oz (350g) onions, peeled and thinly sliced into rings
Pepper
½ level teaspoon salt
½ level teaspoon mixed herbs
1 level teaspoon cornflour

Set the oven to moderately hot, gas mark 5 or 375°F/190°C.

Trim off any excess fat on the meat, then cut into thick strips 2 inches (5 cm) long. Spread the tomato purée thinly over each strip.

Cover the base of a 2 pint (1·1 litre) casserole with half the onion, then add a layer of half the beef followed by the remaining onion. Top with the rest of the meat. Season each layer with pepper and salt and a sprinkling of mixed herbs.

Cover tightly with a lid or foil and bake above the centre of the oven for 2–2½ hours until the meat is tender. No extra liquid is needed as the meat makes its own.

30 minutes before the end of the cooking time, blend the cornflour with a little water and stir into the meat juices to thicken.

Serve half the casserole with a jacket potato which can be cooked in the oven, wrapped in foil, at the same time as the casserole. Cool the other half of the casserole which can be reheated on the following day and served with vegetables.

If liked, bake an extra one or two potatoes and on the following day peel, cube and reheat with the steak and onion mixture.

To freeze: freeze steak and onion mixture in single portions for up to 3 months. Partially thaw and reheat in saucepan.

Savoury Tropical Melon; Steak and Onion Bake; Avocado Supper; Trout with Tomatoes; Kippers with Mushroom Sauce, page 88

AVOCADO SUPPER

1 small avocado

1½ oz (40g) cream cheese

1 tablespoon lemon juice

1 level teaspoon curry powder

3 oz (75g) cooked chicken, cubed

2 walnut halves, chopped

1 level tablespoon mango chutney

Cut the avocado in half, remove the stone, then peel each half.

Cut one half of the avocado into two equal portions. Mash one portion together with the cream cheese, lemon juice and curry powder to form a sauce.

Cube the other portion of avocado and mix together with the chicken, chopped nuts and mango chutney. Slice the remaining half of avocado and arrange on a plate topped with the chicken mixture. Pour the sauce over.

Serve immediately as the avocado may discolour. Or, sprinkle the sliced avocado with lemon juice and arrange with chicken mixture and sauce just before serving.

Not suitable for freezing.

SAVOURY TROPICAL MELON

½ small canteloupe or honeydew melon

2–3 oz (50–75g) ham, cut into strips

1 level tablespoon raisins

1 level tablespoon salted peanuts

1 teaspoon oil

½ teaspoon vinegar

1 stick celery, sliced

¼ punnet mustard and cress

Scoop out the seeds from the centre of the melon. Using a teaspoon take out the flesh and put into a bowl with the ham, raisins, peanuts, oil, vinegar and celery. Mix well and spoon mixture into melon shell. Sprinkle over the mustard and cress and chill well before serving.

Note: use rest of celery in green salads or slice a stick or two and add to the Steak and Onion Bake (page 86). The rest of the packet of ham can be used instead of kippers in the recipe for Kippers with Mushroom Sauce (page 88) or on scrambled egg. Use the rest of the punnet of mustard and cress in

sandwiches, scrambled egg or as a garnish.
Not suitable for freezing.

KIPPERS WITH MUSHROOM SAUCE

7 oz (200g) packet buttered kippers, frozen

2 oz (50g) long grain rice

5 oz (150g) can condensed mushroom soup

3 tablespoons water

2 oz (50g) mushrooms, sliced

Cook the kippers in boiling water according to the directions on the packet. About 12 minutes before the end of cooking, salt the water and add the rice. Continue cooking until both the kippers and rice are cooked.

Meanwhile, place the soup, water and mushrooms in a pan and cook gently for about 5 minutes to cook the mushrooms. Keep hot.

When the fish and rice are cooked, remove the bag of fish from the water and drain the rice. Place the rice on a warm plate, topped with just over half the packet of kippers. Pour over the mushroom sauce.

Note: remaining kippers can be used with scrambled eggs to make a delicious substantial supper dish.

Not suitable for freezing.

DINNER FOR TWO

HOT PRAWN AND WALNUT SALAD

1 oz (25g) butter

4 oz (100g) peeled prawns

2 oz (50g) walnuts, chopped

Pinch of grated nutmeg

1 teaspoon lemon juice

Lettuce leaves

Cucumber slices

Watercress sprigs

Melt the butter in a small saucepan and add the prawns, walnuts, nutmeg and lemon juice. Cook gently for $\frac{1}{2}$ minute. Remove from heat. Add seasoning to taste.

Arrange the green salad vegetables in 2 bowls, then put the prawns on top. Serve immediately with brown bread and butter.

Not suitable for freezing.

BAKED CHICKEN WITH WATERCRESS SAUCE

1 small roasting chicken weighing $2\frac{1}{2}$–3 lb (1·2–1·35 kg) with giblets reserved

1 bunch of watercress

1 lemon

$\frac{1}{2}$ oz (15g) butter or margarine

1 tablespoon oil

4 oz (100g) onion, peeled and sliced

4 oz (100g) fresh or frozen peas

Pepper

1 level teaspoon salt

$\frac{1}{4}$ pint (150 ml) chicken stock, see below

5 oz (150g) carton soured cream

Make the stock: Wash chicken giblets and place them in a pan. Cover with water. Bring to the boil and simmer for 20–30 minutes.

Hot Prawn and Walnut Salad; Baked Chicken with Watercress Sauce; Oven-Baked Lemon Rice; Melon Filled with Jellied Blackberries, page 90

Set the oven to moderate, gas mark 4 or 350°F/180°C.

Trim, wash and chop the watercress reserving a few sprigs for garnish. Slice the lemon and place half inside the chicken.

Heat the butter or margarine and oil in a frying pan. Add the onion to the frying pan and cook until soft. Stir in the chopped watercress and peas and cook for about 2 minutes. Stir in the seasoning and stock. Pour into a 4 pint (2·4 litre) casserole.

Place the chicken on top. Cover with lid or foil and bake above the centre of the oven for 45–50 minutes or until the chicken is tender. Remove the chicken to a serving plate and keep warm.

Purée the cooking liquid in a blender, food processor or foodmill. Bring to the boil in the frying pan or a small pan.

Remove from the heat and stir in the soured cream. Either spoon the sauce over or serve separately. Garnish the chicken with the watercress sprigs and serve on a bed of the Oven-Baked Lemon Rice (see following recipe). Garnish with the rest of the lemon slices. Serve with extra peas.

Not suitable for freezing.

OVEN-BAKED LEMON RICE

6 oz (175g) onion, peeled and sliced
1 tablespoon oil
3 oz (75g) long grain rice
Grated rind of $\frac{1}{2}$ lemon
About 8 fl oz (240 ml) chicken stock
Pepper
$\frac{1}{2}$ level teaspoon salt

In a frying pan, fry the onion in the oil until brown. Add the rice and fry over a medium heat, stirring until it has turned a golden colour. Remove from the heat and stir in the lemon rind, stock and plenty of salt and pepper.

Transfer to a 2 pint (1·1 litre) casserole. Cover with lid or foil and cook below the Baked Chicken with Watercress Sauce (recipe above) for 40 minutes or until tender and the stock has been absorbed.

Fluff up with a fork before serving.

To freeze: freeze for up to 2 months. Thaw and reheat, covered, in moderate oven for 20 minutes.

MELON FILLED WITH JELLIED BLACKBERRIES

$\frac{1}{2}$ large or 1 small honeydew or canteloupe melon

$\frac{1}{2}$ packet of raspberry jelly

4 oz (100g) fresh or frozen blackberries

Cut melon in half and scoop out the seeds.

Reserve melon juice and make up to 3 fl oz (75 ml) with water.

Dissolve the jelly in the juice and water in a pan over heat, then chill until just on the point of setting. Spoon the blackberries through the jelly and chill until set.

Divide the jellied blackberries between the melon halves, and serve.

Note: if frozen blackberries are used, add them to the warm jelly as this will help to speed up the setting.

Not suitable for freezing.

SMALL ROASTS FOR TWO OR THREE

ROAST PORK WITH SAGE

Serve with Apple and Prune Sauce, Diced Potatoes in Soured Cream and Baked Tomatoes (page 91).

Serves 2–3

$1\frac{1}{2}$–2 lb (700–900g) slipper of pork (see note)

1–2 tablespoons oil

2 sprigs of fresh or 1 teaspoon dried sage

Pepper

1 level tablespoon flour

Set the oven to moderate, gas mark 4 or 350°F/180°C.

Roast Pork with Sage

Weigh the meat and calculate the cooking time allowing 35 minutes per lb (450g) plus 35 minutes.

Brush a small roasting tin with oil and sprinkle with the sage. Season the meat with pepper then place in the tin on top of the sage with the scored skin uppermost. Roast uncovered in the centre of the oven for the calculated time or until the meat is cooked.

To obtain a crisp crackling do not baste with the meat juices. If the meat starts to look very dry baste with a spoonful of fresh oil. On completion of cooking, sprinkle salt all over the crackling.

Remove the meat to a serving plate and keep warm.

Remove sage sprigs from the tin. Stir 1 level tablespoon of flour into the meat juices. Place the tin over the heat and gradually stir in ½ pint (300 ml) water, stock or vegetable water. Bring to the boil, stirring, and cook for 1–2 minutes. Taste and add seasoning as necessary.

Note: other suitable cuts of pork are: boned and rolled spare rib; blade bone on or off the bone.

To freeze: slice and freeze as for Roast Beef (page 47) for up to 1 month. Thaw and serve cold.

DICED POTATOES IN SOURED CREAM

| 1 lb (450g) potatoes, peeled and diced |
| 3–4 tablespoons soured cream |
| Salt and pepper |

Cut the potatoes into ½–¾ inch (1–2 cm) cubes. Cook in boiling salted water until just tender. Drain well. Return to the pan and add the cream and seasoning. Gently reheat. Serve.

Not suitable for freezing.

BAKED TOMATOES

Place 2–3 tomatoes in a small greased dish after cutting a cross in the top of each. Brush with a little oil and bake in a moderate oven, gas mark 4 or 350°F/180°C for 15 minutes.

Not suitable for freezing.

APPLE AND PRUNE SAUCE

| 1 large cooking apple, peeled and cored |
| 1 oz (25g) prunes, stoned |
| 1 level tablespoon sugar |
| 1 tablespoon lemon juice |
| 2–3 tablespoons water |

Slice the apple and chop the prunes. Place both in a small saucepan together with the sugar, lemon juice and water. Stew the apples until soft but still in large pieces. Taste and add further sugar if necessary.

To freeze: freeze when cold for up to 3 months. Thaw and serve.

ROAST BACON CARAWAY

Serve with plain, boiled potatoes which have been sprinkled with a little chopped fresh parsley and salt and pepper.

Serves 2–3

| 1–1½ lb (450–700g) joint Danish bacon – collar or streaky bacon |
| 1 tablespoon oil |
| 4 oz (100g) onions, peeled and sliced |
| 1 lb (450g) carrots, peeled and cut into chunks |
| 1 level teaspoon caraway seeds |
| 3 whole cloves |
| 2 level tablespoons soft brown sugar |
| Pepper |
| 1 level tablespoon tomato purée |
| 1 level teaspoon cornflour |

Set the oven to moderately hot, gas mark 5 or 375°F/190°C.

Weigh the piece of bacon and calculate the cooking time allowing 25 minutes per lb (450g).

Brush a roasting tin lightly with oil or fat, place the onions in the centre and put the bacon on top. Roast in the centre of the oven for the calculated time.

Meanwhile, put the carrots into a saucepan with ¾ pint (450 ml) water, the caraway seeds and the cloves. Bring to the boil, cover with lid, and simmer for 15 minutes. Stir in half the sugar and the pepper.

20 minutes before the bacon has finished cooking, remove it from the oven. Pour the carrots and juice over and around the meat and return to the oven to complete cooking.

Remove the bacon to a serving plate and, if a collar of bacon has been used, strip off the skin and string and sprinkle the rest of the sugar over the fat.

With a perforated spoon transfer the vegetables to the plate and arrange around the bacon.

Blend the tomato purée and cornflour to a smooth paste with a little water then stir into the juices in the roasting tin. Put the tin over a moderate heat, bring to the boil, stirring, and cook until thick. Either serve separately or pour over the carrots.

Roast Bacon Caraway

To freeze: slice and freeze bacon, interleaving slices with waxed paper, for up to 1 month. Freeze sauce separately. Thaw and reheat together in pan.

SUNDAY LAMB

Serve with either a green salad or vegetable of choice.

Serves 2

2 lb (900g) joint of boneless lamb for roasting or boned and rolled shoulder

FOR THE MARINADE:

1 level tablespoon oil

⅛ level teaspoon ginger

1 level teaspoon rosemary

1 tablespoon soy sauce

3 level tablespoons French mustard

FOR THE LAMB:

1 lb (450g) potatoes, peeled and thickly sliced

4 oz (100g) onions, thinly sliced

¼ pint (150 ml) water

Pepper

1 level teaspoon salt

1 oz (25g) margarine or butter

Mix the marinade ingredients together and spread over the lamb. Leave in a cool place for at least an hour – overnight if possible.

Set the oven to moderate, gas mark 4 or 350°F/180°C.

Arrange the sliced potatoes and onion in a greased 2½–3 pint (1·5–1·8 litre), shallow ovenproof dish. Pour over the water and the seasonings, then dot with the margarine or butter.

Place the lamb in the centre of the potatoes and cook above the centre of the oven for 1½–2 hours or until the meat is tender and the potatoes are cooked.

Remove the lamb from the dish and allow to stand for about 15 minutes before carving. Return the dish of potatoes to the oven during this 15 minute period.

To freeze: slice and freeze as for Roast Beef (page 47) for up to 2 months. Thaw and serve cold.

BREADS, SCONES, TEA BREADS AND SANDWICHES

There's nothing quite like the taste of fresh bread straight from the oven – it really is cooking at its most satisfying. Even a beginner can turn out fragrant, golden-brown loaves, and if you *do* find it a bit tricky to start with, don't worry. It gets easier all the time, as you learn to know when the dough feels right, whether it has proved long enough, and so on.

Quick tea breads and scones are great favourites of mine, as they are quick and easy to make, they slice well, and are perfect for picnics and tea-time. They taste delicious, too, spread with lots of butter or, for a change, with cream or cottage cheese.

BREADS

Here are lots of lovely recipes for home-made loaves in all shapes and sizes.

Freezing baked bread

All baked bread freezes well provided it is freshly baked when frozen.

Wrap in foil or polythene bags.

White and brown bread keep well for up to six months. Enriched bread and rolls keep for up to four months.

Crisp-crusted loaves and rolls have a limited storage time as the crusts begin to shell off after one week.

Tips for Breadmaking

The Yeast

Easy blend dried yeast is used to make the bread recipes in the large photograph (page 94). It is easy to work with – add it to the flour before adding the water – and is available from most grocers.

Do make sure that you read the instructions on the packet carefully, taking note of the method of adding yeast to the mixture. Remember that some types of dried yeast need to be reconstituted before adding to the flour. See Cottage Loaf and Sticky Buns recipes (pages 98 and 99).

Of course, you can use fresh yeast in recipes, but you'll need twice as much fresh yeast as dried. Fresh yeast needs mixing with water before adding to the flour.

The Liquid

Do measure all liquids very carefully in a measuring jug. If the dough is too slack, knead in another tablespoon or two of flour.

The Mixing

Mix ingredients together with a wooden spoon, in a mixer with a dough hook, or mix in half at a time in most food processors.

The Rising

The dough must be covered during this stage to prevent loss of heat and a skin forming on the surface. Oiled cling wrap is the best and simplest covering.

However long it takes, do allow the dough to double in size before shaping if the recipe requires you to do so. The rising time varies depending on the temperature at which the rising takes place. Be careful of too much heat since this will kill the yeast and give a disappointing result. The covered dough will rise if left in the fridge overnight.

Some white dough recipes only need shaping and proving.

The Proving or second rising

Once again the shaped dough should almost double in size. But remember the richer the

Selection of
Breads

dough, the longer it will take to prove. The dough is at the correct stage for baking if it remains depressed when touched lightly.

saucepan, remove from the heat and add the cold water. Then mix into the flour to form a soft, but not sticky dough.

Knead well for 8–10 minutes until the dough is smooth, then use and shape according to one or more of the white bread recipes.

BASIC WHITE BREAD DOUGH

1½ lb (700g) strong white bread flour

1 level tablespoon caster sugar

1 level tablespoon salt

1 sachet easy blend dried yeast

1 oz (25g) margarine or lard

¾ pint (450 ml) cold water, minus 2 tablespoons

Mix the flour, sugar, salt and yeast together in a large bowl. Melt the margarine in a

FLOURY BAPS

Makes 8

½ quantity basic white bread dough (above)

Knead the bread dough on a lightly-floured surface for 5 minutes. Divide the dough into eight equal pieces and knead. Shape into eight smooth rounds. Place on an oiled and floured baking sheet, in two rows of 4 with a ¾ inch (2 cm) gap between each round. Cover with a piece of oiled cling wrap and

rise in a warm place for 35 minutes or until doubled in size.

With the remaining dough weigh out 1 lb (450g), knead, and shape to fit a greased 2 lb (900g) loaf tin. Divide the remaining dough. Knead and shape into eight 2 oz (50g) balls. Brush the dough in the loaf tin with a little milk. Arrange the balls in two rows of 4 along the top; cover with oiled cling wrap and leave to rise in a warm place for 40 minutes, until doubled in size.

Set oven to very hot, gas mark 8 or 450°F/ 230°C. Remove the cling wrap, and brush both loaves with a little milk or beaten egg.

Bake the 1 lb (450g) loaf tin for 15 minutes, and the 2 lb (900g) loaf tin for 20 minutes. Leave to cool slightly in the tin, before lifting out on to a wire rack.

BLOOMER LOAF

½ quantity basic white bread dough (page 94)

Milk or beaten egg to glaze

1 level teaspoon poppy seeds

Shape the kneaded dough into a flat roll about 9 inches (23 cm) long and place on a greased baking sheet. Brush with milk or beaten egg and sprinkle with poppy seeds. Make diagonal slashes in the surface of the dough and cover with oiled cling wrap. Leave to rise until doubled in size.

Set the oven to very hot, gas mark 8 or 450°F/230°C. Remove the cling wrap and bake towards the top of the oven for 20 minutes. Remove and cool on a wire tray.

leave to rise for 30 minutes or until doubled in size.

Set oven to very hot, gas mark 8 or 450°F/ 230°C. Remove the cling wrap, dust with a little flour and bake for 15 minutes. When cooked, remove from the oven, place on a wire rack and cover with a clean tea towel or cloth. This keeps the crust soft.

TRADITIONAL LOAF

1 quantity basic white bread dough (page 94)

Milk and/or beaten egg to glaze

Turn the dough out on a lightly-floured surface. Weigh out 12 oz (325g) of dough, knead and shape to fit a greased 1 lb (450g) loaf tin. Cover with oiled cling wrap; leave to

GARLIC BREAD

Serves 7

½ quantity basic white bread dough (page 94)

FOR THE FILLING:

2 oz (50g) butter

3 cloves garlic, peeled and crushed

2 level teaspoons fresh parsley, chopped

Cream the butter, garlic and parsley together. Turn the dough out on to a lightly-floured surface, and knead for 3 minutes. Divide the dough into seven equal pieces. Knead, then pat each piece into 4 inch (10 cm) circles. Place a rounded teaspoon of garlic butter in the centre of each circle, wrap the edges over, then roll into seven smooth balls.

Place neatly in a greased 8 inch (20 cm) tin. Cover with a piece of oiled cling wrap and leave to rise for 30 minutes or until doubled in size.

Set oven to very hot, gas mark 8 or 450°F/230°C.

Remove cling wrap and bake for 20 minutes, then leave in the tin for 10 minutes to soak up any butter.

HOT ONION SANDWICH

This is best eaten hot.

Serves 10

$\frac{1}{2}$ **quantity basic white bread dough (page 94)**

FOR THE FILLING:

1 oz (25g) margarine

1$\frac{1}{4}$ lb (600g) onions, peeled and sliced

2 teaspoons lemon juice

Pepper

5 fl oz (150 ml) soured cream

FOR THE TOPPING:

Milk or beaten egg to glaze

2 level teaspoons sesame seeds

Melt the margarine in a large frying pan. Add the onion, lemon juice and pepper and cook for 8 minutes to soften without browning. Move to one side and leave to cool, then stir in the soured cream.

Knead the dough on a lightly-floured surface for 5 minutes. Cut off approximately 12 oz (350g) of dough, and roll out into a 12 inch (30 cm) round. Use to line a lightly-greased 8 inch (20 cm) spring clip tin.

Place the filling in the centre, roll out the remaining dough to a 9 inch (23 cm) round. Place over the onion filling and press the edges together. Cover with oiled cling wrap and leave to rise for 45 minutes in a warm place until doubled in size.

Set oven to very hot, gas mark 8 or 450°F/230°C. Remove the cling wrap, brush the top with a little milk or beaten egg, sprinkle with sesame seeds and bake for 20 minutes.

BASIC BROWN BREAD DOUGH

1$\frac{1}{2}$ lb (700g) wholemeal flour

1 level tablespoon caster sugar

1 level tablespoon salt

1 sachet easy blend dried yeast

1 oz (25g) margarine or lard

$\frac{3}{4}$ pint (450 ml) cold water

Mix the flour, sugar, salt and yeast together in a large bowl. Melt the margarine or lard in a saucepan, remove from heat and add the cold water. Mix into the flour to form a soft, but not sticky, dough.

Knead well for 8–10 minutes until the dough is smooth, then shape into a ball. Return to the bowl and cover with oiled cling wrap and leave in a warm place for about 1 hour or until doubled in size. Remove cling wrap.

Remove from the bowl and knock all the air out of the dough by punching with the fists. Knead for about 5 minutes until smooth, then use according to one of the following brown bread dough recipes.

LARGE BROWN LOAF

$\frac{2}{3}$ quantity basic brown bread dough (above) which has already risen once

Milk or beaten egg to glaze

After the risen dough has been kneaded for the second time, shape into a loaf. Place the dough in a greased 2 lb (900g) loaf tin. Cover with oiled cling wrap and leave to rise until doubled in size for about 35 minutes.

Set the oven to very hot, gas mark 8 or 450°F/230°C. Remove the cling wrap; brush the top with a little milk or beaten egg and bake towards top of oven for 20–30 minutes.

GRANARY BREAD

Makes 2 Granary sticks and 1 Granary tea cake

BASIC RECIPE:

1½ lb (700g) Granary flour

1 level tablespoon caster sugar

1 level tablespoon salt

1 sachet easy blend dried yeast

1 oz (25g) margarine or lard

¾ pint (450 ml) cold water

1 tablespoon milk or beaten egg to glaze

FOR THE TEA CAKE:

4 oz (100g) mixed dried fruit

2 oz (50g) caster sugar

1 oz (25g) margarine

Mix the flour, sugar, salt and yeast together in a large bowl. Melt the margarine or lard in a saucepan, then add the cold water. Pour the liquid into the flour and mix to form a soft dough.

Turn out on to a floured surface and knead for 8–10 minutes until the dough is smooth, then return to the bowl and cover with oiled polythene or cling wrap. Leave for 1 hour or until doubled in size.

Knead well to knock out the air.

Set the oven to very hot, gas mark 8 or 450°F/230°C.

Granary Sticks:
Take one half of the dough and divide in half. Roll each half into a long sausage-shape 12–14 inches (30–35 cm) long. Place on a greased baking sheet and make deep slashes in each loaf with a sharp knife. Cover with oiled polythene or cling wrap and leave to prove for 30 minutes until doubled in size. Remove the cling wrap and brush with milk or beaten egg to glaze and bake above the centre of the oven for 15–20 minutes.

Granary Tea Cake:
Take the other half of the risen dough and knock out the air by kneading. Flatten out the dough on a floured surface, then spread the fruit and sugar evenly over the dough. Lightly knead the dough until the fruit and sugar are evenly distributed, then flatten it out and add the margarine in small dots.

Knead until the dough is smooth, then shape into a ball and place on a greased baking sheet to prove for 30 minutes, covered in oiled cling wrap. The round shape will flatten out slightly.

Remove the cling wrap and brush with milk or beaten egg and bake above the centre of the oven for 25–30 minutes.

OAT BREAD

8 oz (225g) porridge oats

½ pint (300 ml) milk

1 sachet easy blend dried yeast

1 level teaspoon caster sugar

5 tablespoons lukewarm water

12 oz (350g) strong white flour

2 level teaspoons salt

2 tablespoons oil, melted butter or margarine

1 tablespoon milk to glaze

Soak the oats in the milk for 30 minutes. Mix all the ingredients, except the milk to glaze, together to form a soft scone-like dough. Turn the dough out on to a lightly-floured surface and knead until smooth and no longer sticky for about 10 minutes.

Shape the dough into a ball and place in a large floured bowl. Cover with oiled cling wrap and leave to rise until doubled in size for about 1 hour. Knead again for 2 minutes to knock out the air, then divide the dough into two equal portions. Roll each piece into a length about 18 inches (45 cm) long. Join the 2 lengths at one end and plait together, pinching together at the other end. Place on a greased baking sheet, cover with oiled cling wrap and leave to rise until doubled in size.

Set the oven to very hot, gas mark 8 or 450°C/230°C. Remove the cling wrap, brush with milk to glaze, then bake in the centre of the oven for 20 minutes.

Potato Bread;
Cottage Loaf;
Sticky Buns

CHEESE AND HERB LOAVES

Delicious served hot or cold.

Makes 6

FOR THE FILLING:

2 oz (50g) butter

2 level teaspoons tarragon and thyme mustard

1 level teaspoon mixed herbs

1 teaspoon lemon juice

2 oz (50g) Cheddar cheese, finely diced

Pinch of cayenne pepper

$\frac{1}{2}$ quantity basic brown bread dough (page 96) which has already risen once

FOR THE TOPPING:

Milk to glaze

1 oz (25g) Cheddar cheese, grated

Lightly grease six $\frac{1}{2}$ pint (300 ml) loaf tins. Cream the butter, mustard, mixed herbs, lemon juice, diced cheese and cayenne pepper together. Turn the risen dough out on to a lightly-floured surface and knead for 3 minutes. Pat the dough out into a 6 inch (15 cm) round. Place the filling in the centre, wrap the edges around the mixture and knead until the filling is evenly distributed throughout the dough.

Divide the dough into six. Knead each piece into a shape to fit the tins. Cover with a piece of oiled cling wrap and leave to rise in a warm place for 30–45 minutes until doubled in size.

Set oven to very hot, gas mark 8 or 450°F/ 230°C. When the dough has risen, remove cling wrap, brush with a little milk and sprinkle with grated cheese. Bake for 20 minutes. Leave to cool in the tin for 10 minutes, then turn out on to a wire rack.

COTTAGE LOAF

1 level teaspoon sugar

$\frac{3}{4}$ pint (450 ml) tepid (hand hot) milk and water mixed

1 level tablespoon dried yeast

1$\frac{1}{2}$ lb (700g) strong white flour

1 level teaspoon salt

2 oz (50g) lard or white fat

Milk to glaze

Using a fork, whisk the sugar into the tepid milk and water until dissolved. Sprinkle over the yeast and leave in a warm place until there is a good froth on top – 10–15 minutes.

Sift the flour and salt together, then rub in the lard. Make a well in the centre of the flour and pour in the yeast liquid. Mix to a rough dough in the bowl then turn out on to an unfloured surface and knead for a few minutes until the dough is smooth and elastic, or use the dough hook on your mixer. Shape into a ball, place in a floured bowl, cover closely with oiled cling wrap and put in a warm place until the dough has doubled in size – about 45 minutes.

Knead lightly, then cut off a quarter of the dough. Knead both pieces of dough into neat round balls. Place the smaller round on top of the larger and press through the centre of both with a wooden spoon handle. Place on a greased baking sheet and leave to prove for about 20 minutes until puffy.

Set the oven to hot, gas mark 7 or 425°F/220°C.

Brush the loaf with milk and sprinkle a little flour over the top. Bake above the centre of the oven for 20 minutes. Reduce the heat to moderately hot, gas mark 5 or 375°F/190°C and bake for a further 30 minutes or until the loaf is cooked.

POTATO BREAD

Substitute 4 oz (100g) dry mashed potato for an equal weight of flour in the recipe for Cottage Loaf (above). When the dough has risen and doubled in size, knead and place in a greased 2 lb (900g) or two 1 lb (450g) loaf tins. Put to prove until the dough has risen to the top of the tin. Brush with water and sprinkle with cracked wheat or rolled oats.

Bake in a hot oven, gas mark 7 or 425°F/220°C for 30–40 minutes. Remove from tins and return to oven, on a baking sheet, for a further 5 minutes.

STICKY BUNS

Makes 16

2 oz (50g) caster sugar

½ pint (300 ml) tepid milk and water mixed

1 level tablespoon dried yeast

1¼ lb (600g) plain flour

1 level teaspoon salt

2 oz (50g) margarine or butter

1 egg, size 3

2 oz (50g) chopped glacé cherries or sultanas

Stir 1 teaspoon of the sugar into the tepid milk and water. Sprinkle over the yeast and leave until frothy – about 10–15 minutes.

Sift the flour and salt together, then rub in the margarine or butter. Make a well in the centre and stir in the remaining sugar, egg, cherries or sultanas and yeast liquid. Mix to a rough dough with a wooden spoon then work until the dough comes cleanly away from the sides of the bowl. Cover with oiled cling wrap and leave in a warm place until doubled in size.

Turn out the risen dough and gently knock flat. Divide into 16 equal parts and shape each one into a ball. Allow to rest for 5 minutes, then shape each piece into a narrow pear shape. Grease two 8 inch (20 cm) sandwich tins. Fit 8 pieces of dough into each tin, with narrow ends in centre of tin. Put to prove until puffy.

Set the oven to hot, gas mark 7 or 425°F/220°C.

Dust the buns with a little flour then bake in the centre of the oven for 15–20 minutes. Remove the buns from the tins, keeping them together, and allow to cool.

To make the icing: Sift 8 oz (225g) icing sugar into a small basin and stir in enough hot water to make a smooth coating icing. Pour the icing over buns, allow it to set, then break the buns apart before serving.

Scone
Variations

SCONES

All About Scones

Any flour will make good scones but we think that the best and lightest textured ones are made using a mixture of plain flour and baking powder and we have written our recipes accordingly. However, in all the recipes you can use instead, either 8 oz (225g) self-raising flour and 1 level teaspoon baking powder or just 8 oz (225g) self-raising flour. A good scone is also achieved if instead of 3 level teaspoons of baking powder, you use 1½ level teaspoons of cream of tartar and ¾ level teaspoon bicarbonate of soda.

Always sift together the flour and raising agent as this will ensure an even rise; try and add all the liquid in one go for a more even texture. For easy rubbing-in cut the fat into pieces before you start.

If mixing with soured milk, replace the baking powder with 1 level teaspoon bicarbonate of soda and 1 level teaspoon cream of tartar.

Eat scones when they're fresh – they're best eaten whilst still warm from the oven. If you do keep them for a day or two, warm them for a few minutes in the oven before eating, or try them toasted.

BASIC FARMHOUSE SCONES

Makes 7–8

8 oz (225g) plain flour
3 level teaspoons baking powder
½ level teaspoon salt
2 oz (50g) margarine
¼ pint (150 ml) milk

Set the oven to hot, gas mark 7 or 425°F/220°C.

Sift the flour, baking powder and salt into a large bowl. Cut the margarine into pieces and add to the flour. Rub it into the flour until the mixture resembles breadcrumbs. Stir in most of the milk and mix to a soft, not sticky dough using a round-bladed knife. Turn the dough out on to a floured working surface, knead lightly to remove any large cracks then roll out to about ¾ inch (2 cm) thickness.

Cut into triangles, or dip a 2–2½ inch (5–6 cm) cutter in flour then stamp out rounds, cutting them as close to each other as possible so you get as many as you can out of the first rolling. Knead the trimmings then roll out and cut as before.

Place the scones on a greased baking sheet. Brush with a little milk if liked and bake towards the top of the oven for 10–15 minutes. Cool on a wire rack.

Scone Variations

Add any of the following extra ingredients to the basic recipe.

Teatime Currant: After the rubbing-in stage add 1 oz (25g) caster sugar and 2 oz (50g) currants to the mixture.

Coconut: After the rubbing-in stage add 3 oz (75g) desiccated coconut and 1 oz (25g) caster sugar. Reserve 2 level tablespoons of the coconut to sprinkle over the top of each scone after brushing with milk. Use a fluted cutter if preferred.

BANANA & NUT SCONE

Makes 8

8 oz (225g) self-raising flower
2 level teaspoons baking powder
¼ level teaspoon salt
2 oz (50g) margarine
8 oz (225g) banana, peeled and mashed
2 oz (50g) demerara sugar
2 oz (50g) chopped walnuts
4 tablespoons milk

Set the oven to very hot, gas mark 7 or 425°F/220°C.

Sift the flour, baking powder and salt into a bowl. Rub in the margarine until the mixture resembles breadcrumbs. Stir in the mashed banana, sugar, walnuts and enough milk to give a soft, not sticky dough.

On a floured surface, knead lightly to remove the cracks then pat or roll into a large round, ¾–1 inch (2–2·5 cm) thick. Place on a greased baking sheet. Mark into eight wedges cutting to within ½ inch (1 cm) of the base. Bake towards the top of the oven for about 20 minutes or until cooked.

DROP SCONES

Makes 20–22

8 oz (225g) self-raising flour
Pinch of salt
1 oz (25g) margarine
1 oz (25g) caster sugar
1 egg, size 2
9 fl oz (270 ml) milk

Sift the flour and salt into a bowl. Rub in the margarine until the mixture resembles breadcrumbs. Stir in the sugar.

Drop Scones

Make a well in the centre of the dry ingredients. Break in the egg and add the milk gradually, stirring from the centre with a wooden spoon or wire whisk to incorporate the flour and make a fairly thick batter which should just drop from the spoon.

Heat a griddle or heavy-based frying pan until hot (the right temperature has been reached when a hand held 1 inch (2·5 cm) above the surface feels hot or when drops of cold water jump about on the surface before evaporating). Grease the griddle or frying pan using a wad of absorbent kitchen paper dipped in a small amount of melted fat or oil. Drop tablespoonfuls of batter on to the greased surface, leaving 1–2 inches (2·5–5 cm) between each scone.

When bubbles burst on the surface of the scone and the underside is light brown, turn over with a palette knife and cook the other side. Place scones in a clean, folded tea towel to keep warm and soft while cooking the rest. Remember to grease the surface each time.

TEA BREADS

MALT LOAF

8 oz (225g) plain flour and 2 level teaspoons baking powder; or 8 oz (225g) self-raising flour
$\frac{1}{4}$ level teaspoon salt
2 oz (50g) margarine
4 oz (100g) golden syrup
3 oz (75g) malt extract
4 tablespoons milk
1 egg, size 3
4 oz (100g) raisins or sultanas

Set the oven to warm, gas mark 3 or 325°F/160°C. Base line and grease two 1 lb (450g) loaf tins.

Sift the flour, baking powder, if used, and salt together into a bowl. Rub in the margarine until the mixture resembles breadcrumbs.

Melt the syrup and malt extract with the milk in a pan over a low heat.

Beat the egg and add with the liquid to the dry ingredients. Mix to a smooth batter, then stir in the raisins or sultanas. Turn into the tins and bake just above the centre of the oven for about 1 hour.

If the loaves start to over-brown, place a piece of greaseproof paper on the top.

Best kept wrapped or in an airtight tin for a week before cutting as keeping will give a moister, slightly stickier texture.

BUN LOAF

Delicious cut in thick slices and spread with butter.

8 oz (225g) self-raising flour
$\frac{1}{4}$ level teaspoon salt
$\frac{1}{2}$ level teaspoon mixed spice
$\frac{1}{4}$ level teaspoon nutmeg
4 oz (100g) white fat or margarine
4 oz (100g) demerara sugar
12 oz (350g) mixed dried fruit
2 oz (50g) chopped candied peel
1 egg, size 3
6–7 tablespoons milk

Set the oven to moderate, gas mark 4 or 350°F/180°C. Base line and grease a 2 lb (900g) loaf tin.

Sift the flour, salt, mixed spice and nutmeg into a mixing bowl. Rub in the fat until the mixture resembles breadcrumbs. Mix in the sugar, fruit and peel. Add the lightly beaten egg and sufficient milk to mix to a fairly soft consistency. Spoon into the loaf tin and bake above the centre of the oven for about $1\frac{1}{2}$ hours. Cool.

BOILED DATE TEABREAD

Serve on its own as a cake or sliced and thickly buttered.

8 oz (225g) self-raising flour
2 oz (50g) chopped walnuts
3 oz (75g) margarine
5 oz (150g) sugar
8 oz (225g) dates, chopped
$\frac{1}{4}$ pint (150 ml) water
2 eggs, size 3, beaten

Set the oven to moderate, gas mark 4 or 350°F/180°C. Base line and grease a 2 lb (900g) loaf tin.

Mix the flour and nuts in a bowl.

Place the margarine, sugar, dates and water in a pan.

Heat gently until the margarine has melted, then bring to the boil. Stir into the flour together with the eggs and beat until all the ingredients are well mixed.

Pour into the tin. Level the top and bake just above the centre of the oven for about 1¼ hours or until cooked. Cool in the tin for 15 minutes, then turn out.

DATE AND WALNUT LOAF

This loaf improves with keeping, so store for one day before eating.

4 oz (100g) margarine
6 oz (175g) golden syrup
2 oz (50g) black treacle
¼ pint (150 ml) milk
2 eggs, size 3
8 oz (225g) plain flour
2 level teaspoons mixed spice
1 level teaspoon bicarbonate of soda
4 oz (100g) stoned or block dates, chopped
2 oz (50g) walnuts, chopped

Set oven to cool, gas mark 2 or 300°F/150°C. Base line and grease a 2 lb (900g) loaf tin.

Put the margarine, golden syrup and treacle into a saucepan and melt over a gentle heat. Remove from heat and allow to cool slightly, then stir in the milk and beat in the eggs, one at a time.

Sift the flour, mixed spice and bicarbonate of soda into a bowl. Gradually stir in the syrup mixture a little at a time to form a smooth batter, then stir in the dates and

Malt Loaf; Bun Loaf; Boiled Date Teabread; Cheese and Bacon Loaf, page 104

walnuts. Pour into the prepared tin.

Bake in the centre of the preheated oven for $1\frac{1}{2}$–$1\frac{3}{4}$ hours or until the centre is firm and an inserted skewer comes out clean.

Allow to cool in the tin for at least 10 minutes before turning out. Serve sliced with or without butter.

To freeze: wrap and freeze when cold for up to 3 months.

(See photograph on page 109.)

CHEESE & BACON LOAF

Served sliced, with butter.

8 oz (225g) self-raising flour
1 level teaspoon baking powder
3 level teaspoons dry mustard powder
$\frac{1}{4}$ level teaspoon salt
$\frac{1}{4}$ level teaspoon pepper
2 oz (50g) margarine
4 rashers bacon, derinded and chopped
1 egg, size 3
4 oz (100g) Cheddar cheese, grated
$\frac{1}{4}$ pint (150 ml) milk

Set the oven to moderately hot, gas mark 5 or 375°F/190°C. Base line and grease a 2 lb (900g) loaf tin.

Place all the ingredients, reserving 1 oz (25g) cheese for the topping, in a mixing bowl and beat together with a wooden spoon until well mixed. Turn the mixture into the loaf tin. Sprinkle with the rest of the cheese.

Bake in the centre of the oven for 40–45 minutes or until cooked. Cool in the tin for 5–10 minutes before turning out to cool completely.

SANDWICHES

WIDE OPEN SANDWICHES

They look beautiful. They taste sensational – and underneath the mouth-watering toppings of these open sandwiches are tangy, tempting, spicy spreads.

To prepare the bread slices:
Trim the bottom from a large, unsliced sandwich loaf. Using a ruler, make grooves around the loaf at $\frac{1}{2}$ inch (1 cm) intervals with the point of a knife – this makes it easier to slice.

With a serrated knife, cut the loaf lengthways into seven or eight even slices (the number will depend on the loaf but each slice should measure about $7\frac{1}{2}$ inches (19 cm) long by $4\frac{1}{2}$ inches (11 cm) wide). If preferred cut off the crusts. If you need only two slices, wrap and freeze the remaining slices for another time.

Spread each slice with softened butter; this helps prevent the bread from going soggy once the filling is placed on top.

How many they serve:
Each sandwich can be left whole and served as a main course; cut in half and served as a snack or lunch; or cut in three and served for tea. It all depends on the appetite!

Open sandwiches are not suitable for freezing.

CREAM CHEESE AND MACKEREL SLICE

3 oz (75g) cream cheese
1 tablespoon milk
2 tablespoons chopped chives
Pepper
$\frac{1}{8}$ level teaspoon salt
2 long slices buttered bread
4 oz (100g) smoked mackerel
2 teaspoons lemon juice
1 small onion, halved and thinly sliced
2 inch (5 cm) piece of cucumber, sliced
Watercress sprigs

Mix together the cream cheese, milk, chives, pepper and salt, then spread evenly over each slice of bread.

Flake the mackerel into a basin and mix in the lemon juice.

Reserve a few slices of onion for garnish and arrange the rest down the centre of each slice of bread. Arrange a line of sliced cucumber along each side of the onion. Spoon the mackerel down the centre.

Garnish with the remaining onion slices and sprigs of watercress.

HEARTY SALT BEEF WITH SALAD SANDWICH

2 level teaspoons horseradish sauce

2 long slices buttered bread

4 tomatoes, thinly sliced

Salt and pepper

Good pinch of sugar

1 small onion, sliced into rings

2 oz (50g) potato salad with chives

4 slices salt or roast beef

Snipped parsley

Spread the horseradish sauce on each slice of bread.

Place a layer of tomato slices over the horseradish, season and sprinkle with sugar. Follow with a layer of onion rings. Spoon a row of potato salad down the centre of each slice.

Cut the slices of beef into four and fold each slice. Arrange in overlapping rows on either side of the potato salad. Sprinkle parsley over the salad.

CHEESE AND CORN SANDWICH

2 level teaspoons French mustard

2 long slices buttered bread

7 oz (200g) can sweetcorn, drained

2 tablespoons creamy cucumber dressing or mayonnaise

6 slices [3–4 oz (75–100g) wedge] Edam cheese

Watercress sprigs

6 radishes, trimmed and sliced

Spread the mustard evenly over each slice of buttered bread. Mix together the sweetcorn and dressing, then spoon over one long side of each slice. Arrange three slices of cheese, the watercress sprigs and slices of radish on each bread slice.

SWEET AND SOUR CARROT AND EGG SANDWICH

3 level tablespoons mayonnaise or salad cream

1 level tablespoon mango chutney

2 long slices buttered bread

8 oz (225g) carrots, peeled and finely grated

1 level teaspoon sugar

2 teaspoons malt vinegar

Pepper

$\frac{1}{2}$ level teaspoon salt

1 oz (25g) sultanas

4 hard-boiled eggs

4 pineapple rings

Parsley

Mix the mayonnaise and chutney together and spread evenly over each slice of bread.

Mix together the carrot, sugar, vinegar, pepper, salt and sultanas then spoon over the mayonnaise and spread to the edges of each slice.

Cut each egg into four segments and each pineapple ring in half. Arrange in clusters at each end of the carrot-topped bread. Garnish with parsley.

HAM AND CRESS ROLLS

2 tablespoons flavoured mayonnaise

2 long slices buttered bread

1 punnet mustard and cress

4 oz (100g) cottage cheese

Salt and pepper

4 oz (100g) sliced ham

Tube of cheese and onion spread

Paprika

1 tomato, cut in small wedges

Spread the mayonnaise over each slice of bread. Trim two-thirds of the mustard and cress and sprinkle equally over each slice.

Mix the remaining third into the cottage cheese and add salt and pepper to taste. Place one-quarter of the cheese mixture at the end of each slice of ham, and roll up. Cut each roll in half. Place eight small ham rolls on each slice of bread. Pipe cheese spread down the centre and sprinkle with a little paprika. Garnish with tomato wedges.

BACON AND MUSHROOM SANDWICH

About 3 oz (75g) liver and bacon pâté

2 long slices buttered bread

1 teaspoon Worcestershire sauce

1 small bunch spring onions, trimmed

6 small rashers streaky bacon

1 oz (25g) margarine or butter

1 teaspoon lemon juice

3 oz (75g) mushrooms, sliced

Spread the pâté evenly over each slice of buttered bread. Sprinkle over the Worcestershire sauce and work in evenly with a knife.

Save two spring onions for garnish, chop the rest and sprinkle over the pâté. Derind each rasher of bacon and place under the grill. Put the butter, lemon juice and mushrooms into a fireproof or foil dish and grill until the bacon is crispy and the mushrooms just cooked.

Arrange strips of bacon and lines of mushroom slices in alternate lines over each slice of bread. Garnish with a curl of spring onion.

To curl the ends of spring onions: Cut the green part of the onion into long strips. Place in very cold water to curl.

SANDWICH À LA NIÇOISE

2 teaspoons lemon juice

2 long slices buttered bread

4 oz (100g) cooked green beans, cut in half

1 small green pepper, quartered, de-seeded and sliced

1 small, mild onion, finely sliced

7 oz (200g) can tuna fish, drained

1 clove garlic, peeled and crushed

2 tablespoons French dressing

Pepper

$\frac{1}{2}$ level teaspoon salt

2 tomatoes, sliced

4 anchovy fillets

4 black olives, stoned

Sprinkle lemon juice over each buttered bread slice and mix into the butter.

Mix together the beans, pepper, onion, tuna, garlic, dressing, pepper and salt. Arrange the tuna mixture and the tomato slices on each slice of bread.

Slice the anchovies in half lengthways then cut in half. Arrange in a lattice fashion over the tomatoes, placing a piece of olive in the spaces.

SPICY GERMAN SAUSAGE SANDWICH

Finely grated rind of $\frac{1}{2}$ lemon

2 long slices buttered bread

2 large crisp lettuce leaves, shredded

1 stick celery, finely chopped

$1\frac{1}{2}$ inch (4 cm) piece cucumber, diced

1 tablespoon oil

2 teaspoons lemon juice or vinegar

Pepper

$\frac{1}{4}$ level teaspoon salt

2 oz (50g) pepper cheese or other cheese, sliced

4 slices sausage with pistachio

4 slices salami

1 tomato, halved and sliced

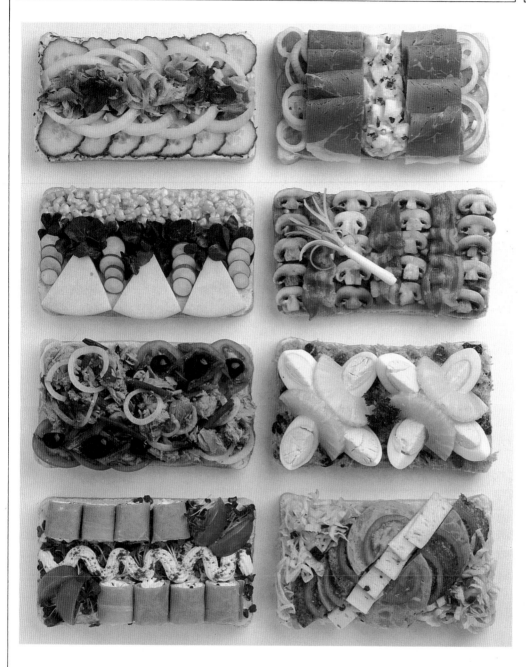

Open Sandwiches

Sprinkle a little lemon rind over each slice of bread and spread evenly into the butter.

Mix together the lettuce, celery, cucumber, oil, lemon juice, pepper and salt.

Spread half over each slice.

Cut the cheese into strips and the sausage and salami in half and arrange with the tomato on each slice.

CAKES, TRAY BAKES AND BISCUITS

Home-made cakes, buns and biscuits are absolutely irresistible! You can't buy them as good as you can bake them, and the traditional country recipes, handed down through the generations, taste as good today as they ever did. In the pages that follow, I'll show you how to bake to perfection. Wholesome, scrumptious and successful – the variety is almost endless – but here are just a few ideas for filling your cupboards with sweet treats. Who knows, you might even start a tradition or two in your own family?

CAKES

GRANDMA'S SEED CAKE

8 oz (225g) plain flour

Pinch of salt

1 level teaspoon baking powder

5 oz (150g) margarine or butter

5 oz (150g) caster sugar

2 eggs, size 3

2 tablespoons milk

3 level teaspoons caraway seeds

Set the oven to moderate, gas mark 4 or 350°F/180°C. Base line and grease a 7–7½ inch (18–19 cm) round cake tin.

Sift the flour, salt and baking powder together in a bowl.

Cream the margarine or butter and sugar together. Separate the eggs and beat the yolks into the creamed mixture. Fold in the flour. Stir in the milk and caraway seeds.

Whisk the egg whites until stiff; fold into the mixture. Put in the cake tin, and bake in the centre of the oven for 1½ hours. Allow to cool in tin for 10 minutes before turning out.

To freeze: wrap and freeze when cold for up to 3 months.

CHOCOLATE POTATO CAKE

Best stored for one day before eating.

6 oz (175g) margarine

6 oz (175g) caster sugar

3 eggs, size 3

5 oz (150g) self-raising flour

1 oz (25g) cocoa

1 level teaspoon baking powder

1½ level teaspoons mixed spice

4 oz (100g) warm, mashed potato

2 fl oz (55ml) milk

3 oz (75g) raisins

1½ oz (40g) flaked almonds

Set oven to moderate, gas mark 4 or 350°F/ 180°C. Base line and grease a 7–7½ inch (18– 19 cm) round cake tin.

Cream margarine with the sugar until soft, then add eggs, one at a time, beating well between each addition. Sift flour, cocoa, baking powder and mixed spice together.

Mix the potato with the milk and fold into the cake mixture together with the flour mixture, raisins and 1 oz (25g) flaked almonds.

Spoon into the tin and level the surface, then sprinkle over the remaining almonds. Bake in the centre of the oven for 1 hour.

Leave to cool in the tin before turning out.

To freeze: wrap and freeze when cold for up to 3 months.

FRUIT AND HONEY SHORTCAKE

12 oz (350g) self-raising flour
Pinch of salt
2 oz (50g) margarine
2 level tablespoons caster sugar
3 oz (75g) currants
5 oz (150g) carton natural yogurt
Milk
FOR THE FILLING:
3 oz (75g) margarine
3 tablespoons honey
1 large or 2 small bananas, sliced

Set oven to moderately hot, gas mark 5 or 375°F/190°C. Grease a deep 8½ inch (21·5 cm) fluted flan tin.

Sift the flour and salt into a bowl. Rub in the margarine until the mixture resembles breadcrumbs. Stir in sugar and currants.

Make the yogurt up to 8 fl oz (240 ml) using milk and stir into the flour mixture. Or, stir in the yogurt and enough milk to give a soft, but not sticky, dough. Knead dough lightly until smooth and either roll out or press out to fit into the tin.

Mark into wedges by making four slits about ¼ inch (5 mm) deep on the top of the dough so that it will be easy to cut into pieces when filled.

Bake in the centre of the oven for 30–35 minutes and then allow to cool.

Meanwhile, make the filling. With a wooden spoon, cream the margarine until

From left: Chocolate Potato Cake; Date and Walnut Loaf, page 103; Fruit and Honey Shortcake; Orange Rock Buns, page 110; Crunchy Sugar-Topped Slices, page 110; Grandma's Seed Cake

soft. Gradually stir in the honey. Split shortcake across middle to form two layers, then spread bottom layer with honey filling and scatter over the sliced bananas. Place top layer over filling.

Not suitable for freezing.

ORANGE ROCK BUNS

These buns are best eaten within two days of baking.

Makes 12 buns

8 oz (225g) self-raising flour

4 oz (100g) soft margarine

2 oz (50g) granulated sugar

4 oz (100g) dried mixed fruit

1 egg, size 3, beaten

Finely grated rind of 1 orange

1 tablespoon orange juice

1 oz (25g) demerara sugar

Set the oven to fairly hot, gas mark 6 or 400°F/200°C.

Put the flour into a bowl and rub in the margarine until it resembles fine crumbs. Stir in the sugar and dried fruit and mix well.

Add the egg, orange rind and juice. Bind together into a stiff dough. Shape into 12 rough balls and place well apart on two lightly-greased baking sheets.

Sprinkle demerara sugar on top of the buns and bake for 15 minutes until pale golden. Leave to cool on the baking sheets for 5 minutes, then transfer to wire cooling trays.

To freeze: wrap and freeze when cold for up to 3 months. Thaw and eat immediately.

CRUNCHY SUGAR-TOPPED SLICES

Cuts into 12 fingers

FOR THE CAKE:

6 oz (175g) butter or margarine

4 eggs, size 3

4 oz (100g) caster sugar

Grated rind of ½ lemon

8 oz (225g) self-raising flour, sifted

FOR THE SUGAR TOPPING:

2 oz (50g) butter

4 oz (100g) caster sugar

Set oven to moderately hot, gas mark 5 or 375°F/190°C. Base line and grease a 7×11×1 inch (18×28×2·5 cm) oblong cake tin.

In a saucepan, gently melt the butter or margarine. Allow to cool.

Whisk the eggs with the sugar until mixture is thick and leaves a trail, then mix in grated lemon rind. Fold in the flour, alternating with the melted butter or margarine.

Spoon the mixture into the prepared tin and level the surface.

For the topping, place thin slivers of butter evenly over the cake and sprinkle generously with the sugar for the topping.

Bake just above centre of the oven for 20–25 minutes. Leave to cool in the tin before cutting into fingers.

To freeze: wrap and freeze when cold for up to 3 months.

EGGLESS EVERYDAY CAKE

12 oz (350g) plain flour

½ level teaspoon salt

1 level teaspoon mixed spice

6 oz (175g) margarine

6 oz (175g) sugar

12 oz (350g) sultanas

½ pint (300 ml) milk and water mixed

2 tablespoons vinegar

2 level teaspoons bicarbonate of soda

2 oz (50g) crunchy nut topping or chopped hazelnuts

Set the oven to warm, gas mark 3 or 325°F/160°C. Base line and grease a 7½ inch (19 cm) round cake tin.

Sift the flour, salt and mixed spice into a bowl. Rub in the margarine until the mixture

Chocolate Chip
Cake, page
113; Lemon
Meringue Cake;
Shortbread
Cheesecake,
page 112;
Eggless
Everyday Cake;
Cider Ring
Cake, page 112

resembles breadcrumbs. Stir in the sugar and sultanas.

Mix together the milk and water, vinegar and bicarbonate of soda then stir into the flour and mix thoroughly with a wooden spoon. Transfer mixture to the tin, hollow out the centre to a depth of about 1 inch (2.5 cm), then sprinkle topping over.

Bake in the centre of the oven for about 1¾ hours or until cooked. Leave to cool in the tin for 10 minutes before turning out.

To freeze: wrap and freeze when cold for up to 2 months.

LEMON MERINGUE CAKE

FOR THE FILLING:

| 2 oz (50g) butter |
| 2 oz (50g) sugar |
| 2 egg yolks, size 3 |
| Grated rind of 1 lemon |
| 2 tablespoons lemon juice |

FOR THE CAKE:

| 3 oz (75g) butter or margarine |
| 3 oz (75g) caster sugar |
| 2 eggs, size 3 |
| 4 oz (100g) self-raising flour |
| ¼ level teaspoon ground ginger |

FOR THE MERINGUE:

| 2 egg whites, size 3 |
| 4 oz (100g) caster sugar |

Set the oven to warm, gas mark 3 or 325°F/160°C. Base line and grease an 8 inch (20 cm) spring clip tin.

Put filling ingredients into a heatproof basin and place over pan of very gently simmering water. Stir until sugar and butter have dissolved and the mixture is thick enough to coat the back of a wooden spoon – the consistency of thick double cream. Cool.

To make the cake, cream the butter or margarine with the sugar until light and fluffy, then add eggs, one at a time, beating well after each addition. Sift the flour with the ground ginger and then fold into the creamed mixture.

Spoon into bottom of prepared tin and level the surface. Spread cooled lemon filling over top.

To make the meringue, whisk the egg whites until stiff, fold in half the sugar and whisk again until stiff. Fold in the remaining sugar. Spoon the meringue on top of the filling, covering it completely.

Bake in the centre of the preheated oven for 1 hour. Test by inserting a skewer into the cake mixture and if it comes out clean, it is cooked – a little of the lemon filling will remain on the skewer, so don't mistake this for uncooked cake.

To freeze: open freeze until firm, then carefully wrap and freeze for up to 3 months. Keep covered whilst thawing.

SHORTBREAD CHEESECAKE

FOR THE SHORTBREAD:
5 oz (150g) plain flour
1 oz (25g) cornflour
2 oz (50g) caster sugar
4 oz (100g) butter
FOR THE CHEESECAKE:
8 oz (225g) cream cheese
3 eggs, size 3, separated
Grated rind and juice of 1 lemon
4 oz (100g) caster sugar
1 oz (25g) plain flour
5 oz (150g) double or whipping cream

Set the oven to warm, gas mark 3 or 325°F/160°C.

Sift the flour and cornflour into a bowl and stir in the caster sugar. Rub the butter into the flour until the mixture resembles coarse breadcrumbs. Knead to form a ball of dough. Cover in cling wrap and chill for at least 30 minutes.

Grease and flour a 7–8 inch (18–20 cm) loose-bottomed, round cake tin. On a floured surface, roll out the dough into a circle and place in the bottom of the prepared tin, pressing it into the sides, if necessary.

Cream the cheese to soften in a large bowl, beat in egg yolks, lemon rind and juice, 2 oz (50g) of the caster sugar, flour and cream.

Whisk the egg whites until stiff, then whisk in the remaining caster sugar. Using a metal spoon, carefully fold 1 tablespoon of the egg white into the cheese mixture to loosen the consistency, then fold in the remainder.

Spoon the mixture on to the shortbread and level the surface. Bake in the centre of the oven for 1½–1¾ hours or until firm but soggy to the touch. It will sink in the middle. Leave to cool in the tin for 1 hour. Loosen the sides of the cake from the tin and push up the base to remove the cake. Dust with icing sugar.

To freeze: do not dust with icing sugar. Freeze for up to 2 months.

CIDER RING CAKE

4 oz (100g) margarine
8 oz (225g) granulated sugar
5 oz (150g) mixed dried fruit
7 fl oz (210 ml) dry cider
1 egg, size 3
10 oz (275g) self-raising flour
Pinch of salt
¼ level teaspoon nutmeg
FOR THE GLAZE:
2 oz (50g) demerara sugar
2 tablespoons dry cider

Set the oven to warm, gas mark 3 or 325°F/160°C.

In a pan heat together the margarine, sugar, fruit and cider. Heat to melt the margarine then bring to the boil. Allow to become cold then beat in the egg. Sift the flour, salt and nutmeg into the cider mixture and mix evenly. Pour the mixture into a greased 2½–3 pint (1·5–1·8 litre) ring tin and bake above the centre of the oven for $1\frac{1}{4}$–$1\frac{1}{2}$ hours or until cooked.

To make the glaze, heat the sugar and cider together for a minute or two until syrupy. Brush over the cake while it is still warm.

To freeze: wrap and freeze when cold for up to 3 months.

CHOCOLATE CHIP CAKE

5 oz (150 g) self-raising flour

$\frac{1}{2}$ level teaspoon salt

4 oz (100 g) ground almonds

4 oz (100g) margarine

6 oz (175g) caster sugar

3 eggs, size 3

$\frac{1}{8}$ teaspoon almond essence

2 tablespoons milk

3 oz (75g) plain chocolate, roughly chopped, or chocolate buttons

Set the oven to moderate, gas mark 4 or 350°F/180°C. Grease a 2 pint (1·1 litre) Kugelhopf tin or, alternatively, a $7\frac{1}{2}$ inch (19 cm) cake tin.

Sift the flour and salt together then stir in the almonds.

Cream the margarine and sugar together. Add the eggs, one at a time, beating well after each addition. Beat in the essence. Fold in the flour, milk and chocolate. Turn the mixture into the tin.

Bake above the centre of the oven for about $1\frac{1}{4}$ hours, or until the mixture is firm and springy to the touch. Cool in the tin for 30 minutes before turning out. Serve sprinkled with a little granulated sugar.

To freeze: wrap when cold and freeze for up to 3 months.

All-In-One Victoria Sandwich, page 114

VICTORIA SANDWICH AND VARIATIONS

ALL-IN-ONE VICTORIA SANDWICH

With this mixture you can fill either two $7\frac{1}{2}$ inch (19 cm) sandwich tins, or one deep $7\frac{1}{2}$ inch (19 cm) cake tin. A very satisfactory but shallower cake can be made using two-thirds of all the ingredients.

6 oz (175g) self-raising flour
1 level teaspoon baking powder
6 oz (175g) soft margarine
6 oz (175g) caster sugar
3 eggs, size 3
2 tablespoons milk
FOR THE FILLING:
Jam of choice
5 oz (150g) whipping cream, whipped
Icing sugar to decorate

Set the oven: for the sandwich tins to moderate, gas mark 4 or 350°F/180°C; for a large cake to warm, gas mark 3 or 325°F/160°C.

Base line and grease the cake tin(s).

Sift the flour with the baking powder into a bowl. Add the margarine, sugar, eggs and milk. Beat the mixture with a wooden spoon for 2–3 minutes, or with electric beaters for 1 minute, until well mixed. Spoon into the cake tin(s).

Bake the two sandwich tins above the centre of the oven for about 35 minutes. Bake the large cake in the centre of the oven for about 1 hour or until firm and springy.

When cold, split if necessary and sandwich together with jam and cream. Sprinkle the top with icing sugar.

To freeze: do not fill. Wrap when cold and freeze for up to 3 months. Thaw and fill as in recipe.

Variations
Chocolate Sponge
1 quantity basic All-in-one Victoria Sandwich mixture (above) made with 5 oz (150g) self-raising flour and 1 oz (25g) cocoa. Make and bake as in basic recipe, sifting cocoa with the flour and baking powder.

QUEEN CAKES
Makes 8–10

$\frac{1}{3}$ quantity All-in-one Victoria Sandwich mixture (left)
2 oz (50g) currants

Make as for Victoria Sandwich, stirring in the currants. Divide the mixture between 8–10 greased, small brioche tins or patty tins and bake in a moderately hot oven, gas mark 5 or 375°F/190°C for 15–20 minutes or until cooked.

To freeze: wrap and freeze for up to 3 months.

MADELEINES
Makes 8–10

4 oz (100g) margarine or butter
4 oz (100g) caster sugar
2 eggs, size 3
$\frac{1}{4}$ teaspoon vanilla essence
4 oz (100g) self-raising flour
1–2 tablespoons milk to mix
TO GLAZE:
6 tablespoons seedless raspberry jam
Juice of 1 lemon
Desiccated coconut
Small pieces glacé cherry

Set the oven to moderately hot, gas mark 5 or 375°F/190°C. Place small discs of grease-proof paper in the bottom of 8–10 dariole or castle moulds, then grease the tins.

Cream the margarine or butter and sugar together. Add the eggs, one at a time, beating well after each addition. Beat in the vanilla. Fold in half the flour then the rest of the flour with enough milk to make a medium-soft consistency.

Fill the moulds just over half full with the mixture. Arrange moulds on a baking tray and bake in the centre of the oven for 15–20 minutes until risen and brown. Cool for 5 minutes before removing from moulds. When cold, cut tops of cakes level.

Queen Cakes;
Choco Top
Hats;
Madeleines;
Sponge Drops;
Almond Puffs,
page 116

Boil the jam and lemon juice together for 15 seconds. Spear each cake in turn on a fork and coat sides and narrow end with glaze. Then roll in desiccated coconut. Stand each one upright in a paper case. Decorate the top with a piece of cherry.

To freeze: do not glaze. Wrap and freeze for up to 3 months. Thaw and decorate as above.

moderately hot oven, gas mark 5 or 375°F/ 190°C for 15–20 minutes.

To make the butter cream, cream the butter until soft and then beat in the icing sugar and cocoa.

Cut a small round out of the centre of each small cake. Pipe a circle of butter cream around the hole, dust the removed piece of cake with icing sugar and place on top of the butter cream.

To freeze: open freeze until firm then carefully pack, and freeze for up to 3 months.

CHOCO TOP HATS

Makes 10

⅓ quantity All-in-one Victoria Sandwich mixture (page 114)

1 tablespoon cocoa

FOR THE BUTTER CREAM:

2 oz (50g) butter

4 oz (100g) icing sugar, sifted

1 level tablespoon cocoa, sifted

Make as for Victoria Sandwich, sifting cocoa with flour and baking powder. Divide between ten paper cases and bake in a

SPONGE DROPS

Makes about 30, or 15 pairs

2½oz (65g) self-raising flour

1 level tablespoon cornflour

2 eggs, size 3

1 egg white

2 oz (50g) caster sugar

FOR THE FILLING:

5 oz (150g) double cream

Set the oven to moderate, gas mark 4 or 350°F/180°C. Line 2–3 baking sheets with ungreased greaseproof paper.

Sift the flour and cornflour on to a square of greaseproof and set aside.

With electric hand-held beaters, whisk the eggs, egg white and sugar together until thick and light and the mixture holds a trail for 5 seconds. Sprinkle the flour over the surface, then fold in using a metal spoon. Spoon the mixture into a piping bag fitted with a $\frac{1}{2}$ inch (1 cm) plain nozzle.

Pipe blobs of the mixture about $1\frac{1}{2}$ inches (4 cm) in diameter on to the greaseproof on the trays. Sprinkle with a little extra caster sugar. Bake for 10–12 minutes until crisp.

Remove from the oven, draw the sheet of greaseproof paper off the tray and place on a damp cloth.

Cool, then sandwich the cakes together in pairs with whipped cream.

To freeze: do not fill. Wrap and freeze for up to 3 months. Thaw and fill.

ALMOND PUFFS

Makes 9

$7\frac{1}{2}$ oz (210g) packet of frozen puff pastry, thawed

3 oz (75g) packet cream cheese

2 oz (50g) ground almonds

$\frac{1}{4}$ teaspoon almond essence

1 oz (25g) caster sugar

1 egg, size 3

A little milk

A few flaked almonds

Set the oven to fairly hot, gas mark 6 or 400°F/200°C.

Roll the pastry out very thinly and cut out nine small rounds with a $1\frac{3}{4}$ inch (4·5 cm) fluted cutter for the lids – the lids are cut first as the first rolling of pastry puffs up most. Transfer the lids to a plate and keep in the fridge until needed.

Cut out a further nine rounds using a 3 inch (7·5 cm) fluted cutter and use to line patty tins.

Put the cream cheese, ground almonds, essence, sugar and egg into a basin. Beat until smooth and well mixed, then divide mixture evenly between lined tins.

Brush lids on both sides with milk and place over filling, lightly pressing edges together. Sprinkle a few flaked almonds on the top.

Bake in centre of oven for 25–30 minutes, until the pastry is well risen and golden brown.

To freeze: pack and freeze for up to 3 months. Thaw and, if liked, reheat in fairly hot oven for 5 minutes.

BASIC TART PASTRY

This quantity will line about 20 patty tins or 14–16 shaped fluted tins

3 oz (75g) self-raising flour

1 oz (25g) cornflour

3 oz (75g) margarine

1 level tablespoon caster sugar

$\frac{1}{2}$ level teaspoon finely grated lemon rind

$\frac{1}{2}$ beaten egg, size 3, or 1 egg yolk and 1 to 2 teaspoons water

If you've a food processor just whizz all the ingredients together for a few seconds.

Otherwise, sift the flour and cornflour together. Cut the margarine into small pieces, then rub it into the flour until the mixture resembles breadcrumbs. Use your fingertips for rubbing in and keep everything cool.

Stir in the caster sugar and lemon rind; then stir in the beaten egg, or egg yolk and water, and bind the ingredients together.

You can roll out and use the pastry immediately, but, if liked, make in advance and store in refrigerator, or properly wrapped in the freezer.

STRAWBERRY TARTS

1 quantity basic tart pastry (page 116)

FOR THE FILLING:

5 oz (150g) whipping or double cream

2 level tablespoons sugar

1 tablespoon orange juice, optional

8 oz (225g) strawberries

Set the oven to fairly hot, gas mark 6 or 400°F/200°C.

Roll out the pastry and cut into rounds with a 2½–3 inch (6·5–7·5 cm) cutter. Line 20 small, deep, fluted tins, or patty tins. Prick the base well, and bake just above the centre of the oven for about 15 minutes. Remove from oven and leave to cool.

Whisk the cream until thick, then whisk in the sugar and, if used, the orange juice.

Hull the strawberries, wash if necessary and dry well. Reserve about four strawberries for decoration. Mash the rest and fold into the cream.

Just before serving, spoon the strawberry cream into the tartlets. Decorate each of the tartlets with slices of strawberry.

Not suitable for freezing.

COCONUT CUSTARD TARTS

1 quantity basic tart pastry (page 116)

FOR THE FILLING:

1 egg, size 3, separated

2 level tablespoons caster sugar

2 level tablespoons cornflour

8 fl oz (240 ml) milk

½ teaspoon vanilla essence

2 oz (50g) coconut

2 oz (50g) green grapes

Set the oven to fairly hot, gas mark 6 or 400°F/200°C.

Roll out the pastry and line the diamond-shaped, individual tins or patty tins. Prick the bases with a fork.

Bake just above the centre of the oven for about 15 minutes. Remove from the oven and leave to cool.

Cream the egg yolk with the sugar, cornflour and a little of the milk until smooth. Heat the rest of the milk to just below simmering, then pour it on to the egg yolk mixture, stirring all the time to ensure a smooth consistency.

Return the custard to the pan and bring to the boil, stirring. Boil gently for 1–2 minutes. Remove from the heat and stir in the vanilla essence.

Whisk the egg whites until stiff, then fold into the warm custard together with 1 tablespoon of the coconut. Leave to cool.

Meanwhile toast the rest of the coconut until golden brown. Halve and seed the grapes.

When both filling and pastry cases are cold, spoon the custard into the cases. Sprinkle over the toasted coconut and decorate with the grapes.

Not suitable for freezing.

MANDARIN CHEESECAKE TARTS

1 quantity basic tart pastry (page 116) made with ½ beaten egg

FOR THE FILLING:

4 oz (100g) cream cheese

½ egg

1 oz (25g) sugar

1 oz (25g) ground almonds

½ teaspoon vanilla essence

FOR THE TOPPING:

11 oz (300g) can mandarin oranges plus juice

1 level teaspoon arrowroot

Sugar to sweeten

Set the oven to fairly hot, gas mark 6 or 400°F/200°C.

Roll out the pastry and line individual, flower-shaped tins or patty tins. Prick the base with a fork.

Mix all the filling ingredients together for about 1 minute or until well mixed. If

Small Tarts, pages 116-9

necessary, add 1 tablespoon of the mandarin juice to make the mixture creamy. Place 1 tablespoon of the mixture on the bottom of each tartlet, and bake just above the centre of the oven for 15 minutes or until the pastry is golden brown.

To make the topping, drain the juice from the mandarin oranges then, in a small pan, blend the arrowroot with a little of the juice, and stir in the rest. Bring to the boil, stirring and boil for half a minute or so until clear.

Remove from the heat and add sugar to taste. Place mandarin orange segments on top and spoon a little of the glaze over the top of each tartlet.

To freeze: do not make topping. Wrap and freeze filled and baked tartlets for up to 2 months. Thaw and complete as in recipe.

RASPBERRY HEARTS

1 quantity basic tart pastry (page 116) – made with the egg yolk and water

FOR THE FILLING:

5–6 level teaspoons raspberry jam

1 egg white, size 3

2 oz (50g) caster sugar

4 oz (100g) fresh raspberries

Set the oven to fairly hot, gas mark 6 or 400°F/200°C.

Roll out the pastry and line individual heart-shaped tins, or cut into rounds and line patty tins. Prick the base with a fork.

Place 1 teaspoon of jam in the base of each tin. Bake just below the centre of the oven for 10 minutes. Meanwhile whisk the egg white until stiff, add the sugar and whisk again until stiff. Spoon into a piping bag fitted with a small star nozzle.

Remove the tartlets from the oven and pipe the meringue in small rosettes round the edge of the pastry cases. Return to the oven and bake for a further 5 minutes until the outside of the meringue feels firm. Allow to cool. Remove from the tins, then arrange raspberries in the centre.

Not suitable for freezing.

BLACK CHERRY CREAMS

1 quantity basic tart pastry (page 116)

FOR THE FILLING:

5 oz (150g) double or whipping cream

1 small carton black cherry yogurt

1 level tablespoon sugar

2 oz (50g) cherries or black grapes, cut into small pieces

Set the oven to fairly hot, gas mark 6 or 400°F/200°C.

Roll out the pastry and line individual boat-shaped tins or patty tins. Prick base with a fork. Bake just above the centre of the oven for about 15 minutes. Remove from the oven and leave to cool.

Whisk the cream until thick, then whisk in the yogurt and sugar.

Fill a piping bag fitted with a small star nozzle and pipe the cream into the pastry cases. Decorate with small pieces of cherry or grapes.

Toffee and Banana Cream Variation: Make as above but use a carton of toffee yogurt instead of the black cherry and add $\frac{1}{4}$ teaspoon butterscotch flavouring with the sugar. Fill the tartlet cases. Decorate with thin halved slices of banana dipped in lemon juice to prevent discolouring.

Not suitable for freezing.

SPICY SYRUP TARTS

Makes 14-16 tarts

1 quantity basic tart pastry (page 116)

FOR THE FILLING:

6 oz (175g) golden syrup

4 oz (100g) fresh breadcrumbs

1 level teaspoon ground ginger

4 teaspoons lemon juice

2 oz (50g) chopped nuts or packet of crunchy topping

Set the oven to fairly hot, gas mark 6 or 400°F/200°C.

Roll out the pastry, cut into rounds with a 3 inch (7·5 cm) cutter, and line individual fluted tins. Prick bases.

Mix together all the filling ingredients except the topping. Fill each pastry-lined tin with $1\frac{1}{2}$ teaspoons of filling. Sprinkle topping over and bake towards the top of the oven for 15 minutes.

To freeze: wrap and freeze when cold for up to 3 months.

JAM TART DESIGNS

1. The Whorl
Here the pastry trimmings are rolled into a long sausage shape before being turned over the jam filled plate – the number of turns depends on how much pastry you have left over.

2. The Star
Cut the pastry trimmings into strips, then place over the pastry as shown. Fill the sections with jam – this is a design where you can use 12 different jams should you wish to show off!

3. The Red Cross
Twist the pastry strips before placing over the base pastry as shown. Traditionally, redcurrant jelly is used for the cross with lemon curd outside.

4. The Split
Divide the two colours of jam with a small strip of pastry.

Jam Tart Designs

5. The Lattice
Twist the pastry trimmings before placing lattice fashion over the jam.

6. The Well
This is the one to make if you've only got a scrap of pastry left or only a spoonful of jam left in one of the jars. The Well looks best if you use two contrasting colours.

7. The Gable
Traditionally filled with syrup (use the recipe for the Spicy Syrup Tarts on page 119). Make 1 inch (2.5 cm) wide cuts round the pastry edge and fold alternate sections inwards.

8. The Woman's Weekly
Well, we just had to have this one in, don't you think? After all we've been going for more than 75 years and we are certainly a tradition!

Make a continuous 'W' with strips of pastry and fill alternate sides with different coloured jams – we should really have used a pink and a blue jam!

9. The Four or Eight
Twist pastry strips and lay them across the pastry base so that the base is divided into sections. Use four or eight different jams to fill the sections.

FINISHING TOUCH

Here are a few simple but effective ways to add a touch of glamour to your cakes. So if you've got spare time after your baking session why not try out one of these ideas.

ORANGE GLACÉ ICING

12 oz (350g) icing sugar, sifted

2–3 tablespoons orange juice to mix

Stir the icing sugar with enough orange juice to give a smooth icing that thickly coats the back of a wooden spoon.

Spread most of the icing over the top of the cake. Allow to dry for a few minutes.

Spoon the remaining icing into a paper icing bag, snip off the end then pipe in a pattern over the top of the cake.

Note: If liked, before icing spread apricot jam over the sides of the cake, roll in chopped nuts or crunchy nut topping and then ice.

Not suitable for freezing.

Creamy
Chocolate
Frosting

CREAMY CHOCOLATE FROSTING

3 oz (75g) margarine or butter

1 lb (450g) icing sugar, sifted

2–3 level tablespoons cocoa or drinking chocolate

4 tablespoons milk

Chocolate brown food colouring

After Eight Mints

Cream the margarine or butter until soft. Stir in the icing sugar and cocoa with sufficient milk to give a smooth, thick butter cream. Add food colouring as necessary.

Use two thirds of the icing to fill and cover the top of the cake.

Spoon the rest into a piping bag fitted with a large star nozzle. Pipe large rosettes round the top edge of the cake. Cut mints in half and press into cake between the rosettes.

To freeze: open freeze until firm then carefully wrap and freeze for up to 3 months.

Orange Glacé
Icing; Creamy
Chocolate
Frosting;
Chocolate and
Cherry Coating

CHOCOLATE AND CHERRY COATING

2½ fl oz (65 ml) whipping cream, whipped

6 tablespoons raspberry jam

4–5 tablespoons chocolate vermicelli

Glacé cherries

Sandwich chocolate Victoria Sandwich cakes (page 114) together with whipped cream. Spread raspberry jam over the top and sides, warming it slightly if necessary. Coat the top and sides with the vermicelli. Decorate the top with glacé cherry halves.

Not suitable for freezing.

TRAY BAKES

CHOCOLATE AND ALMOND FINGERS

Makes 12 slices

6 oz (175g) self-raising flour, sifted
1 oz (25g) cocoa powder, sifted
4 oz (100g) caster sugar
4 oz (100g) sultanas
2 oz (50g) flaked almonds
1 Mars Bar
2 oz (50g) milk chocolate
4 oz (100g) butter

Set oven to moderately hot, gas mark 5 or 375°F/190°C.

Mix the flour, cocoa powder, sugar, sultanas and flaked almonds together. Cut the Mars Bar into $\frac{1}{2}$ inch (1 cm) pieces, place in a small saucepan with the chocolate and butter, and heat gently until melted. Pour on to the dry ingredients and mix well.

Spoon the chocolate mixture into a 7×7 inch (18×18 cm) greased, shallow tin. Spread out evenly and bake for 25 minutes. The top will appear soft to the touch. Leave in the tin to cool and set, then cut into 12 fingers.

To freeze: wrap in foil or polythene bags. Will keep for 2 months.

PINEAPPLE AND COCONUT SLICE

Makes 8 slices

2 eggs, size 3, separated
4 oz (100g) caster sugar
8 oz (225g) can pineapple slices in natural juice
6 oz (175g) desiccated coconut
2 oz (50g) self-raising flour
4 level tablespoons granulated sugar
16 angelica diamonds

Set oven to moderate, gas mark 4 or 350°F/180°C. Grease a 7×7 inch (18×18 cm) shallow tin.

Whisk the egg whites until stiff, add the caster sugar and whisk until stiff again.

Drain the pineapple slices, reserving the juice. Beat the egg yolks and 2 tablespoons of pineapple juice together. Carefully fold the coconut, flour and beaten egg yolks into whisked egg whites. Turn mixture into the tin and level the surface with the back of a spoon.

Cut the pineapple slices into quarters and arrange the pieces in pairs in two rows of 4 on top of the coconut mixture. Bake for 45 minutes until golden and firm to the touch.

Meanwhile gently heat the granulated sugar with 2 tablespoons of pineapple juice until sugar has dissolved. Bring to the boil and boil rapidly for 5 minutes to form a syrup. Allow to cool slightly.

Let the cooked coconut mixture stand for 10 minutes, then brush the pineapple slices on top with a little syrup.

Decorate each slice of pineapple with 2 angelica diamonds, brush lightly with syrup. Leave in tin until cold, then cut into 8 slices.

Not suitable for freezing.

TUNIS TRAY BAKE

Makes 12 slices

FOR THE BASE:
2 oz (50g) margarine or butter
2 oz (50g) caster sugar
1 egg, size 3, beaten
2 oz (50g) self-raising flour
1 oz (25g) ground almonds
2 tablespoons milk

FOR THE TOPPING:
7 oz (200g) bar plain chocolate
$2\frac{1}{2}$ oz (65g) bar milk chocolate

Set the oven to moderate, gas mark 4 or 350°F/180°C. Base line and grease a 7×7 inch (18×18 cm) shallow tin.

Cream the margarine or butter and caster sugar until light and fluffy, then beat in the egg, adding one teaspoon of the flour to prevent the mixture from curdling. Fold in the remaining flour, almonds and milk, then spread evenly in the tin and bake in the centre of the oven for 25–30 minutes or until lightly browned. Leave in the tin to cool.

Gently melt the plain chocolate in a basin standing over a saucepan of hot water. Pour on to mixture in tin, then shake tin to get rid of air bubbles. Leave to set for 2 hours.

With a very sharp knife, cut into 12 slices then remove from the tin and decorate as follows: Melt the milk chocolate in a small basin standing over hot water. Fill a small greaseproof paper piping bag with this melted chocolate and snip off the tip to make a small hole. Pipe a looped pattern on each slice. Leave to set for 1 hour.

Note: Some milk chocolate may become too thick to pipe when melted. If this happens, add half a teaspoon of oil to thin it.

Not suitable for freezing.

PRUNE AND APPLE CRISSCROSS SLICES

Makes 20 slices

FOR THE FILLING:

12 oz (350g) no-need-to-soak prunes, stoned

1 lb (450g) cooking apples, peeled, cored and sliced

$\frac{1}{2}$ pint (300 ml) cold tea

2 oz (50g) sugar

FOR THE PASTRY:

$2\frac{1}{2}$ oz (65g) margarine

$2\frac{1}{2}$ oz (65g) lard

10 oz (275g) plain flour

Water to mix

Set the oven to fairly hot, gas mark 6 or 400°F/200°C. Grease a 7×11×1 inch (18×28×2·5 cm) tin.

Put the prunes, sliced apple, tea and sugar in a pan and simmer for about 10 minutes until prunes and apple have cooked and become a thickish mixture. Stir occasionally to prevent prunes from sticking to the pan. Put on one side to cool.

Rub the fat into the flour until mixture resembles fine breadcrumbs. Bind together with sufficient water to give a soft but not sticky dough.

Roll out the pastry on a lightly-floured surface and line the tin. Crimp edges, turn the prune filling into the pastry case, and level out the surface.

Gather up the scraps, roll out and cut into strips at least 11 inches (28 cm) long and $\frac{1}{4}$ inch (5 mm) wide. Use to decorate the top in a lattice pattern.

Bake for 35 minutes until the pastry is lightly browned. Leave in the tin to cool, then cut into 20 slices.

Not suitable for freezing.

MARMALADE BREAD PUDDING

Makes 16 slices

1 lb (450g) stale bread, with crusts removed

Grated rind and juice of 1 orange

$\frac{1}{2}$ pint (300 ml) milk

8 oz (225g) mixed dried fruit

4 oz (100g) dark brown sugar

3 oz (75g) soft margarine

2 level teaspoons mixed spice

4 level tablespoons marmalade

1 level tablespoon granulated sugar

Set oven to moderately hot, gas mark 5 or 375°F/190°C. Grease a 7×11×1 inch (18×28×2·5 cm) tin.

Cut the bread into small pieces, place in a large bowl with the orange rind and juice and milk. Leave to soak for 15 minutes. Mash with a fork to break up the pieces.

Add the dried fruit, brown sugar, margarine, mixed spice and marmalade to the soaked bread. Mix well together.

Turn into the tin, level out the surface and bake for $1\frac{1}{4}$ hours until firm. Leave in the tin to cool, turn out on to a wire rack and dredge the top with sugar. Cut into 16 slices.

To freeze: wrap in foil or polythene bags. Will keep well for 3 months.

NUTTY ORANGE SLICES

Makes 16 slices

FOR THE BASE:

2 eggs, size 3

8 oz (225g) caster sugar

1 can concentrated frozen orange juice

2 oz (50g) digestive biscuit crumbs

3 oz (75g) chopped nuts

8 oz (225g) chopped dates

2 oz (50g) self-raising flour

FOR THE TOPPING:

5 oz (150g) icing sugar

2 teaspoons water

1 oz (25g) chopped nuts

Set the oven to moderate, gas mark 4 or 350°F/180°C. Base line, grease and lightly flour a 7×11×1 inch (18×28×2·5 cm) tin.

Whisk the eggs until light and fluffy. Whisk in the sugar until thick and mousse-like, then stir in the orange juice until well mixed. Add the biscuit crumbs, nuts and dates. Fold in flour and pour into the tin.

Bake below the centre of the oven for 40–45 minutes, covering with greaseproof paper if it starts to over-brown.

Leave in tin to cool, but loosen edges with a palette knife. Turn on to a wire tray.

Sift the icing sugar into a bowl and mix in the water to make a stiff icing.

Cut the mixture into 16 slices and pour over sufficient icing to cover the top.

Decorate with the chopped nuts, sprinkling them down the centre of each slice.

To freeze: make the base, but do not decorate with the icing. Wrap in foil or polythene bags. Will keep for 2 months.

APRICOT AND BANANA BARS

Makes 16 slices

FOR THE BASE:

8 oz (225g) self-raising flour

2 level teaspoons baking powder

$\frac{1}{2}$ level teaspoon salt

2 oz (50g) soft margarine

1 oz (25g) caster sugar

$\frac{1}{4}$ pint (150 ml) milk

FOR THE TOPPING:

2 oz (50g) margarine or butter

2 oz (50g) soft brown sugar

3 level tablespoons golden syrup

4 oz (100g) digestive biscuits, crushed

2 ripe bananas, peeled and sliced

2 teaspoons lemon juice

15 oz (411g) can apricot halves, drained

2 tablespoons warmed apricot jam

Set the oven to fairly hot, gas mark 6 or 400°F/200°C. Base line and grease a 7×11×1 inch (18×28×2·5 cm) tin.

Sift the flour, baking powder and salt together, then rub in the soft margarine. Stir in the sugar, then add the milk and mix to a soft dough. Roll out to an oblong to fit the tin and press into the base.

Place the margarine or butter, sugar and syrup in a pan and heat gently until melted. Stir in the crushed biscuits and mix well.

Spread the mixture over the base of the tin with a flat-bladed knife.

Toss the sliced banana in the lemon juice and arrange in rows across the tin, alternating with the apricot halves. Bake in the centre of the oven for 30–35 minutes. Leave to cool in the tin and whilst still warm, glaze with the warmed apricot jam which has been melted with a little of the apricot syrup. Cut into 16 slices.

Not suitable for freezing.

FRUIT AND NUT SLICES

Makes 18 slices

3 oz (75g) Brazil nuts

3 oz (75g) walnuts

2 oz (50g) blanched almonds

2 oz (50g) glacé cherries, halved

4 oz (100g) figs, chopped

3 oz (75g) sultanas

2 oz (50g) candied peel

2 oz (50g) self-raising flour

2 oz (50g) brown sugar

2 eggs, size 3

$\frac{3}{4}$ teaspoon vanilla essence

Squeeze of lemon juice

9 glacé cherries, halved for decoration

Set the oven to warm, gas mark 3 or 325°F/160°C.

Chop all nuts roughly. Put in a bowl with 2 oz (50g) cherries, figs, sultanas and candied peel. Mix well. Stir in rest of ingredients, except cherries for decoration. Spread evenly in tin, bake above centre of oven for 1 hour. Remove and leave to cool. Cut into 18. Decorate with halved cherries.

To freeze: wrap in foil or polythene bags. Will keep for 2 months.

NELLIE'S BAKE

Makes 10

FOR THE PASTRY:

8 oz (225g) plain flour

4 oz (100g) lard and margarine, mixed

Water to mix

FOR THE FILLING:

8 oz (225g) Madeira cake crumbs

3 oz (75g) chopped mixed peel

2 oz (50g) chopped raisins or sultanas

Grated rind of 1 lemon

1 tablespoon lemon juice

4 level tablespoons golden syrup

4 tablespoons milk

TO GLAZE:

Milk

A little caster sugar

Sift the flour into a bowl. Rub in the fats until the mixture resembles breadcrumbs. Stir in enough water to give a soft, not sticky, dough. Wrap and chill the pastry in the fridge for 30 minutes.

Set the oven to moderately hot, gas mark 5 or 375°F/190°C.

On a floured surface roll out just over half the pastry and line a 7½ × 7½ inch (19 × 19 cm) shallow sandwich tin.

Make the filling by mixing all the ingredients together, then spoon into the lined tin and spread level. Brush the pastry edges with a little water.

Roll out the rest of the pastry to the size of the tin and place over the filling, pressing the edges lightly together. Trim. If liked, roll out the trimmings and use to decorate the top. Brush the top with milk and sprinkle with caster sugar.

Bake towards the top of the oven for 45–50 minutes or until golden brown.
Cool in the tin then turn out and cut into fingers.

To freeze: wrap in foil and freeze for up to 3 months.

APRICOT AND CORNFLAKE CRUNCHY BAKE

Makes 12

4 oz (100g) margarine

4 oz (100g) caster sugar

2 eggs, size 2

4 oz (100g) self-raising flour, sifted

½ level teaspoon baking powder

2–3 oz (50–75g) dried apricots, chopped

2 oz (50g) plain chocolate buttons

FOR THE TOPPING:

1 oz (25g) butter

3 level tablespoons apricot jam

2 oz (50g) cornflakes

1 oz (25g) demerara sugar

From top:
Banana and
Muesli
Flapjacks, page
128; Iced
Cherry and
Coconut Bars;
Apricot and
Cornflake
Crunchy Bake;
Nellie's Bake,
page 125;
Goosnaugh
Triangles, page
128; Date
Chews, page
128

Set the oven to moderate, gas mark 4 or 350°F/180°C. Grease a 7 × 11 × 1 inch (18 × 28 × 2·5 cm) deep tin.

Place the margarine, sugar, eggs, flour and baking powder into a bowl. Beat together until light and fluffy – 2–3 minutes by hand and 1–2 minutes by electric mixer.

Fold in the chopped apricots and chocolate buttons. Spoon into the prepared tin and level the surface.

Melt the butter and the jam, then stir in the cornflakes and sugar. Sprinkle evenly over the mixture in the tin.

Bake just above the centre of the oven for 35–40 minutes until firm and springy to the touch.
Cool in the tin.

Not suitable for freezing.

ICED CHERRY AND COCONUT BARS

Makes 10

FOR THE PASTRY:

3 oz (75g) lard and margarine, mixed

6 oz (175g) plain flour

Water to mix

FOR THE FILLING:

6 oz (175g) caster sugar

4 oz (100g) desiccated coconut

1 oz (25g) angelica, chopped

4 oz (100g) sultanas

2 oz (50g) glacé cherries, quartered

2 eggs, size 3, beaten

2 level tablespoons self-raising flour

1 tablespoon lemon juice

FOR THE ICING:

2 oz (50g) icing sugar

1–2 teaspoons water

Rub the fats into the flour until the mixture resembles breadcrumbs. Stir in enough water to give a soft, not sticky, dough. Knead lightly then roll out and line a 7½ × 7½ inch (19 × 19 cm) shallow cake tin. Chill in the fridge for 30 minutes if time.

Set the oven to fairly hot, gas mark 6 or 400°F/200°C.

Mix all the filling ingredients together and spread in pastry-lined tin. Level the surface then bake above the centre of the oven for 20 minutes. Reduce the heat to moderate, gas mark 4 or 350°F/180°C and continue baking for a further 20 minutes. Cool in the tin then cut into bars.

Mix the icing sugar and water for the icing, place in a greaseproof bag, cut off the end and pipe a squiggle down each bar.

To freeze: do not ice. Cut and wrap in foil. Freeze for up to 3 months.

GOOSNAUGH TRIANGLES

Makes 16

6 oz (175g) butter

8 oz (225g) plain flour, sifted

$\frac{1}{2}$ level teaspoon ground coriander or caraway seeds

2 oz (50g) caster sugar

Rub the butter into the flour until the two ingredients start to bind together in a ball. Pat the mixture into a $7\frac{1}{2} \times 7\frac{1}{2}$ inch (19×19 cm) shallow sandwich tin.

Mix the coriander or caraway seeds with the sugar and sprinkle over the butter and flour mixture in the tin. Leave it overnight in the fridge and then bake in a moderate oven, gas mark 4 or 350°F/180°C for 20 minutes until firm but not brown.

Allow to cool in the tin. Cut into triangles with a sharp knife when cold.

Keeps well in airtight tin for 1–2 weeks.

To freeze: wrap in foil and freeze for up to 3 months.

BANANA AND MUESLI FLAPJACKS

Makes 16

3 oz (75g) margarine or butter

4 oz (100g) demerara sugar

1 level tablespoon honey

1 large banana, peeled and mashed

1 oz (25g) sultanas

10 oz (275g) muesli

Set the oven to moderate, gas mark 4 or 350°F/180°C. Grease a 7×11 inch (18×28 cm) Swiss roll tin.

Cream the margarine until soft, then beat in the sugar, honey and banana. Stir in the sultanas and muesli. Spoon into the tin and spread level.

Bake towards the top of the oven for 25–30 minutes.

Cut into fingers in the tin while still warm. Then leave to become quite cold before removing from the tin and separating the fingers.

Not suitable for freezing.

DATE CHEWS

Makes 16

1 egg, size 3

1 oz (25g) sugar

2 oz (50g) butter or margarine, melted

8 oz (225g) sugar-rolled chopped dates, see note

1 oz (25g) chopped walnuts

3 oz (75g) self-raising flour

1 tablespoon water

2 level teaspoons sugar

Set the oven to moderate, gas mark 4 or 350°F/180°C. Base line and grease a $7\frac{1}{2} \times 7\frac{1}{2}$ inch (19×19 cm) shallow tin.

Break the egg into a bowl and beat in the sugar and melted butter or margarine.

Stir in the dates, walnuts, flour and water and mix lightly but well. Spread the mixture into the lined tin. Sprinkle the sugar over the top and bake above the centre of the oven for about 30 minutes, until firm and springy to the touch.

Turn out, remove the paper lining and cut into triangles.

Note: If block dates are used, chop finely and add an extra $\frac{1}{2}$ oz (15g) sugar to the recipe.

To freeze: wrap in foil and freeze for up to 3 months.

BISCUITS

FREEZING BISCUITS:

As baked biscuits can be stored for a considerable length of time in an airtight container, it is not necessary to freeze them. However, most unbaked biscuit mixtures freeze well, especially if they can be frozen in rolls of the same diameter as the required biscuit.

BASIC BISCUIT DOUGH

8 oz (225g) plain flour
5 oz (150g) margarine
6 oz (175g) caster sugar
Grated rind of 1 lemon
1 egg, size 4, beaten

Sift the flour into a bowl and rub in the margarine until the mixture resembles breadcrumbs.

Stir in the sugar and lemon rind and enough beaten egg to make a soft but not sticky dough.

Roll the mixture in cling wrap and chill in the refrigerator for approximately 30 minutes before using.

Two-from-one-biscuits: from one batch of the basic biscuit dough above you can easily make these two delicious varieties of biscuit. They are so pretty to look at, too!

Make dough following basic recipe, divide into two and store in cling wrap until required. Freeze any leftover dough for use at a later date.

Set oven to fairly hot, gas mark 6 or 400°F/200°C.

ALMOND DAISIES

Makes 10–12

½ quantity basic biscuit dough (above)
Milk
6 glacé cherries, halved
1 oz (25g) flaked almonds

Set the oven to fairly hot, gas mark 6 or 400°F/200°C.

Make up the basic dough, roll out to ¼ inch (5 mm) thickness and stamp out 10–12 daisy shapes. Place on a baking sheet. Brush with a little milk, then place a halved glacé cherry in the centre of each biscuit and six flaked almond pieces around the cherry.

Bake in the centre of the oven for 7 minutes.

BUTTER CONES AND CURLS

Makes 16

2 oz (50g) butter
2 oz (50g) caster sugar
1 egg white, size 3
2 oz (50g) plain flour
2 teaspoons milk
1–2 oz (25–50g) plain chocolate

Set oven to hot, gas mark 7 or 425°F/220°C.

Cream the butter and sugar until light and fluffy.

Whisk the egg white until stiff. Fold half the egg white and half the flour into the creamed mixture. Fold in the remaining egg white, flour and the milk.

On a cold, lightly-greased baking sheet spoon 3 heaped teaspoons of mixture, well spaced apart. Using the back of a teaspoon, spread each teaspoon of the mixture out to a 3½ inch (9 cm) circle, bake for 3–4 minutes, until the edges are lightly golden.

Meanwhile, grease the outside of 3 cream horn tins. Working quickly, lift and wrap each biscuit round the outside of a cream horn tin. Leave to cool, then lift off and place on a wire rack. Repeat, spreading the mixture on to cold baking sheets each time.

To make the curls, spoon four heaped teaspoons of the mixture on to a cold, lightly-greased baking sheet, well spaced apart. Using the back of a teaspoon, spread each teaspoon of the mixture out to a 2½ inch (6 cm) circle. Bake for 3–4 minutes, until the edges are lightly golden.

Have ready a greased rolling pin. Working quickly, lift and gently curl the biscuits over the rolling pin. When cool, slide on to a wire rack.

Repeat baking and shaping, using the rest of the mixture.

Place chocolate in a small bowl over a pan of boiling water until melted. Dip the cones in chocolate to half cover them. For the curls, fill a small paper icing bag with melted chocolate and pipe lace designs over.

Allow to set before serving or storing in an airtight tin.

NUTTY CHOCOLATE STICKS

Makes 20

½ quantity basic biscuit dough (page 129)

3–4 oz (75–100g) plain chocolate

1 oz (25g) toasted nuts, chopped

Roll out dough into a long sausage shape about ½ inch (1 cm) in diameter and cut into about twenty 3 inch (7·5 cm) lengths. Bake in centre of preheated oven for about 8 minutes. Allow to cool.

Place chocolate in a bowl over a pan of hot water until it has melted. Dip one end of each of the sticks in melted chocolate and place on wire rack.

Sprinkle top side of each stick with chopped nuts before the chocolate sets, as shown in the photograph (opposite).

DELECTABLE FIG ROLLS

Makes 25

4 oz (100g) dried figs

¼ pint (150ml) water

1 tablespoon lemon juice

4 oz (100g) demerara sugar

1 quantity basic biscuit dough (page 129)

Milk for glazing

1 level tablespoon caster sugar

Simmer the figs in the water, lemon juice and sugar for 30 minutes, or until softened.

Allow to cool.

Roll out the chilled dough to ¼ inch (5 mm) thickness.

Cut into strips 3 inches (7·5 cm) wide. Spoon the fig mixture in a neat line ½ inch (1 cm) wide near one side of each strip, dampen the other edge with water.

Gently roll the dough over the fig mixture, forming a long sausage shape with the edge of the dough underneath.

Slice the filled rolls at 1 inch (2·5 cm) intervals and decorate each top with marks made with the blade of a knife. Chill the uncooked rolls for 30 minutes.

Set the oven to fairly hot, gas mark 6 or 400°F/200°C.

Place the chilled rolls on baking sheets, brush with milk and sprinkle with the tablespoon of caster sugar.

Bake in the oven for 10–15 minutes or until the fig rolls are golden brown.

Cool on a wire rack. If you want to make fig rolls in advance, fill the uncooked dough according to instructions and freeze uncooked rolls.

COCONUT COOKIES

Makes 12 biscuits

5 oz (150g) plain flour

2 oz (50g) desiccated coconut

½ level teaspoon salt

4 oz (100g) butter

2 oz (50g) caster sugar

1 teaspoon milk

FOR THE GLAZE:

1 tablespoon milk

½ oz (15g) soft brown sugar

½ oz (15g) desiccated coconut

Set the oven to moderate, gas mark 4 or 350°F/180°C.

Sift the flour, coconut and salt together in a bowl, then add the butter, cut into small pieces. Rub the fat into the flour until the mixture resembles fine breadcrumbs.

Stir in caster sugar. Add milk and knead well until the mixture forms into a ball.

Roll the dough into a sausage-shape approximately 6 inches (15 cm) long. Wrap in foil or cling wrap and chill in the refrigerator for 30 minutes.

Remove the foil or cling wrap and brush with the milk, then roll firmly in the brown sugar and coconut to thoroughly coat the roll of biscuit mixture.

Cut the coconut cookie dough into ½ inch (1 cm) thick round slices and place on a greased baking sheet.

Bake for about 20 minutes until firm and pale golden in colour.

Lift off baking sheets with a palette knife and leave to cool on a wire rack.

MUESLI COOKIES

Makes about 24

4 oz (100g) margarine

3 oz (75g) dark brown sugar

1 oz (25g) golden syrup

3 oz (75g) self-raising flour

1 level teaspoon mixed spice

3 oz (75g) muesli

Set the oven to warm, gas mark 3 or 325°F/ 160°C.

Put margarine, sugar and syrup in a saucepan. Heat gently until margarine melts, stirring occasionally.

Sift the flour and spice together in a bowl. Mix in the muesli, then stir in the melted mixture. Place teaspoonfuls of the mixture on to two greased baking sheets, then flatten out with the back of a spoon. Bake for 15–20 minutes, then leave to cool slightly on the tray before transferring to a wire rack to cool.

CINNAMON BUTTER BISCUITS

Makes 32

6 oz (175g) butter

4 oz (100g) caster sugar

8 oz (225g) plain flour

1 level teaspoon cinnamon

1 oz (25g) granulated sugar

Set the oven to warm, gas mark 3 or 325°F/ 160°C.

Cream the butter and sugar in a bowl until soft and fluffy. Blend in the flour and cinnamon. Using your hands, knead lightly until smooth.

Divide the dough into 2, then roll and shape into two 6 inch (15 cm) sausages. Roll in granulated sugar to coat. Wrap in foil and chill in the fridge until firm or until needed.

Cut each sausage into 16 slices and place on greased baking sheets, allowing room for them to spread.

Bake above the centre of the oven for 25 minutes or until edges of the biscuits are a light golden brown.

BRANDY SNAPS

Makes 30

2 oz (50g) plain flour

½ level teaspoon ground ginger

2 oz (50g) butter or margarine

5 oz (150g) caster sugar

2 oz (50g) golden syrup

FOR THE FILLING, OPTIONAL:

5 oz (150g) double or whipping cream

1–2 tablespoons brandy

Sift the flour and ginger together. Cream the butter or margarine and sugar then beat in the syrup. Stir in the flour. Mix to a smooth and creamy dough. Cover and allow to rest for 1 hour before using.

Set the oven to moderately hot, gas mark 5 or 375°F/190°C. Line two baking sheets with non-stick or Bakewell paper.

Roll teaspoons of the mixture into small balls and put four at a time on a baking sheet. Flatten slightly with the palm of the hand. Bake just above the centre of the oven for about 10 minutes or until a rich golden brown and bubbling. Remove from the oven and cool for a few moments – this allows the mixture to firm up slightly so that the Snaps

Gypsy Creams,
page 134;
Florentines;
Cinnamon
Butter Biscuits;
Brandy Snaps

lift easily from the paper.

Quickly slide a knife under each biscuit and wrap the biscuit round the lightly oiled handle of a wooden spoon – have at least two ready. These Brandy Snaps will cool and harden while the next batch are baking. As soon as they have set firm, slip them off and have the spoons ready for the next ones.

Keep in an airtight tin until ready to use. Serve plain or whisk the cream with the brandy until thick. Spoon into a piping bag fitted with a star nozzle and pipe the cream into each one.

FLORENTINES

Makes 12

2 oz (50g) caster sugar

2 oz (50g) thinly flaked almonds

1 level tablespoon plain flour

1½ oz (40g) butter

1 tablespoon single cream

2 oz (50g) mixed chopped glacé cherries, angelica, candied peel

2 oz (50g) plain chocolate, melted, optional

Set the oven to moderate, gas mark 4 or 350°F/180°C.

Place the sugar, almonds, flour, butter, single cream and the mixed fruits into a small saucepan. Stir over a gentle heat until well mixed – do not overheat. Cool, then chill until firm.

Put rounded teaspoons of the mixture on to well-greased, non-stick baking sheets or baking sheets lined with Bakewell paper. Flatten each heap a little to help it bake in a round shape. Bake just above the centre of the oven for 10 minutes or until just set and golden brown. Allow to cool for 1–2 minutes then lift carefully off the sheet with a knife.

When the Florentines are cold and crisp brush the base of each with melted chocolate, if using, and leave upside down to set.

Not suitable for freezing.

Keep unfilled in an airtight tin for 1–2 weeks.

To freeze: wrap and freeze for up to 3 months.

GYPSY CREAMS

Makes 16

3 oz (75g) margarine
3 level tablespoons golden syrup
6 oz self-raising flour, sifted
1 level tablespoon cocoa powder, sifted
2 oz (50g) sugar
2 oz (50g) rolled oats
2 tablespoons milk
FOR THE CHOCOLATE CREAM:
2 oz (50g) margarine
5 oz (150g) icing sugar, sifted
3 level tablespoons cocoa
1–2 tablespoons evaporated or creamy milk

Set the oven to warm, gas mark 3 or 325°F/160°C.

Melt the margarine and syrup in a pan. Stir in the flour and cocoa then mix in the sugar and rolled oats. Stir in the milk.

Form into 32 balls and place on greased baking sheets. Flatten with a fork dipped in hot water. Bake towards top of oven for about 20 minutes. Cool before removing from sheets. When cold, sandwich in pairs with chocolate cream which is made by mixing all the ingredients together until creamy.

SPECIAL OCCASION CAKES

FREEZING CAKES:

All the basic cakes freeze well. Cakes covered with butter cream can be frozen. Do not freeze cakes covered with satin or fondant icing.

NOVELTY CAKES

BASIC NOVELTY CAKE

Our Basic Novelty Cake is moist and keeps well. Make it a day or two ahead, store in an airtight tin and decorate when needed.

Make in a 7½ inch (19 cm) round cake tin.

8 oz (225g) self-raising flour, sifted
8 oz (225g) caster sugar
4 oz (100g) soft margarine
2 eggs, size 3, beaten
6 fl oz (175 ml) can evaporated milk
½ teaspoon vanilla essence

Set the oven to moderate, gas mark 4 or 350°F/180°C. Base line and grease the cake tin.

Place all the ingredients in a large bowl. Beat together with a wooden spoon or electric beater until pale, and a fairly soft dropping consistency is formed.

Turn into the tin and bake in the centre of the oven for 45–50 minutes until lightly golden and an inserted skewer comes out clean. Leave in the tin to cool slightly, then turn out on to a wire tray.

FONDANT ICING

Makes about 2 lb (900g)

1 lb 12 oz (800g) icing sugar
2 egg whites, size 3
2 tablespoons golden syrup or liquid glucose
2 teaspoons glycerine

Sift half the icing sugar into a large bowl. Beat in the egg whites, golden syrup or liquid glucose, and glycerine.

Work in the remaining sifted icing sugar with the hands until it forms a soft, smooth ball. Wrap tightly in cling wrap until needed.

Note: The icing keeps well in the fridge for a few days, if well covered.

APRICOT GLAZE

3 oz (75g) granulated sugar
3 tablespoons water
4 level tablespoons apricot jam, sieved

Put the sugar and water into a small pan and heat very gently until the sugar has completely dissolved. Stir in the sieved jam. Bring to the boil and boil hard for 1 minute.

Brush the glaze over the cake while still warm. Leave to set firm before icing.

To glaze: cut the cake into the desired shape. Brush each part free of crumbs then place on a cooling rack.

If the cake is to be covered with butter cream it is not necessary to coat with glaze. However, if satin icing is to be used brush all the cake parts with glaze.

Note: The glazing is important, as it seals the cake and stops crumbs from mixing with the icing which would prevent the surplus icing being re-used.

BUTTER CREAM

1 egg, size 3, separated
2 oz (50g) icing sugar, sifted
4 oz (100g) butter or margarine
Flavouring essence (optional)

Whisk the egg white in a medium-sized basin. Stir in the icing sugar then stand the basin over a pan of boiling water and whisk until the icing is stiff and glossy – about 3–4 minutes with an electric beater and a few minutes longer with a rotary whisk. Remove the basin from the pan.

Cream the butter or margarine until soft, then beat in the egg yolk and essence if required.

Gradually mix in the icing to give a soft consistency.

Cover the basin and chill in the fridge for 30 minutes or until softly firm before using.

SATIN ICING

2 oz (50g) white fat (e.g. white Flora)
4 tablespoons lemon juice
1 tablespoon hot water
1 lb (450g) icing sugar, sifted
Food colouring (optional)

Put the fat and lemon juice in a medium saucepan and heat gently until the fat has melted. Take the pan off the heat, add 8 oz (225g) icing sugar and beat well. Return the pan to the heat and cook for 2 minutes only, from the time the mixture begins to simmer at the sides of the pan until it boils gently and bubbles appear all over the surface.

Remove from the heat. Stir in the remaining 8 oz (225g) icing sugar and beat well with a wooden spoon. Beat in the hot water and the colouring.

Pour the icing over the cake, spreading it, if necessary, with a palette knife dipped in hot water.

Scrape up any surplus icing and return it to the pan. If it has started to set, stand the pan over a gentle heat and stir until the icing has melted again. If necessary add a teaspoon or more of water. Pour over uncoated parts of the cake.

KITTY CAKE

Basic Novelty Cake (page 135)
Jam or lemon curd
Basic butter cream (left)

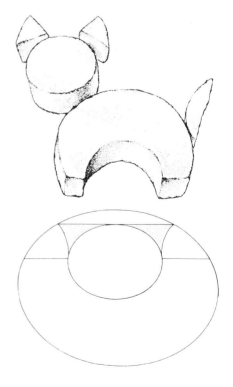

Draw a 4 inch (10 cm) round for the head, shape the other sections around it, then cut out and assemble in a cat shape. Butter cream icing and other decorations produce a perky-looking pussycat!

3 level tablespoons cocoa powder

Brown colouring or gravy browning

TO DECORATE:

1–2 oz (25–50g) coarsely grated chocolate

Strand of thin uncooked spaghetti

Liquorice Allsorts

Cut out a round of greaseproof paper the size of the cake – use the tin as a guide. Draw the pattern shapes as shown on page 136, using a 4 inch (10 cm) round for the cat's head. Cut out the pattern pieces, arrange them on the cake and cut round them with a sharp knife.

If liked, split the cake head and body in half and fill with jam or lemon curd.

Make the butter cream as directed in the basic recipe but beat the sifted cocoa into the butter and egg yolk mixture. If wished, darken the final icing with gravy browning or brown food colouring.

Spread the chocolate butter cream over top and sides of all the cake shapes (not the trimmings). Assemble the cat shapes together on the cake board.

Sprinkle grated chocolate over the top and roughen up the sides with a fork or the point of a knife.

Break the spaghetti into pieces and stick into the sides of the face for whiskers. Place the sweet eyes and nose in position. Add a ribbon, bow and bell.

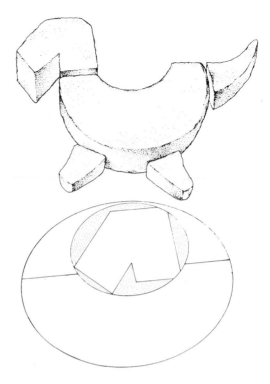

The dragon's head is cut from a 4 inch (10 cm) round and the foot piece split in half to make a pair. Cover the cake with green satin icing and decorate with sweets.

JOLLY GREEN DRAGON

Basic Novelty Cake (page 135)

Jam or lemon curd

1 quantity of apricot glaze (page 135)

1½ quantities of satin icing (page 136)

Apple green colouring

TO DECORATE:

2 packets small colourful sweets

Liquorice Allsorts, cotton wool, stiff card

Using the tin as a guide, cut out a round of greaseproof paper the size of the cake. Draw the pattern shapes on this, marking a 4 inch (10 cm) round first (see diagram). Cut out

the paper patterns, place them on the cake and cut out the pieces with a sharp knife. Cut the piece for the feet through the centre to provide a pair. If liked, split and fill the large cake pieces with jam or lemon curd.

Place the cake pieces on a cooling rack. Make up the glaze and brush all over the top and sides of cake to seal in the crumbs. Leave the glaze to firm and set for 1–2 hours.

Make the satin icing, adding a few drops of green colouring to give the desired depth of colour.

Place a clean tray under the cooling rack and pour the warm icing over the cake body and head. Use a palette knife dipped in hot water to guide the icing over the cake to coat completely. While the icing is still soft press the sweets in position as shown in the photograph, alternating the colours.

Rosie the
Elephant; Jolly
Green Dragon,
page 137; Kitty
Cake, page 136

Scoop the icing from the tray and return it to the saucepan. Reheat it gently, stirring all the time. Add a teaspoon or so of water to get it to the right consistency, then pour it over the tail and legs. Insert the sweets in position on the tail. Leave to set.

Arrange the dragon pieces on a cake board or tray. Place the liquorice pieces in position for eyes. Make mouth and teeth out of card – colouring with black felt tip pen – and smoke from cotton wool supported with a cocktail stick.

ROSIE THE ELEPHANT

Basic Novelty Cake (page 135)

1 quantity apricot glaze (page 135)

1 quantity satin icing (page 136)

Red or pink colouring

TO DECORATE:

Small, colourful sweets for eyes and feet; liquorice comfit for tusk

Fan shaped wafer or biscuit cut in a triangle for the ear

Cut out a round of greaseproof paper the size of the cake, using the tin as a guide. Draw a 4 inch (10 cm) circle, then the pattern shapes on the paper, as shown in diagram opposite, and cut out. Place pattern pieces on cake, cut out shapes.

Make up the apricot glaze. Stand the cake pieces on a cooling rack and brush the glaze all over them. Leave for an hour or so for the glaze to firm and set.

When needed, make up the satin icing and colour it pink. Pour the icing over the head and body, guiding it with a palette knife dipped in hot water to help coat the cake completely. Scoop up excess icing from the tray and return it to the pan. Reheat it gently,

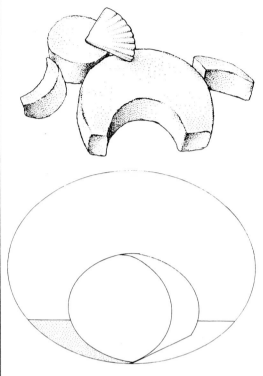

The trunk for Rosie the Elephant is cut from the side of a 4 inch (10 cm) round, the remainder of which forms the head.

adding a teaspoonful or so of water and stirring all the time. Use this to coat the tail, trunk and the wafer or biscuit ear.

When the icing has set, arrange the pieces on a cake board or tray. Position the sweets for the eyes, toenails and tusk and lay the ear on the head.

HOW TO MAKE A PAPER ICING BAG

1

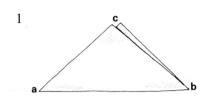

1 Fold a 10 inch (25 cm) square of greaseproof paper in half diagonally. With a sharp knife make a small slit in the exact centre of the folded side.

2

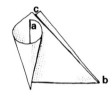

2 Roll point **a** to come in front of point **c**.

3

3 Roll point **b** to come behind **c**.

4

4 Fold down all points to secure the bag. Cut off tip straight across to insert a piping nozzle if needed.

WEDDING CAKES

WEDDING CAKE

Round	6 inch	(15 cm)	7½–8 inch	(20 cm)	10 inch	(25 cm)
Square	5 inch	(13 cm)	7 inch	(18 cm)	9 inch	(23 cm)

Ingredients

Mixed dried fruit	9 oz	(250g)	1 lb 4 oz	(600g)	3 lb	(1 kg 350 g)
Cherries, halved	2 oz	(50g)	4 oz	(100 g)	4½ oz	(125 g)
Peel	2 oz	(50 g)	4 oz	(100 g)	4½ oz	(125 g)
Ground almonds	1 oz	(25 g)	3 oz	(75 g)	6 oz	(175 g)
Plain flour	4 oz	(100 g)	9 oz	(250 g)	1 lb 2 oz	(500 g)
Salt	½ level teaspoon	(2·5 ml)	½ level teaspoon	(2·5 ml)	1 level teaspoon	(5 ml)
Mixed spice	½ level teaspoon	(2·5 ml)	1 level teaspoon	(5 ml)	2 level teaspoons	(10 ml)
Butter	3 oz	(75 g)	6 oz	(175 g)	12 oz	(350 g)
Dark brown sugar	3 oz	(75 g)	6 oz	(175 g)	12 oz	(350 g)
Eggs, size 3	2	2	4	4	9	9
Orange juice	1 tablespoon	(15 ml)	2 tablespoons	(30 ml)	5 tablespoons	(75 ml)
Orange rind	1 level teaspoon	(5 ml)	2 level teaspoons	(10 ml)	1 level tablespoon	(15 ml)
Gravy browning	1 teaspoon	(5 ml)	2 teaspoons	(10 ml)	1 tablespoon	(15 ml)
Brandy, sherry or sweet wine (optional)	2 tablespoons	(30 ml)	4 tablespoons	(60 ml)	6 tablespoons	(90 ml)

Baking times

	3¼–4 hours		4–4¼ hours		4½–5¼ hours	

Approximate number of servings

	25–30		40–45		70–80	

Almond paste

Icing sugar	4 oz	(100 g)	7 oz	(200 g)	9 oz	(250 g)
Caster sugar	4 oz	(100 g)	7 oz	(200 g)	9 oz	(250 g)
Ground almonds	8 oz	(225 g)	14 oz	(400 g)	1 lb 2 oz	(500 g)
Eggs, size 3	2	2	2	2	2½–3	2½–3
Almond essence	¼ teaspoon	(1 ml)	½ teaspoon	(2·5 ml)	1 teaspoon	(5 ml)
Lemon juice	¼ teaspoon	(1 ml)	½ teaspoon	(2·5 ml)	1 teaspoon	(5 ml)

Apricot jam

Sieved apricot jam	4 tablespoons	(60 ml)	5 tablespoons	(75 ml)	6 tablespoons	(90 ml)

Sherry or rum

	1 tablespoon	(15 ml)	2 tablespoons	(30 ml)	3 tablespoons	(45 ml)

Moulded icing

Icing sugar, sifted	1 lb 12 oz	(800 g)	1 lb 12 oz	(800 g)	3 lb 8 oz	(1 kg 600 g)
Egg whites from size 3 eggs	2	2	2	2	4	4
Liquid glucose	2 level tablespoons	(30 ml)	2 level tablespoons	(30 ml)	4 level tablespoons	(60 ml)
Glycerine	2 teaspoon	(10 ml)	2 teaspoons	(10 ml)	4 teaspoons	(20 ml)

Royal icing

Egg whites from size 3 eggs	2	2	This amount of royal icing is sufficient for all three tiers of your cake. If you decide to make a one- or two-tier cake, halve the quantities given here
Glycerine	1 teaspoon	(5 ml)	
Icing sugar, sifted	14 oz	(400 g)	

Note: A 3 tier cake will look more attractive if there is a 2 inch (5 cm) difference in cake sizes between the tiers, eg. 6 inch (15 cm), 8 inch (20 cm) and 10 inch (25 cm). Similarly, with a 2 tier cake have a 3 inch (7.5 cm) difference between the size of the cake tiers, eg. 6 inch (15 cm) and 9 inch (23 cm).

Extras

8 inch (20 cm) round silver cake board

10 inch (25·5 cm) round silver cake board

12 inch (30 cm) round silver cake board

1–2 tablespoons rum, sherry or sweet wine

No. 8 small star nozzle, No. 1 plain nozzle

8 round hollow pillars

8 wooden skewers

1 quantity of royal icing (see chart on page 140)

Rose-pink food colouring

3 small circles of foil

12 silver leaves

3 inch (7·5 cm) fluted cutter

1½ inch (4 cm) plain cutter

Wooden toothpicks

Fine paintbrush

Greaseproof paper

Glass-headed pins

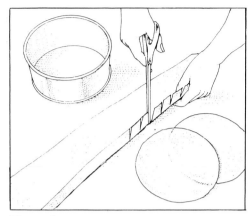

Diagram 1

Time Plan

3–4 months before the wedding: Make the cakes, wrap, and leave them to mature.

3 weeks before: Apply the almond paste and leave to dry out for 1 week.

Approximately 2 weeks before: Cover the cakes with moulded icing. Pipe the shell border. Leave to dry for 24 hours.
Attach the pink frills. Leave to dry for 24 hours.
Attach the white frills. Pipe on the pink dots.
Make the carnations, leave to dry out for 3 days.
Make the centres. Position the skewers and pillars.

On the day: Assemble the cake on its pillars about 2–3 hours before it is needed.

Lining the round cake tins

Brush the tin with melted lard. Cut out two rounds of greaseproof paper the size of the base of the tin, place one in position and brush with melted lard. Cut a doubled strip of greaseproof paper, 2 inch (5 cm) deeper than the tin and long enough to go round the inside of the tin.

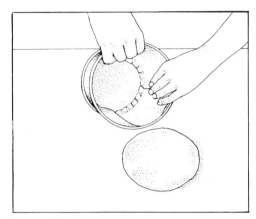

Diagram 2

Turn the folded edge up 1 inch (2·5 cm), then make slanting cuts to the crease at 1 inch (2·5 cm) intervals (see diagram 1). Fit this paper strip inside the tin so that the snipped edge fits neatly into the base (see diagram 2). Place the other round of paper on top and brush the entire lining with melted lard.

The mixture

Wash the sticky syrup from the cherries and dry them thoroughly on kitchen paper. Mix the halved cherries into the mixed dried fruit and peel, and add the ground almonds.

Sift the flour, salt and mixed spice together and stir a third of it into the dried fruit.

Beat the butter to a soft cream (you may find this easier to do with your hand rather than with a wooden spoon as the warmth helps to soften the butter more quickly).

Add the brown sugar and continue beating until the mixture is very light and fluffy. Beat the eggs together, then add them gradually to the creamed mixture, beating well between each addition. Stir in the fruit and remaining dry ingredients a little at a time, alternating with the orange juice and rind and gravy browning.

Turn the cake mixture into the prepared tin – it should be about two thirds full. If you are making all three cakes together, put half the mixture into the largest tin, then divide the rest between the other two tins so that the finished level of each tin is identical. An easy way to test that all tins are exactly the same is to insert a skewer into the mixture, then measure this level. When all the cakes are exactly the same depth, smooth over the surfaces and hollow out the centres fairly deeply, so that the cakes will rise evenly.

Bake the largest cake first, the other two cakes can be baked later, either together or separately, for the mixture will come to no harm if it is left in a cool place overnight.

Baking times

All the cakes are cooked on the centre shelf of a cool oven, but if baking two cakes at once try to position them as centrally as your oven allows; gas mark 1 or 275°F/140°C for 1 hour, then the heat is reduced to very cool, gas mark ½ or 225°F/110–120°C for the rest of the baking time.

Follow the baking times given in the chart, page 140, but do remember these are a guide only. As ovens vary, start testing about 30 minutes before the cakes are due to come out of the oven.

To test if the cakes are cooked, warm a skewer or steel knitting needle and push it into the centre of the cake; if it comes out clean the cake is ready but if any mixture sticks to the skewer, cook the cake for a little longer and then test again.

When the cakes are cooked leave them in their tins overnight to cool completely, then turn them out of the tins leaving on the greaseproof paper linings. If liked, brandy, sherry or sweet wine can be painted on to the cakes at this stage. This does enhance the flavour and keeping qualities of the cakes. Use 2 tablespoons for the top layer, 4 tablespoons for the middle layer and 6 tablespoons for the base.

Wedding Cake

Wrap the cakes separately in another layer of greaseproof paper, then tightly in foil or store them in airtight tins (not plastic containers) sealed with adhesive strapping. Store the cakes in a cool place. Their flavour improves with keeping, and they should be at their best after about three months.

Almond Paste

Make the almond paste using the quantities set out in the chart on page 140 for the 6 inch (15 cm) round, 7½–8 inch (20 cm) round and 10 inch (25 cm) round, following mixing instructions.

Mix the ingredients for each cake separately as a smaller amount is easier to handle, and overhandling the mixture makes it oily.

Sift the icing sugar into a bowl, and add the caster sugar and almonds, and stir these together. Beat the eggs together with the almond essence and lemon juice, and add this to the mixture to make a fairly stiff dough, a little softer than that of short crust pastry. Keep the almond paste in a plastic bag if it is not to be used immediately as it will form a hard crust if left uncovered.

Covering the cakes: Remove the foil and greaseproof paper from the cakes and, using a sharp knife, trim to level the top of the cake if necessary. Turn the cake upside down so that the base becomes the top as this will give the cake a good, flat working surface.

Clear working surface of crumbs, ensure cakes are free from them also. The method for covering all three cakes is identical.

Cut paste in half, keep one half covered. Sprinkle working surface with caster sugar, roll half the paste to the size of the cake top and, using the tin as a guide, trim to fit.

Brush top of cake with warmed, sieved apricot jam, then place cake on to the almond paste, jam side down. When you are quite sure it has stuck, turn cake back up the right way. Measure the circumference of the cake by encircling it with a piece of string.

Roll the remaining almond paste into a long sausage shape the length of the string, flatten the roll evenly with a rolling pin and trim the strip to the exact depth of the paste-topped cake (see diagram 3), then roll this up like a Swiss roll. Brush the sides of the cake with warmed, sieved apricot jam, then unwind the roll of paste round the sides of the cake so that it adheres (see diagram 4). Press firmly to the cake, especially at joins,

then take a clean jam jar and roll this round the sides of the cake to make them absolutely straight (see diagram 5).

Cover the cake with a clean tea-towel and leave it in a cool, dry, airy place for about a week, so that the almond paste dries and hardens.

Covering the cake with moulded icing

The method for covering each tier of the cake is identical.

Paint the rum on to the almond paste. This will stick the moulded icing to the cake. Sherry or sweet wine can be used instead if you prefer.

On a surface dusted with icing sugar, roll

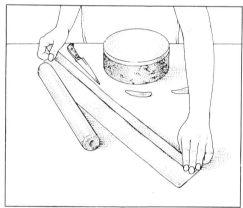

Diagram 3

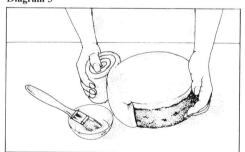

Diagram 4

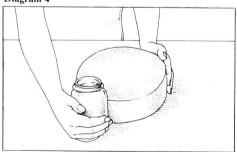

Diagram 5

out a quantity of moulded icing to a circle large enough to completely cover the cake with 1 inch (2·5 cm) over at the base. To cover the 10 inch (25·5 cm) cake, for instance, you will need a circle approximately 19 inches (47·5 cm) across.

Carefully lift the icing on the cake using both hands. Smooth the icing over the cake right down to the board with the flat of your hand. Do not pleat the icing, but press it well on to the sides of the cake, making a frilled edge on the cake board (see diagram 6). Cut the frill away with a sharp knife and wrap the trimmings immediately in a heavy-duty plastic bag. Quickly smooth over the top and sides of the cake with the flat of your hand (see diagram 7).

Do not touch the cake with your fingers as this will cause ridges to form. If any air bubbles appear, burst them with a pin and smooth over the pin hole. An icing smoother can be used to smooth the top and sides for a really professional finish. Any bumps, cracks or ridges can be smoothed out at this stage while the icing is soft.

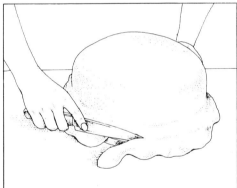

Diagram 6

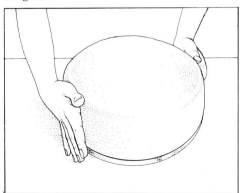

Diagram 7

Keep all the remaining trimmings tightly-covered in strong, non-porous plastic bags. These will be needed for the frills and carnations. It is important to use a thick plastic bag, and to seal it well, as this will prevent the icing from drying out.

Piping the shell border

Make a paper icing bag (see page 139) and place the No. 8 small star nozzle in it. Fill with white royal icing (page 148) and neatly fold over the edge.

Pipe a neat border of shells between the cake and the board on all three cakes. Keep the remaining royal icing in a covered plastic container for the pink dot border.

Mark the sides and top of cake

For the side-pattern: It is important to mark the sides of the cake to get the positioning of the frills right. To do this, cut a strip of greaseproof paper long enough to go round the outside of the covered cakes, and meet exactly. Fold the strip in half widthways, in half again, and in half again, making eight equal sections. Using glass-headed pins, pin the strip round the cake through the eight folds, about 1 inch (2·5 cm) from the base of the cake. Make sure the pinholes are big enough to be seen, then remove the paper. Repeat the markings on all three cakes (see diagram 8).

For the pillars: Cut a circle of greaseproof paper the size of the top of each cake. Fold the paper in half, then in half again to make four equal sections.

For the 10 inch (25·5 cm) cake, measure 2½ inches (6 cm) from the centre along one of the straight folds, and mark with a dot.

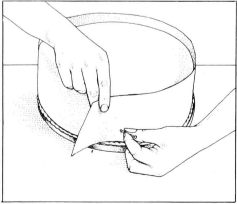

Diagram 8

Repeat with the other three folds. Mark out the top of the cake by placing the paper centrally on the cake and marking through the four holes with a pin. Make a similar circle for the 8 inch (20 cm) cake, but measure 2 inches (5 cm) from the centre and mark out in the same way (see diagram 9).

To make the frills

Gather all the scraps of icing together and knead into a ball. Cut the ball in half, colour one half pink and leave the remainder white. Wrap tightly in two heavy duty plastic bags until ready to use.

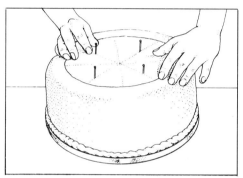

Diagram 9

For the pink frills: Take a small ball of pink icing and roll out thinly on a surface dusted with icing sugar.

Using a 3 inch (7·5 cm) cutter, cut out a round, then cut out centre using a 1½ inch (4 cm) plain cutter (see diagram 10). Using a wooden toothpick, roll round the edge with a backward and forward motion until edge becomes thin and fans out (see diagram 11).

Attach the frills to the side of the cake as follows: Dip the paintbrush into plain water

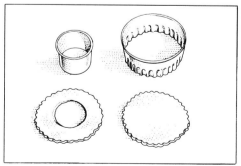

Diagram 10

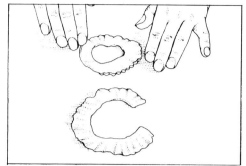

Diagram 11

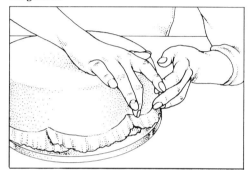

Diagram 12

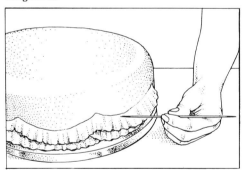

Diagram 13

and paint a curved line between two of the marks on the side of the cake. Press a piece of frilled icing on to the moistened side of the cake between the two points (see diagram 12).

Carefully lift the bottom edge of the frill with the dry tip of the paintbrush to make it stand out. Trim away icing to form a neat edge. Make the frills and attach them one at a time. Repeat with the other seven frills. Complete the other two tiers of the cake. Leave the pink frills to dry out for 24 hours.

For the white frills: Paint the side of the cake with plain water, again about ½ inch (1 cm) above the pink frills, following the curve.

Press a white frill to the cake with your fingers, then trim the edge away neatly with a sharp knife to form a point at either end. Mark with a skewer or knitting needle to form a line of tiny dots (see diagram 13).

Lift the bottom edge of the white frill away from the pink frill so that it stands out in pretty folds. Use the dried tip of the paintbrush again to do this. Make the remaining frills overlapping each join, and finishing neatly with a sharp knife.

To pipe the pink dots

Colour the remaining royal icing pink with the rose-pink food colouring to match the pink frill. Fill a paper icing bag, fitted with a No. 1 plain nozzle, with pink icing and fold the end over. Neatly pipe three small dots above the point of each frill. Finish all three cakes in this way.

To make the carnations

Roll out a small ball of the pink icing on a surface dusted with icing sugar and cut out a circle using the 3 inch (7·5 cm) fluted cutter. Roll a wooden toothpick round the edges to make fluted frills all round (see diagram 14). Fold in half, then into quarters, pinch the base and fan out to form a carnation.

Stand in an egg box lined with small circles of foil to dry for 3 days. Make nine pink and six white flowers, plus two extra of each colour in case of any breakages.

To arrange the flowers, roll a ball of the

remaining white icing to the size of a golf ball. Press on to a small circle of foil, and spread to cover the edges of foil. Make a raised point in the middle. Press two pink and two white carnations into the icing, alternating the colours then press a pink carnation on to the top (see diagram 15). Position the flowers to cover any gaps, then insert four silver leaves between the flowers. Repeat with the other two centres and leave to dry out for 24 hours.

Inserting the wooden skewers and assembling the pillars

As both of our cakes are covered in a soft icing, the tiers do not stand directly on to the pillars, they only appear to do so. A skewer is placed inside each hollow pillar to bear the weight of the tiers.

The skewers are inserted through the marked positions on the cake using the pointed end to make a hole. The skewer is then removed, the pointed tip cut off (to prevent it piercing the cakeboard) and the pillar attached to the other end of the skewer (there is a small round hole in the pillar for the skewer). The skewers and pillars are then re-inserted into the cake.

The pillar should fit directly flat on to the cake. If it is too high, the wooden skewer will need to be trimmed down with a sharp knife. Trim all four skewers to the same length and insert in the cake (see diagram 16). Repeat the process with the middle tier.

The skewers and pillars can be left in the cake until needed, then the cake can be quickly and easily assembled on the day.

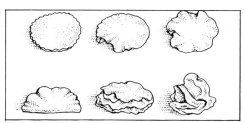

Diagram 14

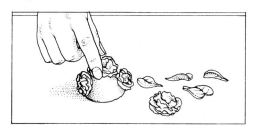

Diagram 15

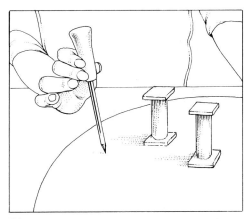

Diagram 16

CHRISTMAS CAKE

CHRISTMAS ROSE CAKE

7½–8 inch (20 cm) round basic Wedding Cake (see page 140)

FOR THE MOULDED ICING:

1 lb 12 oz (800g) icing sugar, sifted

2 egg whites, size 3, lightly beaten

2 level tablespoons liquid glucose

2 teaspoons glycerine

3 level tablespoons apricot jam, sieved

Cornflour for rolling out the icing

FOR THE ROYAL ICING:

1 egg white, size 3, lightly beaten

8 oz (225g) icing sugar, sifted

Yellow, orange and green food colouring

12 inch (30 cm) cake board

1 reel, ¾ inch (2 cm) wide white satin gift tie

Make and bake the cake as given on pages 141–2. If there is time, store, wrapped in greaseproof and foil, for 6 weeks.

Cover the cake with almond paste if the iced cake is to be kept for more than 4–5 days. Leave to dry for at least 48 hours before icing.

Make the moulded icing: Place 1 lb 8 oz (700g) of the icing sugar into a bowl and add the egg whites, glucose and glycerine. Mix to a fairly stiff dough with a wooden spoon. Turn out on to a surface sprinkled liberally with the remaining 4 oz (100g) of icing sugar. Knead until smooth.

Cover the cake: Weigh 1 lb 4 oz (600g) of the moulded icing. Keep the remainder tightly wrapped in cling wrap in a cool place to prevent a crust from forming.

Place the cake on a 12 inch (30 cm) cake board and paint it with the 3 level tablespoons of jam.

Roll out the 1 lb 4 oz (600g) of moulded icing on a surface dusted with cornflour to a circle approximately 16 inches (40 cm) in diameter.

Carefully lift the icing on to the cake (see diagram 1), trim edges to fit and then smooth down all around with the fingers.

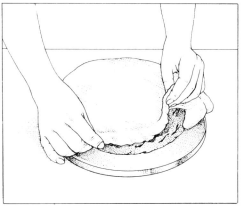

Diagram 1

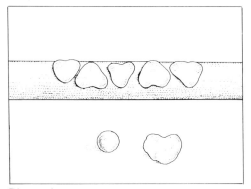

Diagram 2

Any bumps or cracks can be smoothed over quite easily at this stage with the reserved icing.

Make the royal icing: Place the egg white in a clean, dry bowl and gradually beat in the sifted icing sugar with a wooden spoon until smooth and thick. Store the royal icing in a small plastic container with a tight fitting lid until needed.

Divide the rest of the moulded icing as follows: 5 oz (150g) for the Christmas Roses, 1 oz (25g) for the ivy leaves, 2 oz (50g) for the candle and flame, 4 oz (100g) for the twisted border.

Make the Christmas Roses: Divide the 5 oz (150g) moulded icing into 20 balls of various sizes: 5 large balls [about 1½ inches (4 cm) in diameter], 5 medium balls, 5 medium/small balls and 5 small balls.

Divide each ball into 5 smaller balls, flatten out each ball into a heart-shaped petal. Place the petals over a rolling pin or jam jars on their sides, covered with grease-

Diagram 3

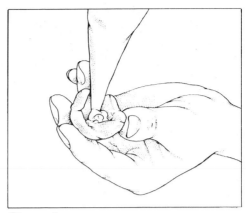

Diagram 5

Diagram 4

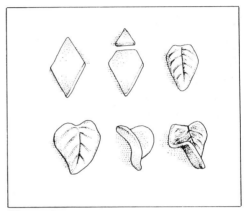

Diagram 6

proof or non-stick paper, and leave for 24 hours to dry in a cool place (see diagram 2).

When dry, join 5 petals together with a dab of royal icing and leave to set in an egg carton lined with foil (see diagram 3). When the petals are dry, paint the centres with yellow food colouring and leave to dry (see diagram 4). When the centres are dry, colour 2 oz (50g) royal icing with orange food colouring and pipe in the stamens (see diagram 5) with a small greaseproof paper bag, snipped at the point to make a small hole. Leave to dry for 1 hour.

Make 5 large roses, 5 medium roses, 5 medium-small roses and 5 small roses following the above instructions.

Make the ivy leaves: Roll out the 1 oz (25g) moulded icing set aside for the ivy leaves thinly and cut into 20 small diamond shapes. Cut away the top of each leaf, then make the veins by indenting with a sharp knife. Press out the edges with the thumb, then twist the

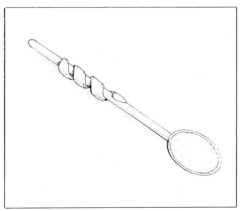

Diagram 7

ends and leave to dry for 24 hours. When dry, paint each leaf with green food colouring (see diagram 6).

Make the candle and flame: Roll out the 2 oz (50g) moulded icing set aside for the candle and flame into a strip 12 inches (30 cm) long

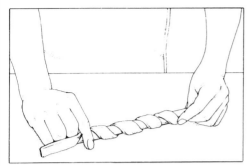

Diagram 8

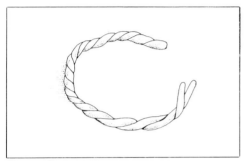

Diagram 9

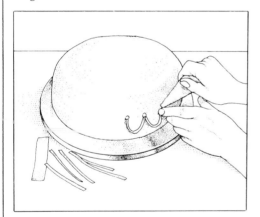

Diagram 10

by ½ inch (1 cm) wide. Cover the handle of a wooden spoon with greaseproof or non-stick paper. Carefully wind the strip loosely around the handle of the spoon, trim top and bottom neatly and leave to dry for at least 48 hours (see diagram 7 on page 149).

Shape the trimmings into a flame shape and leave to dry with the candle.

To remove the paper, carefully slide both paper and icing off the spoon, then twist each end of the paper in opposite directions and remove (see diagram 8). Paint a flame in the centre of the flame shape with yellow food colouring and attach the flame to the top of the candle with a small blob of royal icing. Leave candle and flame to dry for 2 hours.

If you should accidentally break the candle when removing from the spoon, it can be mended with a dab of royal icing and left to dry for 24 hours.

Make the twisted border: Divide the moulded icing set aside for the twist into two. Roll each portion out into a long thin sausage 36 inches (90 cm) long. Carefully roll both sausages into a twist and press down the ends (see diagram 9). Place the twist around the bottom of the cake and neaten the join with a sharp knife while still soft.

To attach the ribbon: Divide the white satin tie into strips measuring ⅛ inch (3 mm) wide by 3 inches (7·5 cm) long. You will need 24 strips. Place 2 oz (50g) white royal icing in a small greaseproof paper icing bag with a medium-sized hole snipped at the point. Carefully attach the loops with a spot of royal icing at 1½ inch (4 cm) intervals as shown in diagram 10.

Keep any trimmings of white moulded icing together in a ball wrapped in cling wrap; these will be needed to stand the candle in.

Complete the cake: Place the candle centrally in the cake in the ball made from scraps and trimmings. Place the five large roses around the base of the candle. Fan out the medium, medium-small and small roses into a trail, keeping the medium-small roses in the centre and ending with the smaller roses on the outer edge of the cake. Make five trails of roses and position 4 leaves in between each set. Attach the trails of roses and leaves to the cake with the remaining royal icing, as shown in the main colour picture.

Christmas Rose Cake

ENTERTAINING

Lunch and dinner parties are a popular way to entertain friends and family. In this section there are recipes for starters, for main courses and finally for desserts. In this way you can pick and choose and change the menu to suit your tastes and the occasion.

Planning the menu

Plan the menu so that one or two of the courses can be prepared beforehand and then served cold or reheated at the last minute. Many dishes actually improve from being made in advance. Also, when planning the menu choose dishes which contrast in flavour, colour and texture – so there are not too many creamy ones, or too many rich, spicy or bland.

STARTERS

First courses should be light and simple. In fact, they should do no more than whet the appetite. They're the food that gets everyone talking! All the dishes are easy to make and some can be prepared in advance to save you time on the day.

CURRIED MANGO SLICES

Serves 4

---

5 oz (150g) double cream

2 tablespoons apricot jam

$\frac{1}{2}$ level teaspoon mild curry paste

2 large ripe mangoes

Place double cream in a bowl. Mix together the sherry, apricot jam and curry paste and rub through a sieve. Add to the cream.

Beat until the mixture becomes thick enough to coat the back of a spoon. Cover with cling wrap and place in the fridge until required.

Just before serving, peel the mangoes and cut into slices.

Place slices in four individual serving dishes and spoon the curried cream over.

Note: Sauce keeps well in the fridge for 1–2 days so long as the cream is fresh and the bowl well covered.

Not suitable for freezing.

SUMMER FRUIT CORNUCOPIA

Serves 4

---

2 small melons, Honeydew, Ogen or Galia

4 oz (100g) white grapes, washed

4 oz (100g) black grapes, washed

1 kiwi fruit, peeled and thinly sliced

4 strawberries, sliced

4 tablespoons fresh orange juice

4 tablespoons port, optional

Cut melons in half lengthways (from top to bottom) and remove the seeds. Cut grapes into small bunches using scissors and place in centre of melons. Place melons on plates. Cut each kiwi fruit slice in half and arrange with sliced strawberries on sides of plates.

Chill until required. Pour a tablespoon each of orange juice and port, if used, into the centre of the melon just before serving.

Not suitable for freezing.

ORIENTAL BACON ROLLS WITH SPINACH

Serves 4

10 rashers streaky bacon, derinded

8 oz (225g) chicken livers

1 tablespoon runny honey

1 tablespoon tomato ketchup

1 tablespoon vinegar

1 tablespoon oil

$\frac{1}{2}$ level teaspoon oregano

Good pinch of pepper

8 oz (225g) fresh spinach, trimmed and washed

Using the back of a round-bladed knife, stretch each bacon rasher and then cut each rasher in half. Place a piece of chicken liver on each bacon rasher and roll up.

In a flat dish, mix together the honey, tomato ketchup, vinegar, oil, oregano and pepper. Place bacon rolls on top and leave overnight in the fridge, turning rolls once, after a few hours.

Remove bacon rolls from marinade. Reserve marinade. Take four skewers and place five bacon rolls on each skewer. Turn grill on to high and grill for 10–12 minutes, turning once during cooking.

Place spinach in serving dish, pour the marinade over and toss. Place bacon rolls on top. Serve immediately, or, if preferred, grill bacon rolls before guests arrive and keep hot in a warm oven.

Not suitable for freezing.

TOMATO PROVENÇAL SOUP WITH CROUTONS

Tomato Provençal Soup is delicious served hot or cold.

Serves 6

8 oz (225g) onions, peeled and finely chopped

2 tablespoons oil

8 oz (225g) can tomatoes, chopped

$1\frac{1}{2}$ pints (900 ml) chicken stock

$\frac{1}{2}$ level teaspoon salt

Good pinch of pepper

$\frac{1}{4}$ level teaspoon dried basil

1 level teaspoon granulated sugar

1 lb (450g) fresh tomatoes, skinned and de-seeded

2 slices white bread, crusts removed

Oil for frying

3 tablespoons chopped parsley

Fry the onion in the oil for about 5–10 minutes until soft. Add canned tomatoes, stock, salt, pepper, basil and sugar. Chop the fresh tomatoes and add to the pan. Bring to the boil, cover, and simmer for about 30 minutes.

Meanwhile, cut the bread with crusts removed in half diagonally and then cut again into small triangles.

Heat the oil in a frying pan and fry the bread for 1–2 minutes, turning once, or until the bread is golden brown on both sides. Drain on absorbent paper.

Just before serving stir the parsley into the soup and serve with croutons.

To freeze: freeze when cold for up to 1 month. Thaw and serve hot or cold with the croutons.

CRISP AND CREAMY CRAB MILLE-FEUILLE

Serves 4

$7\frac{1}{2}$ oz (210g) frozen puff pastry, thawed

8 oz (225g) cream cheese

2 tablespoons tomato ketchup

$\frac{1}{4}$ level teaspoon salt

Good pinch of pepper

Dash of Tabasco

6 oz (175g) can dressed crab or salmon, drained

1 punnet mustard and cress

Set oven to fairly hot, gas mark 6 or 400°F/ 200°C.

Roll out pastry to a rectangle just larger than 15×8 inches (37·5×20 cm), then trim edges to make a rectangle 15×8 inches 37·5×20 cm) exactly. Cut into three strips

each 5×8 inches (13×20 cm), place on a baking sheet, prick well with a fork and bake for 15–20 minutes until golden brown. Allow to cool, then trim edges to neaten.

Meanwhile, place cream cheese in a bowl and beat with a wooden spoon until soft. Stir in the ketchup, salt, pepper, Tabasco and crab or salmon.

Using a pair of scissors, cut off the mustard and cress and snip roughly with the scissors.

Split each piece of pastry horizontally, reserving one perfect piece for the top. Spread each of the other pieces with a fifth of the cream cheese mixture and sprinkle with a fifth of the mustard and cress. Layer up in a sandwich fashion, pressing well together, and place plain pastry layer on top.

Serve in thickish slices.

Dinner party tip: Cook the pastry layers and make the filling the day before to save time. Assemble the layers 3–4 hours before the dinner party. The filled slice will sink slightly during this time.

Not suitable for freezing.

MAIN COURSES

The main course is the dish that shows off your culinary skills at their best, and leaves everyone just enough room for dessert!

If you're not used to entertaining, you may like to serve a dish which can be prepared in advance.

It's a good idea to try out a recipe before you serve it on a special occasion. You'll feel more cool and confident on the day.

GREEN PEPPERED STEAK

Serves 4

| 1 level teaspoon prepared English mustard |
| 4 fillet steaks, each weighing 6–8 oz (175–225g) |
| 1 level tablespoon green or black peppercorns |
| 1 tablespoon oil |

| 1 oz (25g) butter |
| 1 tablespoon brandy, optional |
| 5 fl oz (150 ml) double cream |
| Watercress |

Spread the mustard on both sides of the steaks. Place peppercorns in between a folded piece of tin foil and crush them with a rolling pin.

Using the fingers, press the peppercorns into both sides of the steaks.

Heat the oil with the butter in a 10 inch (25·5 cm) frying pan and when bubbling hot, fry the steaks for 3–4 minutes on each side for a medium-cooked steak or according to taste. Remove steaks from pan and keep hot. Stir in the brandy, if used, and then the cream and bring to the boil.

Pour the creamy sauce over steaks and serve immediately.

Serve with Duchesse Potatoes (below) and extra mustard. Garnish with watercress.

Not suitable for freezing.

DUCHESSE POTATOES

Serves 4

| 2 lb (900g) potatoes |
| 2 oz (50g) butter |
| 2 eggs, size 3, beaten |

Peel the potatoes and cook in boiling salted water until tender. Drain well, then place in a bowl and mash thoroughly to remove all lumps. Beat in the butter until it has melted and is well combined, then thoroughly beat in the eggs. Season well.

Set the oven to fairly hot, gas mark 6 or 400°F/200°C.

Fit a large piping bag with a No. 10 star nozzle. Fill the piping bag with the mixture then pipe about 20 rosettes on to two greased baking trays. Bake towards top of the oven for 20–25 minutes or until lightly browned.

To freeze: the potatoes can be piped on to the baking trays and open-frozen. To cook from frozen, set the oven to fairly hot and bake for 40–45 minutes or until lightly browned.

From top: Summer Fruit Cornucopia, page 152; Crisp and Creamy Crab Mille-Feuille, page 153; Oriental Bacon Rolls with Spinach, page 153; Tomato Provençal Soup with Croutons, page 153; Curried Mango Slices, page 152

CELEBRATION GUARD OF HONOUR

Serves 4–6

1 Guard of Honour with 12–14 cutlets
1 oz (25g) butter
Bunch of fresh herbs made with one sprig each of parsley, thyme, rosemary, and sage
2 oranges
$\frac{1}{4}$ pint (150 ml) stock
2 level teaspoons cornflour
4 level tablespoons redcurrant jelly
Sprig of parsley

Ask your butcher to make up a Guard of Honour using best end of neck of lamb.

Set oven to moderately hot, gas mark 5 or 375°F/190°C.

Place meat in roasting tin and place butter inside. Tie bunch of herbs together with string and place inside Guard of Honour. Cook in the centre of the oven for 20 minutes per lb (450g) if you prefer meat slightly pink. Cook for a further 20 minutes if you prefer lamb well done. Baste occasionally.

Meanwhile, finely grate the rind and squeeze the juice from one of the oranges. Grate a little rind from the other orange to garnish the sauce and using a knife carefully remove the rind and cut the flesh into slices. Reserve and use as garnish.

Blend stock and cornflour together in a saucepan until smooth. Add redcurrant jelly and the grated rind and juice from one orange. Bring to the boil, stirring, and boil gently for 1 minute or until all the jelly has dissolved.

When meat is cooked, remove herbs from centre of lamb, place fresh piece of parsley inside and put on a serving plate and keep warm. Pour meat juices into sauce, reheat and pour in gravy boat and sprinkle with the reserved grated orange rind.

Place a cutlet frill on the end of each chop, and place on serving plate. Garnish with orange slices as shown (opposite). Serve immediately with peas.

Dinner party tip: The sauce can be made well in advance so you only have to add meat juices before serving.

Not suitable for freezing.

LEMON TARRAGON CHICKEN

Serves 4

1 oz (25g) flour
$\frac{1}{4}$ level teaspoon salt
Good pinch of pepper
4 large chicken breasts, skin removed
2 tablespoons oil
$\frac{1}{4}$ pint (150 ml) white wine
$\frac{1}{2}$ pint (300 ml) water
1 chicken stock cube
1 level teaspoon dried tarragon
4 oz (100g) button mushrooms, halved
1 lemon
2 level teaspoons cornflour
1 tablespoon water

Mix together the flour, salt and pepper and coat the chicken breasts thoroughly.

Heat oil and fry chicken for about 10 minutes or until golden brown on both sides. Add any remaining seasoned flour and stir in the wine, water and stock cube, tarragon and mushrooms. Bring to the boil, cover and simmer gently for 35 minutes or until chicken is cooked.

Meanwhile, using a zester, remove the rind from the lemon in long thin strips or grate finely and reserve. Keep covered to prevent drying.

When chicken is cooked, blend the cornflour and water together to make a smooth paste and stir into sauce. Bring to the boil, stirring, and cook for 1 minute. Spoon into serving dish and sprinkle with reserved lemon rind.

Serve with broccoli and hollandaise sauce, and Duchesse Potatoes (page 155) if liked.

Dinner party tip: The chicken dish can be prepared the day before, cooled quickly and kept in fridge. Reheat thoroughly in pan, adding a little more wine and water if the sauce is too thick.

Not suitable for freezing.

PORK EN CROUTE WITH CRANBERRY STUFFING

Serves 4

1½ lb (700g) pork fillets

1 lb (450g) frozen puff pastry, thawed

1 egg, size 3, beaten

FOR THE STUFFING:

1 medium onion, peeled and chopped

2 green eating apples, peeled and cored

4 level tablespoons cranberry sauce

¼ level teaspoon salt

Good pinch of pepper

½ level teaspoon dried thyme

Set oven to fairly hot, gas mark 6 or 400°F/200°C.

Place pork fillets on top of each other to form a thick sausage shape and tie with string to secure. Place in a roasting tin and cook for 45 minutes, then remove from oven and allow to become cold. Remove the string.

Meanwhile, make the stuffing. Place onion in bowl, quarter apples and slice and add to the bowl with the cranberry sauce, salt, pepper and thyme. Mix well.

On a lightly-floured surface, roll out pastry to a 14 inch (35 cm) square, trim edges and reserve trimmings for decoration. Place stuffing mixture on top of pastry, leaving a 4 inch (10 cm) border and place pork on top. Brush pastry edges with some of the beaten egg and fold them over the pork, tuck in the pastry ends and press to seal. Place the roll, join side down, on a baking sheet and brush all over with more beaten egg. Re-roll the trimmings and cut diamond-shaped leaves for decoration and place on top. Brush with remaining beaten egg.

Bake in centre of oven for 35–40 minutes until golden brown. Serve with French beans.

Dinner party tip: Cook meat and make up filling the day before and leave covered, overnight, in the fridge. The following day, the pastry can be rolled out and croûte made 2–3 hours before cooking.

Not suitable for freezing.

GOLDEN SEAFOOD PLATTER

This is definitely not a dish for those who don't like spicy food!

Serves 4

1 lb (450g) monk fish

8 oz (225g) large prawns, preferably raw

3–4 tablespoons oil

Salt and pepper

3–4 tablespoons brandy

1 level tablespoon curry powder

1 clove garlic, peeled and crushed

5 oz (150g) double cream

6–8 tomatoes, skinned and cut into segments, with seeds removed if liked

1 small can pimentos, drained and sliced

Few drops Tabasco sauce

TO GARNISH:

Shredded lettuce

Lemon wedges

Trim the monk fish, removing any black skin and membrane. Cut into largish chunks. Peel the prawns if fresh.

Heat the oil and fry the fish and prawns quickly. Add seasoning to taste.

Spoon the brandy over and light with a match – but do take care. When the flames have died down add the curry powder and garlic and stir. Add the cream, tomato segments and sliced pimentos. Bring to the boil and simmer slowly for 2–3 minutes. Add Tabasco and more seasoning to taste. Serve with or on a bed of boiled rice.

Dinner party tip: Cook the rice as usual, stir in 1 oz (25g) butter, then spread out on ovenproof serving dish. Cover with foil and keep hot in low oven. Prepare fish mixture as above, but simmer for 1–2 minutes only. Leave until required, then reheat for 1–2 minutes and spoon into centre of rice. Garnish with shredded lettuce and lemon segments.

Not suitable for freezing.

HAM MOUSSE

A can of consommé and madeira can be used instead of the consommé and port.

Serves 6

| 1 lb (450g) boiled ham |
| 8 oz (225g) liver pâté |
| 5 tablespoons cold water |
| 1½ level tablespoons gelatine |
| ½ pint (300 ml) very hot water |
| 10 oz (275g) can condensed consommé |
| Sliced radishes |
| 2 level teaspoons paprika |
| 1–2 tablespoons port |
| 5 oz (150g) double cream |
| Salt and pepper |

TO GARNISH:

| Tomato wedges |
| Asparagus |

Mince the ham (and fat) or use the food processor. Mix in the liver pâté thoroughly.

Put the cold water into a measuring jug and sprinkle over the gelatine. Leave for a few minutes until the mixture swells and becomes spongy. Pour over the hot water and stir until the gelatine has dissolved. When cool but still liquid, stir in consommé. Pour ¼ pint (150 ml) of the consommé liquid into a 3 pint (1·8 litre) ring mould which has been rinsed with cold water. Arrange radish slices decoratively over the bottom, leave to set. Meanwhile, add the rest of the consommé to the ham mixture. Stir in paprika, port and cream. Taste and add salt and pepper as necessary. Leave to half set, then carefully spoon the mixture over the jellied base. Leave the mould in the fridge to set.

To serve, quickly dip the mould in hot water and turn out on to a serving dish. Garnish with tomatoes and asparagus.

Lunch party tip: Make mousse the day before and leave in fridge until required.

To freeze: cover tightly and freeze in the mould for up to 1 month. Leave cover in place to thaw.

DESSERTS

It arrives when everyone is feeling relaxed and well fed – a delicious dessert to be the crowning delight of a memorable meal.

LIME SYLLABUB

Serves 4

| 5 oz (150g) double cream |
| 2 egg whites, size 3 |
| 2 oz (50g) caster sugar |
| Grated rind and juice of 2 limes |
| ¼ pint (150 ml) white wine |
| Angelica |

Whisk cream until thick. Whisk egg whites until stiff, then fold in sugar, rind and juice from the limes, white wine and cream. Spoon into four tall glasses and place in fridge for 2 hours to chill. (Continue stirring mixture in main bowl while spooning out to prevent separating.)

When chilled the mixture should separate out into two layers: cream mixture at the top and wine at the bottom.

Cut angelica into 8 thin strips and use to decorate syllabub.

Dinner party tip: The syllabub should be made the day before and left in the fridge until required. Decorate with the angelica an hour or so before serving.

Not suitable for freezing.

TROPICAL FRUIT EXTRAVAGANZA

Serves 4

| 1 lb (450g) strawberries, hulled and halved |
| 3 oz (75g) caster sugar |
| 3 passion fruit |
| 8 oz (225g) lychees, peeled, halved and stones removed |
| 1 lemon |
| 3 kiwi fruit |
| 8 oz (225g) kumquats |

Layer up the strawberries and caster sugar in a large bowl. Cut passion fruit in half, scoop out centres and add to the bowl with the prepared lychees.

Using a zester, remove rind from lemon in long strips and add to the bowl. Squeeze the juice from the lemon and pour in the bowl. Cover with cling wrap and place in fridge overnight or for 4–5 hours to allow the juice to develop.

Just before serving, peel the kiwi fruit and slice and then wash and quarter the kumquats. Stir into the rest of the fruit and leave in fridge until required.

Not suitable for freezing.

COFFEE REFRIGERATOR CAKE

Serves 4–6

$\frac{1}{4}$ pint (150 ml) strong coffee made with $1\frac{1}{2}$ level tablespoons coffee and 2 tablespoons coffee essence

2–3 tablespoons brandy

28 sponge finger biscuits

10 oz (275g) double cream

2 tablespoons milk

Angelica

In a shallow dish combine the coffee and brandy.

Dip the sponge fingers one at a time in the coffee and arrange seven, side by side, on a serving plate.

Whisk half the double cream with 1 tablespoon milk together until the mixture just holds its shape. Use a little to spoon over the sponge fingers. Repeat using the rest of the sponge fingers and all the coffee and cream, allowing seven sponge fingers for each layer.

Cover and chill in the fridge overnight or for several hours.

Whisk remaining cream with 1 tablespoon milk until mixture holds its shape. Spread a little over the top of the layered cake.

Spoon the rest into a piping bag fitted with a large star nozzle, then pipe shells of cream over the top.

Decorate with pieces of angelica.

To freeze: open freeze until firm. Freeze in container for up to 1 month.

GOLDEN WALNUT TART

Serves 8–10

FOR THE PASTRY:

6 oz (175g) plain flour

2 oz (50g) margarine

2 oz (50g) lard

1 tablespoon lemon juice

Water to mix

FOR THE FILLING:

8 oz (225g) golden syrup

$\frac{1}{2}$ level teaspoon salt

2 teaspoons vanilla essence

4 oz (100g) soft brown sugar

3 oz (75g) butter, melted

3 eggs, size 3, beaten

6 oz (175g) walnuts

Sift the flour into a bowl, rub in the fats until mixture resembles fine breadcrumbs. Bind together with the lemon juice and sufficient water to form a soft but not sticky dough. Roll in cling wrap and chill for 30 minutes.

Set oven to moderately hot, gas mark 5 or 375°F/180°C. Grease a 9 inch (23 cm) round, loose-bottomed flan tin.

On a floured surface roll out the dough and use to line the flan tin. Trim and crimp then stand it on a baking sheet.

Mix the golden syrup, salt, vanilla essence, sugar and melted butter together. Stir in the eggs until well mixed. Reserve 8 walnut halves for decoration, then coarsely chop the remaining walnuts. Fold the chopped walnuts into the syrup mixture and turn into the pastry case.

Bake just above centre of the oven for 20 minutes. Remove tart from the oven, decorate with the walnut halves, and bake for a further 20–25 minutes, until firm.

From top:
Coffee Refrigerator Cake; Lime Syllabub, page 159; Golden Brandy Snaps, page 163; Tropical Fruit Extravaganza, page 159; Golden Walnut Tart; Strawberry-Filled Chocolate Case, page 162; Grape Crème Brûlée, page 162

If the top begins to over-brown, cover with greaseproof paper.

Dinner party tip: The pastry case may be prepared the day before and completed and baked on the day.

To freeze: wrap in foil and freeze. Thaw for at least 4 hours. Reheat in a warm oven for 15–20 minutes, if served warm.

STRAWBERRY-FILLED CHOCOLATE CASE

Serves 6

8 oz (225g) plain chocolate, broken into squares

2 tablespoons water

2 level teaspoons gelatine

1 lb (450g) strawberries, hulled

$\frac{1}{2}$ level teaspoon vanilla essence

3 level tablespoons icing sugar, sifted

1 egg white, size 3

5 oz (150g) double cream

1 level tablespoon redcurrant jelly

2 teaspoons water

Line the base and sides of an 8 inch (20 cm) spring clip tin with greaseproof paper and grease lightly.

Place chocolate in a bowl, place over a pan of boiling water and heat until chocolate has melted. Using a pastry brush, paint some of the chocolate evenly over the base and 2 inches (5 cm) up the sides of tin. Leave to cool and harden in the fridge and then continue painting and leaving the chocolate to cool and harden until you have an even layer over the case and all the chocolate has been used up. Leave until firm and then remove from tin.

Place water in a cup and sprinkle the gelatine over and allow to become spongy.

Place half the strawberries in a liquidizer or pass through a sieve to make a purée. Stir in the vanilla essence and icing sugar. Place cup of gelatine into a pan filled with 1 inch (2·5 cm) of water and heat to dissolve the gelatine. Stir into strawberry purée. Put in

fridge to half set.

Whisk egg white until stiff and then whisk cream until thick and fold both ingredients together into the half-set purée. Carefully spoon into chocolate case and place in fridge to set and become firm.

Slice remaining strawberries and arrange on top of set purée. Place redcurrant jelly and water in a small saucepan and heat until smooth. Brush over strawberries to glaze and place dessert in fridge until required.

Dinner party tip: Make the chocolate case 2–3 days in advance and leave in the fridge. Fill the chocolate case the day before required. Cover and leave in the fridge. Decorate and glaze the case 2–3 hours before the party and leave in the fridge until required.

Not suitable for freezing.

GRAPE CRÈME BRÛLÉE

Serves 6

6 oz (175g) green grapes, washed

10 oz (275g) double cream

5 oz (150g) carton natural yogurt

4 egg yolks, size 3

3 level tablespoons caster sugar

1$\frac{1}{2}$ teaspoons vanilla essence

3 oz (75g) demerara sugar

Cut the grapes in half and remove the seeds. Divide the grapes between 6 individual ramekin dishes, reserving 6 halves for decoration. Stand the dishes on a flat tray.

Warm the cream to just below boiling, remove from the heat and stir in the natural yogurt.

In a heatproof bowl lightly beat the egg yolks, caster sugar and vanilla essence until smooth. Pour the warmed cream, in a steady stream, on to the egg yolk mixture, stirring.

Stand the bowl over a pan of gently boiling water. Cook, stirring occasionally, for about 10 minutes, until mixture thickly coats the back of the spoon. Pour the mixture evenly over the grapes in each ramekin dish and chill until cream is cold and set.

Heat a hot grill, sprinkle the demerara sugar over the set cream and grill for 2 minutes, until the top is golden brown.

Chill well, then place half a grape on top of each dish before serving.

Dinner party tip: The Crème Brûlée can be prepared to the first chilling stage the day before. On the day, sprinkle with demerara sugar, grill and chill well before serving.

Not suitable for freezing.

GOLDEN BRANDY SNAPS WITH RICH CREAM

Makes 30

Brandy snaps (page 132)

10 oz (275g) double cream

1–2 tablespoons brandy

2 level tablespoons icing sugar, sifted

Stem of crystallized ginger, optional

Make brandy snaps according to recipe.

Whisk the cream until stiff, then stir in the brandy and icing sugar. Spoon the cream into a dish and serve with the Brandy Snaps.

A chopped or finely-sliced stem of crystallized ginger may be used to decorate the top of the cream.

Dinner party tip: The Brandy Snaps may be prepared a few days in advance and stored in an airtight tin until ready to eat.

SUMMER BUFFET

Preparing food for a summer buffet – whether it's a wedding reception or an anniversary celebration – can sometimes be a daunting affair. But with plenty of advance planning and preparation you can certainly save time and space and feel quite confident on the day.

Of course it's easier if you have a freezer as the menu can be prepared even further ahead. But for those of you without a freezer, here is a handy plan to help make the best use of your time. Do try to resist the temptation to set out food hours in advance. It's better to have one or two extra hands to put out food at the last moment.

Quantities

Each recipe is enough for 20 helpings, and it is assumed each guest will sample 4 savouries, 2 sweets and a slice of cake. We suggest you choose 4 savoury recipes from those below and make them along with the sweet recipes and cake.

There's enough punch for 1 glass each. The choice of other drinks is your own. A sparkling Saumur adds as much verve to the occasion as champagne but is cheaper!

Time plan for busy cooks without freezers

■ **5 days before**: Make and complete the Nutty Gem Florentines. Store in an airtight tin.

■ **4 days before**: Make and complete the Two-tone Truffles, store in an airtight tin. Make Midsummer Dream Cake (cake only). Cool and wrap in foil.

■ **3 days before**: Make lemon buttercream filling for the cake and the fondant icing. Fill and cover the cake.

■ **2 days before**: Make the butters for the Rainbow Sandwiches, cover and keep in the fridge. Make the Spanish Quiche Slices, cover and keep in the fridge.

■ **1 day before**: Coat and cook the Curried Party Drumsticks. Cool, cover and keep in the fridge. Make and cook Special Sausage and Herb Rolls. Cool, cover and keep in fridge or a cool larder.

Cook the cocktail sausages and cover. Make the Creamy Tomato Dip, cool and keep in the fridge or a cool larder.

Make the tuna topping for the Tasty Tuna Twirls, cover and store in the fridge. Soften butters for Rainbow Sandwiches and make up and wrap. Cover with a damp cloth and press.

Chill the wine and lemonade. Decorate the Midsummer Dream Cake.

SAUSAGES WITH CREAMY TOMATO DIP

Serves 20

1½ lb (700g) cocktail sausages

FOR THE DIP:

1 oz (25g) margarine

8 oz (225g) onion, peeled and sliced

15 oz (420g) can tomatoes

2 level tablespoons tomato purée

1 level teaspoon oregano

Pepper

8 oz (225g) cream cheese

TO GARNISH:

Watercress

Set oven to fairly hot, gas mark 6 or 400°F/200°C.

Put the sausages in a roasting tin and bake for 30–40 minutes until evenly browned. Turn sausages during cooking.

Meanwhile, make the dip; melt the margarine and gently fry the onion until soft. Stir in the tomatoes, tomato purée, oregano and pepper. Cook for 5 minutes; allow to cool.

Place the cooled tomato mixture in a liquidizer or food processor with the cream cheese and blend until smooth.

Pour into a dish; serve warm or cold.

Push a cocktail stick in each sausage, and place in the dip. Garnish with a few sprigs of watercress.

To freeze: cook the sausages, allow to become completely cold, then wrap in foil and freeze. For the dip, place in a firm container, cover and freeze. Thaw. Reheat sausages in fairly hot oven if liked. Arrange in dishes as above.

RAINBOW SANDWICHES

Makes 40 (2 each)

FOR THE SAVOURY BUTTER:

8 oz (225g) butter, softened

2 bunches watercress

1 level tablespoon tarragon and thyme mustard

Pepper

FOR THE CHEESY BUTTER:

4 oz (100g) butter, softened

8 oz (225g) Cheddar cheese, grated

3 level tablespoons mayonnaise

2 level tablespoons tomato relish

Pepper

½ large brown sliced loaf

1 large white sliced loaf

TO GARNISH:

Mustard and cress

Make the savoury butter: cream the butter until soft. Trim the watercress, then very finely chop. Beat into the butter with the mustard. Season to taste with pepper.

Make the cheesy butter: cream the butter until soft, then beat in the cheese, mayonnaise, tomato relish, and season to taste with pepper.

On a large working area, lay five slices of white bread in a row. Line up four more rows, alternating white and brown bread. Leave the top row plain, then spread the cheesy butter over the remaining two rows of white bread.

Spread the savoury butter over both rows of brown bread.

Working in columns, stack the slices of bread, ending with the unspread white bread. This will make five stacks. Wrap each stack individually in greaseproof paper. Place on a board or tray and cover with a clean damp tea-towel. Place a board on top and leave overnight.

To serve, cut off the crusts and slice each stack in half. Cut each half in four to make eight fingers.

Arrange the sandwiches on a serving plate and garnish with small bunches of mustard and cress.

The sandwiches can be cut up to 3 hours

before required, provided they are covered with a clean, damp tea-towel.

To freeze: place each stack in a plastic bag, or wrap individually in foil and freeze. The sandwiches will not need pressing. Allow 6 hours to thaw at room temperature.

TASTY TUNA TWIRLS

Makes 20

1 oz (25g) margarine
8 oz (225g) onion, peeled and sliced
1 level tablespoon cornflour
5 oz (150 g) carton natural yogurt
2 tablespoons milk
1 tablespoon lemon juice
$\frac{1}{2}$ level teaspoon thyme
Pepper
7 oz (200g) can tuna fish, drained
TO GARNISH:
20 small cheese biscuits
Parsley
Sliced smoked salmon (optional)

Melt the margarine, add the onion and gently fry until soft. Mix the cornflour into the yogurt, and stir into the onion with the milk, lemon juice, thyme and pepper. Cook, stirring, until mixture thickens. (This is a very thick mixture.)

Remove from the heat and cool slightly, then stir in the tuna fish. Liquidize or place the mixture in a food processor and blend until smooth. Allow to become cold.

Fit a piping bag with a large star nozzle. Fill the piping bag and pipe small rosettes, about the size of walnuts, on to the biscuits. Garnish with a small piece of parsley, and a small roll of smoked salmon, if desired.

Note: the filling may be piped on to the biscuits about 4 hours before required.

To freeze: line a baking sheet with foil. Pipe 20 small rosettes straight on to the sheet. Open freeze until firm, then lift off into a foil container or foil-lined box. To thaw, lightly butter the biscuits, place a rosette on each biscuit and leave at room temperature for 1–2 hours before garnishing.

SPANISH QUICHE SLICES

Serves 20

FOR THE PASTRY:
12 oz (325g) plain flour
Pinch of salt
3 oz (75g) margarine
3 oz (75g) lard
Water to mix
FOR THE FILLING:
2 oz (50g) butter
$1\frac{1}{4}$ lb (600g) potatoes, boiled and cubed
8 oz (225g) onion, peeled and chopped
1 clove garlic, peeled and crushed
1 level teaspoon Marmite
1 large red pepper, de-seeded and diced
4 oz (100g) frozen peas
$1\frac{1}{2}$ level teaspoons salt
$\frac{1}{4}$ level teaspoon pepper
$\frac{3}{4}$ pint (450 ml) milk
3 eggs, size 3
4 oz (100g) Cheddar cheese

Set oven to fairly hot, gas mark 6 or 400°F/200°C.

Sift flour and salt into a bowl. Rub in the fats until mixture resembles fine breadcrumbs. Add enough water to give a soft, but not sticky dough. Cut dough in half and knead until smooth. Roll out both pieces of dough and line two 8 inch (20 cm) loose-bottomed flan tins. Place in fridge to chill.

Meanwhile make the filling; melt the butter in a frying pan, add the potatoes, onion and garlic and cook for 10–15 minutes or until the onion is soft. Remove from the heat and stir in the Marmite, red pepper, peas, salt and pepper.

Divide mixture between the two lined cases and level the surface. Beat milk and eggs together well. Pour half into each flan case, sprinkle with the cheese and bake in the oven for 45 minutes or until golden brown. Allow to cool. Refrigerate and cut each quiche into 10 slices when cold.

To freeze: can be cooked and frozen. Defrost overnight in the fridge. Refresh if necessary by cooking in a fairly hot oven for 15 minutes.

A Summer Buffet

CURRIED PARTY DRUMSTICKS

Serves 20

5 level tablespoons plain flour

5 level tablespoons parmesan cheese

5 level teaspoons paprika

5 level teaspoons curry powder

2½ level teaspoons salt

2 eggs, size 3

20 chicken drumsticks, skin removed

Set the oven to fairly hot, gas mark 6 or 400°F/200°C.

Mix together the flour, parmesan cheese, paprika, curry powder and salt and place on a large plate. Using a fork, beat eggs for about 15 seconds until well mixed. Dip drumsticks in beaten egg and then coat with flour mixture. Place in a lightly-greased roasting tin and bake for 55–60 minutes or until chicken is cooked. Remove from oven to allow to cool.

To freeze: drumsticks can be cooked and then frozen. Thaw overnight in the fridge or a cool place. No need to refresh.

SPECIAL SAUSAGE AND HERB ROLLS

Serves 20

3 oz (75g) packet parsley and thyme stuffing mix

½ pint (300 ml) boiling water

1½ lb (700g) sausagemeat

2 level tablespoons chopped fresh parsley

8 spring onions, trimmed and chopped

Pepper

½ level teaspoon salt

1 egg, size 3, beaten

1 lb (450g) packet puff pastry

Milk

TO GARNISH:

Watercress

2 inch (5 cm) piece of cucumber, sliced

Set oven to fairly hot, gas mark 6 or 400°F/200°C.

Put the stuffing mix into a bowl, stir in the water, and leave for 10 minutes.

Mix the sausagemeat, parsley, spring onions, and seasoning into the stuffing. Add the beaten egg, and mix together.

Cut the puff pastry into four and thinly roll out each quarter into a rectangle 6×12 inches (15×30 cm). Divide the sausage mixture into four and spoon a quarter evenly down the centre of each pastry strip. Brush the edges with a little milk, and roll up into four long shapes.

Trim the ends of each sausage roll and place on a baking sheet. Make nine diagonal cuts about ¼ inch (5 mm) deep along each sausage roll. Brush with milk and bake for 35 minutes.

Arrange on a bed of watercress and cucumber. Slice for easy serving.

To freeze: when cold wrap individually in foil and freeze. Allow to thaw at room temperature for about 6–7 hours before required. If liked, refresh in moderate oven for 10–15 minutes.

NUTTY GEM FLORENTINES

Serves 20

4 oz (100g) caster sugar
1 oz (25g) hazelnuts, chopped
1oz (25g) blanched almonds, chopped
4 oz (100g) mixed angelica, preserved ginger and glacé cherries, chopped
2 level tablespoons plain flour
3 oz (75g) butter
2 tablespoons single cream

Place all the ingredients in a saucepan. Stir over a gentle heat until well mixed. Do not overheat. Cool, then chill mixture in fridge until firm.

Set oven to moderate, gas mark 4 or 350°F/180°C. Spoon 5–6 level teaspoons of mixture on to a well-greased, non-stick baking sheet, or a baking sheet lined with non-stick paper.

Bake just above the centre of the oven for 10 minutes or until just set and golden brown. Remove from oven. Allow to cool for 1–2 minutes, then lift carefully off the sheet with a round-bladed knife and fold over a greased rolling pin. Leave until set and crisp, then slide off on to a cooling rack.

Repeat using the remaining mixture.

Store in a completely airtight tin for up to 1 week.

Not suitable for freezing.

TWO-TONE TRUFFLES

Makes 40

BASIC TRUFFLE MIXTURE:

1 lb (450g) cake crumbs
14 oz (400g) can condensed milk

FOR THE FLAVOURINGS:

3 oz (75g) chocolate, melted
1 tablespoon rum
2 oz (50g) desiccated coconut
1 teaspoon vanilla essence
1 oz (25g) icing sugar
2 oz (50g) chocolate-flavoured sugar strands

Place the cake crumbs in a bowl and bind together with the condensed milk. Divide the mixture in two.

Stir the melted chocolate and rum into one half, cover and leave to stand for 30 minutes.

Stir the coconut and vanilla essence into the remaining half of the truffle mixture. Roll into 20 small balls, about the size of walnuts. Put the icing sugar in a small jar or container. Add truffles, one at a time, and shake until completely coated. Place in sweet paper cases.

When the chocolate truffle mixture is firm enough to handle, roll into 20 small balls, and coat with the chocolate-flavoured sugar strands in the same way as for the coconut truffles.

The truffles may be stored in an airtight tin for up to 5 days.

To freeze: place the finished truffles in a rigid, covered container. Freeze for up to 2 months. To thaw, place the truffles in small paper cases, redusting the coconut truffles with icing sugar, if necessary. Allow to thaw for 2 hours at room temperature.

MIDSUMMER DREAM CAKE

FOR THE CAKE:

14 oz (400g) butter

14 oz (400g) caster sugar

3 lemons

7 eggs, size 3

1 lb (450g) self-raising flour

$\frac{1}{4}$ pint (150 ml) milk

FOR THE LEMON BUTTERCREAM FILLING:

8 oz (225g) butter or margarine

1 lb 4 oz (550g) icing sugar, sifted

4 tablespoons lemon juice

2 egg yolks

FOR THE FONDANT ICING:

2 oz (50g) powdered glucose

1 oz (25g) white vegetable fat

2 tablespoons hot water

2 egg whites, size 3

2 teaspoons fresh lemon juice

2 lb 4 oz–2 lb 6 oz (approximately 1 kg) icing sugar, sifted

Cornflour for rolling out the icing

Set oven to moderate, gas mark 4 or 350°F/180°C. Grease a 10 inch (25·5 cm) round cake tin, base line with greaseproof paper and grease.

Place butter and sugar in a large bowl. Finely grate the rind from the 3 lemons and add to bowl. Squeeze the juice from all the lemons and reserve. Cream butter, sugar and rind until light and fluffy. Beat in the eggs, one at a time, adding a little flour if the mixture begins to curdle. Sift in the flour and pour in the milk. Fold the mixture together carefully and spoon into the prepared tin. Make a hollow in the centre to ensure even rising.

Bake in the centre of the oven for about $1\frac{1}{2}$–$1\frac{3}{4}$ hours until firm and springy to the touch and a skewer, when inserted, comes out clean. About 30 minutes after the beginning of cooking cover the top of the cake with greaseproof paper to prevent the cake from becoming too brown.

Cool in the tin, then remove and wrap tightly in greaseproof paper and foil until ready to use.

Note: the cake can be made up to 3 days before the party.

To freeze: freeze for up to 2 months. Thaw in wrapping.

For the lemon buttercream filling: cream the butter or margarine until soft. Gradually add the icing sugar together with the lemon juice and egg yolks until the mixture is soft and smooth.

Trim the top of the cake if peaked and then, if liked, invert the cake so that the bottom becomes the top.

Cut the cake into three layers. Make sure the filling is soft and spreadable before dividing it equally and spreading evenly over the bottom two layers. Sandwich the cake together.

Note: the buttercream can be made and kept covered in the fridge for 3 days before using.

For the fondant icing: place powdered glucose into a small saucepan with the fat and water. Heat gently, stirring, until the fat melts. Meanwhile, lightly beat the egg whites with the lemon juice in a large mixing bowl. Stir in the melted glucose mixture and gradually add the icing sugar to give a soft, but not sticky, manageable paste. Knead until smooth and cover in cling wrap until required.

To cover the cake: place the cake on a 12 inch (30 cm) cake board. Reserve a piece of icing about the size of a walnut and cover. (Use this when making the Silk Flower Decorations.) Roll out the fondant icing on a surface dusted with cornflour to a circle about 12 inches (30 cm) in diameter.

Carefully lift the icing on to the cake and roll the top surface flat and level using a rolling pin. Dust hands with cornflour and smooth and gently ease and press the icing down the sides of the cake using the fingers.

This is a very pliable icing and by rubbing the icing gently with the fingers it is easy to mould the icing to the shape of the cake.

Note: the fondant icing can be kept, covered in cling wrap, for 1 day before being used to cover the cake.

SILK FLOWER DECORATIONS

½ teaspoon lemon juice
3 yards (2·7 metres) thin pink ribbon
14 pink sprigs of heather
1 yellow sprig of heather
4 dark pink forget-me-nots
2 light pink forget-me-nots
2 yellow and pink blossoms
2 lilac roses

Cut two pieces of ribbon long enough to go around the cake. Place the reserved walnut-sized piece of fondant icing in a small bowl and mix to a paste with the lemon juice. Put the two ribbons around the side of the cake, securing with the icing paste and place nine of the pink heathers at equal intervals around the sides, using icing paste to secure.

Place remaining flowers together, arranging them in an attractive posy. Twist the stems together; cover with remaining pink ribbon. Secure with small knot and bow. Trim the edges of the ribbon and place in centre.

Note: the cake can be assembled the day before the party.

ROSY SUMMER PUNCH

Serves 20

Two 1¾ pint (1 litre) bottles rosé wine, chilled
2½ pint (1·5 litre) bottle lemonade, chilled
¼ pint (150 ml) cherry brandy
2 inch (6 cm) piece cucumber, sliced
8 oz (225g) strawberries, hulled and halved

Pour wine into punch bowl. Stir in lemonade and brandy. Add cucumber and strawberries and serve.

CHRISTMAS DINNER

Dickens knew that turkey and Christmas are inseparable. So they are, and here is a wonderful, traditional turkey dinner to feast a large family party.

MENU FOR 6–8

Roast Stuffed Turkey
Bacon Rolls and Tiny Sausage Kebabs

Crispy Sausage Balls
Spicy Stuffing
Giblet Gravy

Bread Sauce
Cranberry and Tangerine Sauce

Roast Potatoes and Onions
Honeyed Carrots and Parsnips
Nutty Topped Sprouts

Christmas Pudding
Sweet White Sauce and Orange
Brandy Butter

CHRISTMAS DINNER PLAN

Pre Christmas Eve: If frozen, put the turkey to thaw. Make the breadcrumbs. Make the cranberry sauce.

Christmas Eve: Make the lemony stuffing for the turkey, the crumbly spicy stuffing, the bread sauce and the giblet stock.

Prepare the sausages and bacon rolls and leave in the fridge. Make the sausage balls, coat with stuffing and leave in the fridge.

Peel the carrots and parsnips, cut in chunks; trim sprouts, peel onions, and keep vegetables in separate plastic bags in the fridge. Peel potatoes and keep in water with a squeeze of lemon juice. Gently fry the nuts.

Re-cover Christmas Pudding. Make brandy butter.

Christmas day:

5½–6 hours before required: Stuff the turkey. Cover with foil. Set oven.

5 hours before: Put turkey in oven to cook.

2½ hours before: Put onions round turkey. Put the water for the potatoes and the pudding on to boil. Lay the table.

2 hours before: Parboil the potatoes in batches. Drain and put to roast. Put the Christmas Pudding on to boil.

Christmas
Dinner

1½ hours before: Remove the foil from the turkey, turn the turkey roasting tin, baste. Re-set the oven to hot, gas mark 7 or 425°F/220°C. Place crispy, spicy stuffing in the oven.

1 hour before: Test the turkey and, if cooked, remove it from the oven and keep warm. Re-position the shelves. Put in the bacon and sausage kebabs and the sausage balls. Make the gravy.

45 minutes before: Put water on to boil for the carrots, then add them. Cook the sprouts. Add the parsnips to the carrots to cook. Complete the bread sauce. Complete the sauce for the sprouts.

20–30 minutes before: Turn out the Christmas Pudding. Dish all foods.

10 minutes before: Have a drink!

Note: IF the turkey is completely thawed and

If the stuffing is completely cold and If there is sufficient room in the fridge, the turkey can be stuffed on Christmas Eve and kept in the fridge overnight.

ROAST STUFFED TURKEY

10–12 lb (5–5.4 kg) oven-ready turkey, fresh or frozen
2 oz (50g) butter or margarine
1 level teaspoon salt
3 bay leaves
FOR THE LEMONY STUFFING:
8 oz (225g) dried white breadcrumbs (see note)
Finely grated rind of 1 large lemon
2 heaped tablespoons chopped parsley
1 level teaspoon dried marjoram
2 eggs, size 3
5 oz (150g) butter or margarine, softened
1 level teaspoon salt
1/4 level teaspoon pepper

Make sure the turkey has thawed completely. Remove the giblets from the bird as soon as possible.

Note the oven-ready weight of the turkey and add on 1 lb (450g) to allow for weight of the stuffing. Then calculate the cooking time allowing 20 minutes per lb (450g).

Wipe the bird inside and out and pluck out any large pin feathers. If liked, for easier carving remove the wishbone before stuffing and cooking.

Season body cavity with salt and place bay leaves inside.

Mix all the stuffing ingredients together binding them with the eggs and softened butter. The stuffing will appear crumbly but when squeezed should hold together in lumps. If not, add more butter or another beaten egg.

Remove 2–3 tablespoons of stuffing to coat the sausage balls and use the rest to stuff the neck end of the turkey. Pull the neck skin over the opening and secure it underneath the bird with a skewer.

Use any remaining stuffing to make balls or spoon into the body cavity. Place the turkey on its side in a large roasting tin and spread the butter over the skin. Arrange bacon rinds (see recipe for Bacon Rolls, page 172) over the leg. Cover the turkey completely with foil.

Set the oven to moderate, gas mark 4 or 350°F/180°C.

Put the turkey to roast below the centre of the oven and cook for the time which has been calculated. Turn the turkey on to its other side half-way through the cooking.

Remove the foil about 30 minutes before the end of cooking and sit the turkey on its back to allow the turkey to brown evenly.

To test if the turkey is cooked, pierce the thickest part of the thigh with a skewer; if the juices are almost colourless the turkey is ready; if they are tinged pink, continue to cook a little longer.

Note: The day or two before Christmas Eve buy a large white loaf and make into breadcrumbs. Spread the breadcrumbs out on one or two baking or roasting tins and dry them in a very low oven – or when you have switched the oven off after cooking. You will need about half the breadcrumbs for the lemon stuffing. Use the rest for other Christmas cooking.

ROAST ONIONS

1½–2 lb (700–900g) small onions
A little oil

Peel the onions and coat with oil. About 2–2½ hours before serving, place the onions round the turkey. Baste during cooking. Arrange around the turkey to serve.

ROAST POTATOES

5 lb (2·3 kg) potatoes, peeled
Oil or lard
Salt

Cut the potatoes into even sizes. Cook them in boiling salted water for 7 minutes. Drain in a colander. Shake the colander and roughen up the surface of the potatoes – this helps to give the potatoes a crisper coating.

Place the oil or lard in the tin and heat to melt if necessary. Add the potatoes and roll each one in the fat so that they are well coated. Sprinkle with salt.

Place on a shelf above the turkey 2 hours before serving time. After removing the turkey, continue cooking in the same place but at gas mark 7 or 425°F/220°C until brown. Turn the potatoes in the fat during cooking, adding more fat as necessary.

CRUMBLY SPICY STUFFING

3 oz (75g) margarine

1 level teaspoon nutmeg

1 level teaspoon ginger

6–8 oz (175–225g) onion, peeled and chopped

8 oz (225g) brown or white breadcrumbs

2 oz (50g) ham, diced

4 oz (100g) dried apricots, soak for 2 hours or use pre-soaked ones

2 oz (50g) sultanas

Pepper

1 level teaspoon salt

1 egg, size 3, beaten

Melt the margarine, stir in nutmeg, ginger and onions and cook for about 5 minutes to soften the onion.

Add the breadcrumbs and fry until lightly browned and beginning to crisp. Stir in the ham, apricots, sultanas and seasoning. Cook for a minute or so.

Remove from the heat and stir in the egg. Turn into a greased, 8 inch (20 cm), pie plate or dish. Bake in a hot oven, gas mark 7 or 425°F/220°C for an hour. Use a spoon to serve.

BACON ROLLS AND SAUSAGE KEBABS

8 large rashers back bacon

8 chipolata sausages

Derind the bacon. Using the flat side of the blade of a knife, stretch each bacon rasher then cut in half crossways. Roll each bacon half into a roll. Twist each sausage in half to make two smaller ones.

Thread bacon rolls and sausages alternately on to skewers.

Place in a lightly-greased, shallow tin or dish and brush with oil.

Place the tin just below the centre of a hot oven, gas mark 7 or 425°F/220°C for 40–45 minutes.

Turn or baste once during cooking. Placing on skewers makes the turning easy.

CRISPY SAUSAGE BALLS

12 oz (325g) sausagemeat

2–3 tablespoons lemon and parsley stuffing (see Roast Stuffed Turkey, page 171)

Divide the sausagemeat into 8 pieces and roll each piece into a ball. Press some stuffing mix into each ball until completely coated. Place in the same tin as the Bacon and Sausage Kebabs. Cook in a hot oven, gas mark 7 or 425°F/220°C for 40–45 minutes. Baste once, if necessary.

GIBLET GRAVY

Wash the giblets, put in a pan and cover with water – about 2 pints (1·1 litres). Simmer for 45 minutes–1 hour.

When the turkey is cooked, transfer it to a serving plate together with the onions.

Blend 3–4 level tablespoons of flour to a smooth paste with water. Stir the paste into the juices in the tin. Stir in half the strained giblet stock. Place the tin over the heat and bring to the boil, stirring all the time. Reduce the heat and add more giblet stock to correct the consistency. Taste, and add seasoning as necessary. Add a little gravy browning to colour.

HONEYED CARROTS AND PARSNIPS

1½ lb (700g) carrots, peeled

1½ lb (700g) parsnips, peeled

3 tablespoons thin honey

Salt and pepper

Cut the carrots and parsnips into ¾–1 inch (2–2·5 cm) chunks.

Cook the carrots in boiling salted water for 30 minutes until tender.

Add the parsnips after 15 minutes of cooking. When both vegetables are tender, drain. Add honey and seasoning and gently turn vegetables over in honey until coated.

Turn into a serving dish and keep warm.

NUTTY TOPPED SPROUTS

3 lb (1·35 kg) sprouts, trimmed and washed

Salt and pepper

¼ level teaspoon nutmeg

FOR THE SAUCE:

4 oz (100g) mixed nuts, Brazils, hazelnuts, almonds, walnuts, coarsely chopped

1 oz (25g) butter or 2 tablespoons oil

¼ level teaspoon nutmeg

4 tablespoons cream, preferably double

Either cook the sprouts in boiling salted water for 20 minutes or until just tender or, if pans are in short supply, place in a steamer, sprinkle with salt, pepper and nutmeg and place over the pan in which the carrots and parsnips are cooking. Steam for about 20 minutes or until just tender.

Meanwhile, make the sauce: gently fry the nuts in the butter or oil and nutmeg for about 3 minutes, stirring occasionally.

Just before serving, stir the cream into the nuts and reheat for a few seconds – do not boil – then spoon over the sprouts.

BREAD SAUCE

1 medium onion

20 whole cloves

1 pint (600 ml) milk

1 small bay leaf

8 oz (225g) bread, after crusts have been removed

Ground nutmeg

Salt and pepper

1 oz (25g) butter, or 1–2 tablespoons cream

Peel the onion, then stud one half with cloves. Put the onion, clove side down, in a pan and pour over the milk. Add the bay leaf. Heat the milk to just below boiling point and keep it at this temperature for 3–5 minutes. Remove the pan from the heat and leave to infuse for 2 hours.

Remove the crusts from the bread and cut the bread into cubes. Bring the milk back to the boil, remove the onion and bay leaf and reserve the onion. Beat in the bread and nutmeg, and add salt and pepper to taste. Remove from the heat. Return the onion to the pan and leave overnight.

Remove the onion, then reheat for 2–3 minutes adding further seasoning to taste, the butter or cream, or both!

CRANBERRY AND TANGERINE SAUCE

2 tangerines or satsumas

1 lb (450g) fresh or frozen cranberries

7 fl oz (210 ml) water

About 6 oz (175g) sugar

Grate the rind of the tangerines, or satsumas, and put in a pan together with the cranberries and water. Bring to the boil and simmer gently until the fruit is tender – about 5 minutes.

Stir in the sugar and cook gently for about 5 minutes to dissolve the sugar and thicken the mixture.

Remove all the white pith from the tangerines. Roughly chop the fruit, remove any pips, then stir the fruit into the cranberries.

Heat through, then cool and spoon into a serving dish.

This will keep well in a covered container in the fridge for 4–5 days.

CHRISTMAS PUDDING

Makes one 3 lb (1·35 kg) pudding to serve 8

4 oz (100g) self-raising flour

2 level teaspoons mixed spice

$\frac{1}{2}$ level teaspoon nutmeg

Good pinch of salt

3 oz (75g) fresh breadcrumbs

3 oz (75g) shredded suet

4 oz (100g) dark brown sugar

8 oz (225g) raisins

8 oz (225g) sultanas

2 oz (50g) chopped mixed peel

$\frac{1}{2}$ cooking apple, peeled and grated

4 oz (100g) carrot, peeled and grated

2 eggs, size 3

1 level tablespoon treacle

A good $\frac{1}{4}$ pint (150 ml) milk or ale

1–2 tablespoons rum or brandy

Sift the flour, mixed spice, nutmeg and salt into a bowl. Add the breadcrumbs, suet, sugar, dried fruit, chopped peel, grated apple and carrot.

Lightly mix the eggs and treacle and stir into the mixture with the ale or milk. Mix well for at least 5 minutes. Mixing is an important part of the Christmas pudding and should be done very thoroughly. Get everyone in the family to give a hand.

Spoon into a well-buttered, $2\frac{1}{2}$ pint (1·5 litre), pudding basin. Cover with buttered foil and tie securely. Steam for 4 hours.

When cold, remove the foil and pour over the rum or brandy. Re-cover with fresh, ungreased foil and store in a cool place.

On Christmas morning, re-cover with greased foil and steam briskly for 2 hours. Remember the pudding will darken after the second steaming.

Just before you sit down to dinner, take the pudding out of the pan and remove the covers. Invert the pudding on to a large plate leaving the basin in position around the pudding, and stand the plate over the pan of boiling water.

To flame the pudding, pour 1–2 tablespoons rum or brandy into a small pan and warm gently. Pour evenly over the pudding and light immediately. Use a taper as a cigarette lighter can be dangerous.

Pressure cooking: Fill the pan with $3\frac{1}{2}$ pints (2·1 litres) boiling water. Steam for 30 minutes then cook for $2\frac{1}{2}$ hours at high pressure. Reduce pressure slowly.

ORANGE BRANDY BUTTER

4 oz (100g) butter, softened

8 oz (225g) icing sugar, sifted

2 tablespoons brandy

Finely grated rind and juice of $\frac{1}{2}$ orange

Cream the butter and icing sugar together then gradually beat in the brandy, orange rind and juice.

The butter can either be put into a small dish or piped in large rosettes and chilled in the freezer or ice-making compartment until 30 minutes before required.

SWEET WHITE SAUCE

4 level tablespoons cornflour

3–4 tablespoons sugar

$1\frac{1}{4}$ pints (750 ml) milk

Mix the cornflour and sugar in a basin. Stir in just enough cold milk to give a smooth paste. Heat the rest of the milk to boiling point then immediately pour into the paste, stirring all the time. Return to the pan, bring back to the boil, stirring, and cook for half a minute. Remove from the heat and, if liked, stir in a drop or two of vanilla essence.

PRESERVING

This is a branch of cookery I love. If you want high-quality preserves and pickles, full of flavour and goodness, you have to make them at home. Apart from being fun, it's an excellent way of saving money. There's no special season for preserving as far as I'm concerned and, given any excuse, I can be found filling jar upon jar with colourful jams and chutneys.

One tip I would pass on, however, – when trying a new recipe, make a small quantity first, to be sure that you and the family like it!

JAMS AND JELLIES

TIPS FOR JAMS & JELLIES

1. To test for setting point, a sugar thermometer can be used. When the temperature reaches 222°F the jam is ready. But I find the saucer test is best and most reassuring: put a few saucers in the fridge so that the test sample of jam can be cooled as quickly as possible. Take the pan off the heat. Spoon 1 tablespoon of jam or jelly on to the chilled saucer and cool for a few minutes. Then, push the jam or jelly with a finger; the jam should wrinkle or frill if setting point has been reached. If not, return the pan to the heat and boil briskly for a few more minutes.

Note: When testing for a set with a thermometer always stir the jam well before taking a reading.

2. Use a large saucepan or preserving pan if you're making large quantities.

3. Choose slightly under-ripe rather than over-ripe fruit. Prepare fruit, taking care to remove all bruised and damaged pieces as these spoil the colour and flavour of the jam.

Stones may be removed beforehand or during cooking, when they float to the surface and can be removed with a slotted spoon.

4. Granulated sugar is excellent. Caster and brown sugar are not recommended because they produce a lot of froth. Always weigh the sugar as it is now sold in 1 kg bags and not the familiar 2 lb.

5. Fruit should be cooked slowly in water until completely tender, adding acid such as lemon juice during this stage, if required.

6. When the fruit is soft the contents of the pan should be reduced by a good third before adding sugar. This ensures the correct proportion of water to sugar in the finished preserve.

7. The sugar must be completely dissolved before the jam is boiled rapidly to reach setting point. Test after 5 minutes. No jam should need boiling for longer than 25 minutes.

8. Scum should only be removed at the end of cooking as it is wasteful to remove any before. A knob of butter can be added to the boiling jam to reduce the scum.

9. So that the fruit will not rise in the jars, some jams must cool for 10–15 minutes.

10. Warm jam jars by putting them in a low oven for 15 minutes, then fill them right to the brim. Put a waxed disc on at once, waxed side down, pressing carefully to remove all air bubbles. Place the lid, glass stopper or Cellophane cover on when the jam is either very hot or cold – not when jam is warm. When jam is cold, label with name and date.

11. Store jars in a cool, dry place away from strong light.

12. When making jelly don't squeeze the jelly bag or you will have a cloudy mixture. If you scald the jelly bag or cloth with boiling water first, the juice will run through and not be absorbed by the fabric.

13. There are new pectin and jam sugars in the shops. If you decide to buy, do follow the manufacturer's recipes carefully.

What went wrong and why:

Mouldy jam: results from over-ripe fruit; slow or insufficient boiling with sugar; cold or damp jars; incorrect covering – the waxed discs should be put on when the jam is very hot or cold; poor storage.

Jam does not set or a syrupy jam or jelly: results from lack of pectin (the fruit could have been over-ripe, in which case the normal pectin has deteriorated); insufficient boiling or over-boiling past setting point; insufficient acid in fruit or lemon juice. Jelly can be affected if the strained juice is left too long before using.

Jam crystallises: due to over-boiling with the sugar; too much sugar has been used; sugar not dissolved completely.

FREEZER JAMS

Freezer jams are uncooked, and can be stored in the freezer for 3–6 months.

Fresh, ripe fruit is essential for these jams, which are brightly coloured and retain the delicious flavour and aroma of fresh fruit. The jams contain a large proportion of sugar and the yield for each lb (450g) of fruit is high, so do not make more than one batch at a time.

It's best to pack the jams in small quantities in freezer-proof plastic containers with tight-fitting lids, allowing ½ inch (1 cm) headspace for expansion of the frozen jam. Freezer jams keep for up to one year in the freezer.

Jams should be thawed for 1 hour before serving, and after opening they should be stored in the refrigerator and quickly used up.

Freezer jam has a soft consistency and is not as firm as a cooked jam. They also make delicious fruit sauces for ice-cream and desserts.

STRAWBERRY FREEZER JAM

Makes 3–3½ lb (1·35–1·6 kg)

1½ lb (700g) ripe strawberries, washed and hulled and well drained

2 lb (900g) caster sugar

4 fl oz (100 ml) liquid pectin

Mash the strawberries and stir in the sugar. Leave to stand for 24 hours or until the sugar has completely dissolved.

Add the liquid pectin and stir well together for 3 minutes. Pour into small freezer containers, leaving ½ inch (1 cm) headspace for expansion. Leave for 3 hours at room temperature and then refrigerate for 2 hours or until the jam has gelled. Cover, label and store in the freezer until required.

STRAWBERRY AND ORANGE JAM

Makes 2–2½ lb (900g–1·2 kg)

1½ lb (700g) strawberries, hulled

1 large orange

1½ lb (700g) granulated sugar

A knob of butter

Wash the strawberries only if necessary. Put them into a large pan. Finely grate the rind from the orange, then add it to the strawberries with the juice from the orange.

Simmer over a gentle heat for about 15 minutes until the fruit is soft, the juice is released from the strawberries and the mixture is reduced by a good third.

Add the sugar and stir well until it is completely dissolved. When every grain of sugar has dissolved, bring the jam to the boil and boil rapidly for about 15 minutes. Test for a set.

If there is a lot of scum, remove as much as liked before stirring in the butter. Stir well to mix the butter evenly. Leave the jam to stand for 10 minutes, then stir and pour into clean, warmed jars. See Jam Tip 10 (page 175) for covering and labelling.

LEMON AND CARROT JAM

Makes about 6½ lb (3 kg)

4 large lemons, weighing 1½ lb (700g)

1 lb (450g) carrots

3–4 pints (1·8–2·4 litres) water

4 lb (1·8 kg) granulated sugar

Slice lemons thinly, removing pips. Cut slices into segments. Scrape and grate carrots. Put into a large bowl with the water and leave to soak overnight.

Put into a large pan and cook until the lemon is soft and mixture has reduced by half, about 45 minutes–1 hour. Stir in the sugar and stir to dissolve – do not allow to boil at this stage. When all the sugar has dissolved, bring to the boil and boil until setting point is reached. Leave to cool for 5 minutes.

Pour into clean, warmed jars. See Jam Tip 10 (page 175) for covering and labelling.

SEEDLESS APPLE AND BLACKBERRY JAM

Makes about 2½ lb (1·2 kg)

1 lb (450g) cooking apples

1 lb (450g) blackberries

2 pints (1·1 litres) water

¾ level teaspoon mixed spice

2 tablespoons lemon juice

Granulated sugar (see recipe)

Knob of butter

Wash apples and cut out any bruises. Do not peel or core. Cut apples into slices and put in a preserving pan or large saucepan. Pick over blackberries and add them to the apples. Add the water, mixed spice and lemon juice. Bring to the boil, reduce heat to a simmer and cook until soft.

Rub the mixture through a sieve or fine Mouli (food mill) to get rid of the seeds.

Strawberry and Orange Jam

Measure the pulp and return it to the pan. For every pint (600 ml) of juice allow 1 lb (450g) of granulated sugar.

Heat the pulp and sugar gently to dissolve the sugar, adding a good knob of butter to lessen the scum. Bring to the boil and boil rapidly to setting point.

Pour into clean, warmed jars, see Jam Tip 10 (page 175) for covering and labelling.

PEAR AND LEMON CONSERVE

Makes 3½–4 lb (1·6–1·8 kg)

4 lb (1·8 kg) pears

2 lb (900g) granulated sugar

2 lemons

Peel the pears, cut into quarters or halves and remove the cores. Place in a large bowl with the sugar, mix well and leave to stand overnight, or for at least 8 hours.

Cut lemon in ⅛ inch (3 mm) thick slices. Cut slices into small wedge-shaped pieces, and remove any pips. Place the pears, sugar and lemons in a preserving pan and bring to the boil, then simmer very gently for 2 hours, stirring occasionally with a wooden spoon. The pieces of pear should remain whole, and the syrup should take on a light pink colour and be thick. A few drops of pink food colouring may be added.

Carefully place the pears into clean, warmed jars, then pour the syrup over. Cover and label, as in Jam Tip 10 (page 175).

RHUBARB CONSERVE

Makes 5 lb (2·3 kg)

2 large lemons, weighing about 4 oz (100g) each

2 large thin-skinned oranges, weighing about 6 oz (175g) each

¾ pint (450 ml) water

3 lb (1·35 kg) rhubarb

3 lb (1·35 kg) granulated sugar

2 oz (50g) raisins

2 oz (50g) walnuts, roughly broken

A knob of butter

Squeeze the juice from the lemons and oranges and keep on one side. Place the squeezed halves in a pan and cover with cold water, then bring to the boil and boil gently for 5 minutes – this removes some of the bitter flavour. Drain, then slice the lemons and oranges into thin shreds.

Trim and wash the rhubarb, removing the bruised parts, and cut it into approximately 1 inch (2·5 cm) chunks; put them into a large pan with the orange and lemon shreds, the water and the fruit juices and cook over a gentle heat until the rhubarb is very soft. Increase the heat and boil until the volume of the fruit has been reduced to two-thirds, stirring occasionally.

Add sugar and stir over a gentle heat until dissolved. Add the raisins, walnuts and butter, which will help prevent scum forming. Bring the jam to the boil and boil rapidly, stirring occasionally, for about 10–15 minutes, then test for setting. If not set, return the jam to the pan and continue boiling for a little longer.

Leave the conserve to cool in the pan for 10 minutes before pouring into warm, clean jars, see Jam Tip 10 (page 175).

PENNY-WISE PEEL MARMALADE

Makes 4½–5 lb (2–2·3 kg)

8 oz (225g) fresh mixed peel, e.g. grapefruit and/or tangerine, orange, pomelo, see note

2 lemons, washed

3 pints (1·8 litres) water

¾ pint (450 ml) fresh orange juice (from a carton)

3 lb (1·35 kg) granulated sugar

Cut peel into thin strips. Cut lemons into quarters lengthwise, remove pips, then slice thinly. Tie pips up in 'J' cloth or muslin.

Place cut peel in a pan [at least 6 pints (4 litres)] with lemon, water and bag of pips.

Cover and simmer for about 2 hours until each type of peel disintegrates when pressed.

Remove bag of pips, stir in orange juice. Bring to the boil (do not cover) and cook rapidly for 5–7 minutes to reduce liquid by almost a half.

Turn off the heat then add the sugar to the pan and stir until all the sugar crystals have completely dissolved.

Bring to the boil and boil for 1 minute. Turn off the heat and test for setting point according to Jam Tip 1 (page 175).

Allow marmalade to cool for 10 minutes, then pour into clean, warmed jars, right to the top. Cover and label as Jam Tip 10 (page 175). Store in a cool, dry place.

Note: As you eat the fruit reserve the peel and keep in a plastic bag in the fridge until you have the required amount.

CHUTNEYS

TIPS FOR CHUTNEYS

1. The fruit and vegetables used to make chutney may be bruised and imperfect but never mouldy or rotten, as this will spoil the flavour and the keeping quality of the chutney. Always cut off bad parts.

2. The vinegar and sugar preserve the chutney, so always use the amounts recommended in the recipe. Malt vinegar and brown sugar produce a richer-looking chutney whereas granulated sugar and white distilled vinegar give a lighter, brighter look. The flavour of the chutney will also be slightly different depending on the type of sugar and vinegar used.

3. With vinegar mixtures always use an aluminium or stainless steel pan – never a copper or brass one.

4. Most chutneys are cooked for a long time to reduce the mixture down to a pulp. The correct consistency is reached when you can draw a wooden spoon across the pan base and see a line, showing that there is no free liquid left.

5. Always pour chutney into clean, warmed pots while hot. (Warm the jars by putting them in a low oven for 15 minutes.)

6. When cold, cover with a vinegar-proof lid which could be made of glass, plastic or coated metal. Jam cellophane covers are not enough, as they allow the vinegar, i.e. the preservative, to evaporate, causing the chutney to shrink and dry out. Label with name and date.

7. Store chutney in a cool, dry, dark place. Try to keep it for 3–4 months before eating, as this will give sufficient time for the flavours to blend and mellow.

What went wrong and why:

The chutney shrinks and dries out: due to storing in a warm place and the covering not being airtight.

The chutney ferments and goes mouldy: could be due to insufficient cooking: too much water or too little vinegar has been left in the mixture.

Penny-wise Peel Marmalade

AUTUMN CHUTNEY

If preferred, any 6 lb (2·7 kg) weight combination of fruit and vegetables can be used instead of the ones here.

Makes about 6 lb (2·7 kg)

2 lb (900g) windfall or cooking apples

2 lb (900g) pears

2 lb (900g) red tomatoes

8 oz (225g) dried apricots

8 oz (225g) chopped dates

2 lb (900g) soft brown sugar

1 pint (600 ml) malt vinegar

1 level teaspoon cayenne pepper

2 level teaspoons mixed spice

1 level tablespoon salt

1 level teaspoon pepper

Peel and core the apples and pears, and cut into small pieces. Skin and roughly chop the tomatoes and remove the seeds if liked.

Put the apples, pears, tomatoes and remaining ingredients into a large pan or preserving pan and bring to the boil. Simmer gently for about 2 hours until the fruit and vegetables are tender and the chutney thick.

Pour the chutney into clean, warmed jars and cover as in Chutney Tips 5–6 (page 179).

SPICY APPLE CHUTNEY

Makes 7 lb (3·2 kg)

4 lb (1·8 kg) cooking apples

2 lb (900g) onions

2 level teaspoons cinnamon

1 level teaspoon ginger

2 pinches ground cloves

1 level tablespoon salt

1 pint (600 ml) malt vinegar

6 oz (175g) sultanas

2 lb (900g) granulated or brown sugar

Peel, quarter and core the apples then slice them into a large pan. Add the peeled and chopped onions, all the spices, salt and vinegar. Bring to the boil, cover pan with lid and simmer for 30–40 minutes, until the fruit has pulped down. Remove the lid and boil the chutney to evaporate excess liquid, stirring occasionally.

Add the sugar and sultanas and heat gently to dissolve the sugar, stirring all the time. Bring to boil and boil, stirring, until mixture is thick (see Chutney Tip 4, page 179).

Pour into clean, warmed jars. When cold, cover as in Chutney Tips 5–6 (page 179).

GREEN TOMATO CHUTNEY

Makes about 4 lb (1·8 kg)

12 oz (325g) green tomatoes

8 oz (225g) cooking apples, peeled, cored and chopped

12 oz (325g) onions, peeled and chopped

12½ fl oz (390 ml) light malt vinegar

12 oz (325g) brown sugar

1½ level tablespoons cornflour

3 level teaspoons ground ginger

¼ level teaspoon turmeric

1 level teaspoon salt

½ level teaspoon pepper

Halve the tomatoes and cut them into fine segments. Put into a large saucepan with the apple and onions. Add ½ pint (300 ml) vinegar and the sugar, and boil for 5 minutes.

Blend the cornflour to a smooth paste with the rest of the vinegar, then stir in the ginger, turmeric, salt and pepper. Add to the tomatoes in the pan and boil again for 2–3 minutes stirring constantly, then remove pan from heat.

Spoon the mixture into warm, clean jars; when cold, top with a vinegar-proof cover.

TOMATO AND ONION CHUTNEY

Makes about 3 lb (1·35 kg)

4 lb (1·8 kg) tomatoes

1 lb (450g) onions, peeled and roughly chopped

1 level tablespoon salt

½ pint (300 ml) malt vinegar

1 level teaspoon mixed spice

1 level teaspoon paprika

A pinch of cayenne pepper

12 oz (350g) soft brown sugar

Place half the tomatoes in a large bowl, cover with boiling water and leave for 10–15 seconds. Pour off the hot water and replace with cold. Drain, then remove the skins and repeat with the remaining tomatoes.

Chop all the tomatoes roughly and put them in a large saucepan or preserving pan with the onions, salt, vinegar, spices and cayenne pepper. Simmer over a low heat for 35 minutes until the vegetables are cooked and the flavours have started to blend. Increase the heat and boil to evaporate some of the liquid, stirring occasionally, until the mixture is a thick, pouring consistency. Add sugar and stir to dissolve, then bring to the boil and boil, stirring frequently, for 20–30 minutes or until the chutney is thick, with no excess liquid.

Cool slightly then pour into clean, warmed jars. Pot and cover as in Chutney Tips 5–6 (page 179).

UNCOOKED CHUTNEY

Makes 2 lb (900g)

1 large green pepper

1 large red pepper

1 lb (450g) cooking apples, peeled and cored

8 oz (225g) onion, peeled and quartered

3 oz (75g) raisins

Juice of 1 lemon

2 oz (50g) dark brown sugar

1 level teaspoon salt

Freshly ground black pepper

2 level teaspoons paprika

4 drops Tabasco sauce

De-seed the green and red peppers and cut in half. Using the double-bladed knife attachment of a food processor, chop the peppers for about 10 seconds. Place in a bowl.

Change the blade to the grating disc, but do not clean the bowl. Grate the apple and onion and add to the peppers. Mix in the raisins, lemon juice, sugar, salt, pepper, paprika and Tabasco. Place in cleaned jars and label.

This chutney will keep for 3 weeks and should be kept in the refrigerator.

If you do not own a food processor: Coarsely grate the peppers, apple and onion by hand, then mix in with the other ingredients as above.

PICKLES

TIPS FOR PICKLING

1. Before pickling raw vegetables in vinegar it is necessary to reduce their water content either by brining or salting them. Too much natural liquid will dilute the vinegar, preventing preservation.

Cooking drives off liquid, so cooked vegetables need not be brined.
2. Block, cooking or table salt can be used. Table salt contains a special chemical to keep it free-running which may cloud the vinegar.
3. Vegetables must be rinsed well under cold, running water and drained thoroughly to prevent saltiness in the final pickle.
4. Pack the vegetables into clean jars to within 1 inch (2·5 cm) of the top. Leave a space at the top of the jar so the vinegar does not touch the lid. Label when cold.
5. Pickles taste best when they are left for a month or two before using.
6. When making a sweet pickle it is important to reduce the spiced syrup to thicken it before pouring over the fruits. During storage the syrup will draw out some of the

natural juices of the fruit and vegetables and reduce the concentration. If the vinegar syrup is too weak it will not preserve the fruit and the pickle will go mouldy.

What went wrong and why:

The pickles discolour and mould grows: the jar has not been covered properly and the vinegar has evaporated, exposing the vegetables. Make sure that there is $\frac{1}{2}$ inch (1 cm) of pickling vinegar above the vegetables.

The pickles fermented: vegetables may have been under-brined with too little salt or for too short a time. Weak vinegar and bad pieces of fruit or vegetable included in the pickle also result in deterioration.

Yellow spots on pickled onions: due to the formation of a harmless substance. The onions can still be eaten.

SPICED VINEGAR

Makes about $1\frac{3}{4}$ pints (1 litre)

2 pints (1·1 litres) malt vinegar
3–4 inch (7·5–10 cm) stick cinnamon
10 whole cloves
1 level teaspoon blade mace
1 level dessertspoon whole allspice
3 bay leaves
1 level tablespoon mixed pickling spice or 1 infusion sachet

Put all the ingredients into a pan; an enamel one for preference, but an aluminium one will do. Bring to the boil and simmer for 2–3 minutes.

Immediately remove from the heat and pour into a bowl. Cover and leave to infuse for at least 3 hours or preferably overnight. Strain and use.

BREAD AND BUTTER PICKLE

Makes 3 lb (1·35 kg)

2 cucumbers, each weighing about $1\frac{1}{4}$ lb (600g)
$1\frac{1}{2}$ lb (700g) onions

1 large green pepper, optional
2 level tablespoons salt
$1\frac{3}{4}$ pints (1 litre) spiced vinegar (left)
2 level tablespoons pickling spice
3 small bay leaves
6 oz (175g) granulated sugar

Leaving the skin on, slice the cucumbers thinly; peel and thinly slice the onions. Cut the top off the pepper and remove the seeds, then slice thinly. Put the vegetables in a large bowl, sprinkle each layer with salt. Leave for 2 hours to extract some of the juices, then rinse the salt off under cold running water; drain and shake dry.

Dissolve the sugar in the spiced vinegar. Heat slightly if necessary. Fill clean jars with the vegetables, packing them in neatly. Strain the vinegar then pour it over the vegetables to cover. Top each jar with a vinegar-proof cover or plastic-lined lid and leave to stand for 2 weeks before using.

Note: The pickle will lose some colour on storing.

CLEAR MIXED PICKLE

Makes about 4 lb (1·8 kg)

1 lb (450g) shallots or pickling onions, peeled
1 medium cauliflower [about $1\frac{1}{2}$ lb (700g)]
1 large cucumber
1 large red pepper, de-seeded and sliced
1 oz (25g) salt
3 pints (1·8 litres) spiced vinegar (left)
$\frac{1}{2}$ oz (15g) pickling spice

Peel the shallots and cut the cauliflower into small sprigs. Peel the cucumber and cut into cubes.

Mix all the vegetables together in a large bowl. Sprinkle over the salt, mix well and leave to stand overnight.

Drain off the liquid, rinse (see Pickling Tip 3) and pack the vegetables into jars. Pour over the spiced vinegar and put some pickling spice in each jar.

Cover tightly. Keep for 2–3 months before using.

RED CABBAGE PICKLE

Makes about 3–4 lb (1·35–1·8 kg)

1 firm red cabbage weighing about 3 lb (1·35 kg)

6 oz (175g) salt

2 pints (1·1 litres) spiced vinegar (page 182)

Trim the cabbage, quarter, then shred finely discarding the core. Layer the cabbage with the salt in a large bowl. Leave for 24 hours.

Rinse thoroughly under cold running water. Drain very well.

Put into a basin, cover with spiced vinegar. Leave for a further 24 hours, stirring occasionally. Pack into jars, top up with vinegar, cover.

Spiced Orange Slices, page 184; Sweetcorn Relish, page 184; Red Cabbage Pickle; Clear Mixed Pickle

SWEETCORN RELISH

Makes about 2½ lb (1·2 kg)

1½ lb (700g) red or green tomatoes, skinned and quartered

2 red peppers, de-seeded and chopped

1 yellow pepper, de-seeded and chopped

8 oz (225g) cooking apples, peeled, cored and sliced

2 cloves garlic, peeled and crushed

11 oz (300g) can sweetcorn, drained

1 level tablespoon salt

1 pint (600 ml) distilled malt vinegar

1½ oz (40g) mixed pickling spice

12 oz (350g) granulated sugar

Place the tomatoes, peppers, apple, garlic, sweetcorn, salt and ½ pint (300 ml) vinegar in a pan. Tie the pickling spice in a piece of muslin and also add to pan.

Bring to the boil and simmer for about 20 minutes. Add the sugar and remaining vinegar and cook for a further 15–20 minutes or until the correct consistency is reached.

Remove the bag containing the pickling spice before potting, and label when cold.

CARROT AND RUNNER BEAN CHUTNEY

Makes 4–5 lb (1·8–2·3 kg)

1 lb (450g) carrots, peeled and sliced

1½ lb (700g) onions, peeled and chopped

1¼ pints (750 ml) distilled vinegar

1 oz (25g) cornflour

1½ level tablespoons turmeric

5 level tablespoons dried mustard powder

2 lb (900g) runner beans, sliced diagonally

1 lb (450g) demerara sugar

Cook the carrots and onion in 1 pint (600 ml) of vinegar for about 15 minutes until tender. Mix the cornflour, turmeric and mustard with a little vinegar to a smooth paste and

add to the pan with the beans. Bring to the boil and simmer for 10 minutes.

Add the remaining vinegar and the sugar and cook for another 15 minutes.

Bottle and cover when cold with Porosan skin or lids.

PICKLED ONIONS

2 lb (900g) small pickling onions, (silverskin are ideal)

2 oz (50g) salt

1 pint (600 ml) malt vinegar

½ oz (15g) whole pickling spice

Peel the onions, put them into a glass or earthenware bowl and sprinkle with salt. Leave overnight.

Put the vinegar and spices into a pan and bring to the boil. Immediately pour the vinegar and spices into a glass or earthenware basin. Leave to stand in a warm place or in a pan filled with hot water for at least 2 hours. Cover the basin with a plate during this time.

Rinse the onions well under cold water then pat dry. Pack into wide-necked jars. Strain the vinegar then pour it over the onions to cover completely. Cover the jars with vinegar-proof covers or plastic-lined lids. Label with name and date.

Keep for 2 months before using.

SPICED ORANGE SLICES

Makes about 2 jars

6 thin-skinned oranges

½ pint (300 ml) distilled malt vinegar

1 lb (450g) granulated sugar

10 whole cloves

4 whole allspice

Two 2 inch (5 cm) pieces stick cinnamon

Wash the oranges, then cut across the fruit into ¼ inch (5 mm) thick slices. Remove any pips. Place the slices in a 7–8 inch (18–20 cm) saucepan and just cover with cold water. Bring to the simmer, then cover with lid and simmer for about 1 hour until the skin and pith are tender – test with a fork. (Cook gently so as not to break up the slices.)

With a slotted spoon, lift the orange slices from the pan and place in a large mixing bowl. Throw away the cooking water.

Place the rest of the ingredients in the pan and heat gently to dissolve the sugar. Replace orange slices and simmer gently for about 30 minutes or until glazed.

With the slotted spoon, transfer the orange slices and spices into wide-necked jars.

Boil the remaining syrup until reduced by half. Pour the syrup over the fruit – it should cover the slices. Cover when cold.

MUSTARD PICKLE

Makes 6–7 lb (about 3 kg)

1 cauliflower weighing about 1 lb (450g)
1 lb (450g) onions, peeled
1 lb (450g) courgettes, trimmed and washed
3 red peppers, de-seeded
1 lb (450g) runner or French beans
1 oz (25g) salt
2 pints (1·1 litres) white vinegar
1 lb (450g) granulated sugar
2 level tablespoons dry mustard powder
1 level tablespoon turmeric
2 level teaspoons ground ginger
Two 11 oz (300g) cans sweetcorn, drained
2 oz (50g) cornflour

Divide the cauliflower into tiny sprigs. Cut the onions in half from root to tip, then cut each half from root to tip into ½ inch (1 cm) thick slices.

Thinly slice the courgettes and red peppers. String the beans, then cut into ½ inch (1 cm) diamonds. Place all the vegetables in a large bowl. Sprinkle with salt and leave to stand overnight.

Next day, wash the vegetables and drain well. Put the vinegar, reserving 5 tablespoons for later, and the sugar into a very large pan. Heat gently until the sugar has dissolved.

In a small basin blend the mustard, turmeric and ginger to a smooth paste with a little of the hot vinegar, then add to the pan, together with the vegetables and sweetcorn.

Mix well, then simmer for about 15 minutes until the vegetables are almost cooked. With a slotted spoon, lift out the vegetables into a large bowl.

Blend the cornflour to a smooth paste with the reserved vinegar. Stir into the spicy vinegar in the pan. Bring to the boil, stirring, and cook for 5 minutes, stirring all the time until the sauce is thick and smooth. Pour the sauce over the vegetables and mix well together. Spoon into clean, warmed jars to within 1 inch (2·5 cm) of the top. The vinegar should not touch the lid. See Chutney Tip 6 (page 179) for covering and labelling. The flavour of the Mustard Pickle will improve if it is stored for 6 weeks.

INDEX